AMERICAN INDUSTRIAL POLICY

Also by William R. Nester

AMERICAN POWER, THE NEW WORLD ORDER, AND THE
  JAPANESE CHALLENGE
ENDS OF THE EARTH
EUROPEAN POWER AND THE JAPANESE CHALLENGE
INTERNATIONAL RELATIONS: Geopolitical and Geoeconomic
  Conflict and Cooperation
JAPAN AND THE THIRD WORLD: Patterns, Power, Prospects
JAPANESE INDUSTRIAL TARGETING: The Neomercantilist Path
  to Economic Superpower
JAPAN'S GROWING POWER OVER EAST ASIA AND THE
  WORLD ECONOMY: Ends and Means
POWER ACROSS THE PACIFIC: A Diplomatic History of
  American Relations with Japan
THE FOUNDATIONS OF JAPANESE POWER: Continuities,
  Changes, Challenges
THE WAR FOR AMERICA'S NATURAL RESOURCES

American Industrial Policy

Free or Managed Markets?

William R. Nester
Professor of Political Science
St John's University
New York

St. Martin's Press
New York

AMERICAN INDUSTRIAL POLICY
Copyright © 1997 by William R. Nester
All rights reserved. No part of this book may be used or reproduced
in any manner whatsoever without written permission except in the
case of brief quotations embodied in critical articles or reviews.
For information, address:

St. Martin's Press, Scholarly and Reference Division,
175 Fifth Avenue, New York, N.Y. 10010

First published in the United States of America in 1997

This book is printed on paper suitable for recycling and
made from fully managed and sustained forest sources.

Printed in Great Britain

ISBN 0–312–16592–7

Library of Congress Cataloging-in-Publication Data
Nester, William R., 1956–
American industrial policy : free or managed markets / William R.
Nester.
p.   cm.
Includes bibliographical references and index.
ISBN 0–312–16592–7 (cloth)
1. Industrial policy—United States.   I. Title.
HD3616.U47N47   1997
338.973—dc20   96–35137
                                                              CIP

Contents

Introduction:
The Great Debate – Free
or Managed Markets?

I want to unleash the magic of the marketplace!

Ronald Reagan

I do not want to see the Government pick winners and losers.

George Bush

Nothing in our economic policy is so deeply ingrained, and so little reckoned with by economists, as our tendency to wait and see if things do not improve by themselves.

John Kenneth Galbraith

I do not know much about the tariff, but I know this much, when we buy manufactured goods abroad we get the goods and the foreigner gets the money. When we buy the manufactured goods at home we get both the goods and the money.

Abraham Lincoln

The dogmas of the quiet past are inadequate to the stormy present. The occasion is piled high with difficulty, and we must rise to the occasion. As our case is new, so we must disenthrall ourselves and then we shall save our country.

Abraham Lincoln

1

What is the government's proper role in the economy? Do free or managed markets best promote economic development? Who can best pick industrial winners and losers, the government or the private sector?

During the mid-1990s, politicians and the public rallied around two starkly different answers. President Clinton and other "new Democrats" argued that government could nurture economic development through policies that invested in education, infrastructure, and strategic industries, while insisting on reciprocal trade relations with foreign countries. Loudly denouncing that perspective, Representative Newt Gingrich and "radical Republicans" pushed through Congress a "Contract with America" program that attempted to dismantle or reduce virtually all federal programs except those of the Pentagon and turn over their duties either to the states or to the private sector.

These conflicting visions are as old as the American Republic. During the 1790s, Treasury Secretary Alexander Hamilton and Secretary of State Thomas Jefferson were the leading voices in the same debate. Like today's New Democrats, Hamilton argued that government could and should guide the nation's economic development by nurturing industry and trade. Inspiring today's radical Republicans, Jefferson asserted that the government that governs least, governs best; markets rather than officials should determine the nation's economic fate.

Although this debate has alternately raged and ebbed ever since, in many respects it has been a charade. The real issue has not been whether government should develop the economy, but rather how and where it should do so. From Hamilton through Clinton the federal government has conducted industrial policies designed to develop the economy. Although Congress initially rejected Hamilton's call for a comprehensive industrial policy, over the next 150 years it enacted a series of tariffs, invested in canals, ports, and roads, gave away public land to entrepreneurs and homesteaders, promoted or inhibited trade, conquered and developed new territories, imposed an income tax, passed antitrust laws, and experimented with a central bank, all of which helped some regions, industries, firms, technologies, families, and individuals more than others.

And all of that happened before 1933 when Franklin Roosevelt stepped into the White House and proceeded to create the modern presidency and welfare state. During World War II when the federal government directed the nation's economy, it had never expanded so quickly or run as efficiently. To fight the Cold War, Democrats and Republicans worked together to expand a vast military–industrial complex that developed an array of industries and technologies. In the mid-1960s, President Lyndon Johnson further expanded Washington's economic and social duties with a range of new programs. And by the late 1960s, as European, Japanese, and other foreign industries became ever more formidable rivals, Washington has increasingly stepped in to protect threatened American industries and firms.

Washington's industrial policies are hardly unique; virtually every other government around the world does the same. Yet, in many ways America's industrial policies are distinct from those of other countries. Perhaps the biggest difference is that "industrial policy" is a dirty word for most American political and economic leaders. As Chalmers Johnson put it, Americans differ from other peoples in "their commitment to the market mechanism as the supreme arbiter of economic decisions, their reliance on adversarial rather than cooperative public–private relations, and their greater devotion than other peoples' to free trade."[1] While Americans may indeed extensively practice industrial policies, they preach such mythical cultural icons as Horatio Alger who transformed himself from "rags to riches" through hard work and ingenuity unaided by others, especially government. According to this ideal, economies develop from the efforts of rugged individuals asserting themselves in free markets; government only impedes progress.

Given the power of the "rugged individual" myth, why then do any industrial policies exist? Human nature explains the discrepancy. Most Americans may genuinely believe in the Horatio Alger ideal and resent it when their taxes go to programs which support others. But those same people often receive generous federal aid of various kinds, and shrilly whine whenever their subsidy is threatened. Washington heavily subsidizes farmers, ranchers, miners, and loggers; protects such industries as automobiles, steel, and semiconductors;

bails out the savings and loan system; underwrites the medical system, and so on. According to Stuart Bruchey, a "persistent theme in the nation's economic development" is "the incorrigible insistence of private citizens that government encourage or entirely provide those services and utilities either too costly or too risky to attract unaided private capital."[2] Is that an unreasonable request? Yes or no, depending on where one stands in the industrial policy debate.

Like it or not, today even the most "rugged" of individuals cannot do without some government help. Yet, not so long ago when most Americans lived on farms, they could subsist on their own. Industrialization, urbanization, and integration into a global economy created a host of new socioeconomic problems with which individuals and families could not cope. Guy Peters maintains that today virtually all Americans agree that Washington has at least four broad economic duties – maintaining "economic growth, full employment, stable prices, and a positive balance of payments."[3]

This discrepancy between cultural ideals and modern needs helps explain another key difference between American and foreign industrial policies. In no other democratic industrial country are industrial policies more politicized than in the United States. Political power rather than national interests determines America's industrial winners and losers. Industries such as agriculture and textiles may contribute little to the nation's wealth, jobs, or economic future but have enormous political clout and thus enjoy the lion's share of direct subsidies and protection from imports. While Washington does promote winners such as aerospace, computers, weapons, and semiconductors, its industrial policies target an unusually large share of losers.

The term "industrial policy" has two major meanings. One is a comprehensive, long-term government plan for developing the entire economy. The other is the means by which a government attempts to develop a specific industry. Although the United States lacks the former, it has literally hundreds of the latter. Every nation has industrial policies whether they are comprehensive or fragmented, or whether officials admit the practice or not. Governments employ industrial policies either because they aid development, because the politically powerful demand them, or through some combination.

The freer and more competitive a market, the shorter the outlook of its participants. No national economy has freer markets than those of the United States. In such a Darwinian world, business leaders do anything they can get away with to ensure their immediate survival and boost quarterly profits rather than carefully planning for their firms' expansion a decade, a quarter-century, or even a century down the road. The Japanese deride America's economic system as promoting "excessive competition," and in their industrial policies try to avoid it at all costs.

THE INDUSTRIAL POLICY DEBATE

All along, the debate between Hamiltonians and Jeffersonians (or their contemporary equivalents Clinton and Gingrich) has both reflected and inspired the views of economists. Neoclassical economists agree with Jefferson's notion that the government governs best which governs least. At the very most, Washington must confine itself to fine-tuning the overall economy by manipulating interest rates, taxes, and public spending. Taking Hamilton's view, political economists reply that not all industries, investors, or consumers have equal economic power, and thus Washington should target those which can best develop the economy.

The Neoclassical Economic Argument

The theoretical basis of neoclassical economics is really quite simple. It has evolved from the 1776 publication of Adam Smith's *Wealth of Nations*.[4] Smith argued that government must confine itself to defense, justice, and the "general welfare" while allowing entrepreneurs to supply goods and services demanded by the populace. When individuals are free to pursue their selfish ambitions, they inadvertently aid the entire society, a process Smith calls the "invisible hand."

David Ricardo's *Political Economy* (1819) expanded Smith's ideas with the concept of "comparative advantage" whereby states, like individuals, specialize in making or marketing those things which they can best make or market, and then trading those products for other things they need from other countries.[5] Ricardo's famous example to illustrate comparative advantage compared Britain and Portugal. Both countries could, with difficulty, produce enough sheep and grapes to satisfy their needs. Yet, Britain specializes in raising sheep and Portugal in cultivating grapes because those are the activities best suited to their respective climates. They then trade their surplus to each other. The freer the trade, the more each country can benefit from cheap and abundant products from the other. The composition of a nation's economy does not matter. As Michael Boskin, the former Reagan Council of Economic Advisors' Chair, put it, "I don't care whether America makes computer chips or potato chips."

Economists go so far as to laud America's mostly one-sided free trade policies whereby foreign firms can dump their products freely in the United States while the products of American firms are limited and sometimes completely shut out of foreign markets. They believe that if foreign firms dump their products in the United States and drive American firms into bankruptcy and workers into unemployment lines, the nation should write them a thank you note for providing American consumers with cheap products. Likewise, if a foreign government imposes trade barriers that block American exports to that market, it is only hurting the purchasing power of its own citizens. The last thing that Washington should do, the neoclassical economists warn, is to retaliate against foreign predatory industrial and trade policies. In effect, the economists advocate unilateral economic disarmament. If the United States deregulates its own markets, other countries may follow suit and those that do not only hurt themselves.

Classical economists like Smith and Ricardo were fatalistic about business cycles of growth and depression. As President Warren Harding put it in 1921, "There has been vast unemployment before and there will be again. There will be depression and inflation just as surely as the tides ebb and flow."[6] John Maynard Keynes disagreed. In his 1936 book *The General Theory of Employment, Interest, and Money*, he argued that business cycles could be smoothed out by government spending. Depressions were caused by low demand for goods and services. A government could stimulate a depressed economy by spending more and cutting taxes. Inflation occurs when there is too much demand for goods and services. Governments can curb inflation by cutting back their own spending and raising taxes.[7] Keynes gave a theoretical basis to Roosevelt's New Deal experiments designed to overcome the Great Depression. Every administration since Roosevelt's has accepted the "neoclassical economic" idea that the economy can be fine-tuned by manipulating government spending, taxes, and interest rates, although they have differed greatly on the relative merits of each means.

Critics blast classical and neoclassical economics alike on many grounds. The central criticism is that while the economists may use a scientific methodology, their theories find little basis in the real world. Adam Smith and David Ricardo devised their theories and assumptions during the agrarian age when industrialization was just beginning. Although since then industrialization has transformed the world, their followers have maintained the same assumptions. Robert Kuttner knocks those economists for whom "deductive reasoning tends to crowd out empirical inquiry.... Suggest that perhaps industrial policy does some good, and you might make the op-ed page of the *New York Times*, but you won't get tenure." Clyde Prestowitz, Alan Tonelson, and Robert Jerome point out that the neoclassical economists "are not stupid. But their faith has driven them to make the cardinal mistake of most zealots and ideologues: they assume that if their dogma does not accurately explain reality, then reality should change to fit their dogma." Or, as Laura Tyson succinctly asserts, "free trade is not necessarily and automatically the best policy."[8]

In the real world, it very much does matter what a nation produces. Ricardo developed his comparative advantage theory when Britain was largely an agrarian economy, hence his emphasis on natural resources endowments in determining specialization. This "static" conception of comparative advantage has recently been swept away by a "dynamic" one suited for the industrial and post-industrial worlds. In Ricardo's model, Portugal could not do much more with its grapes than press them into wine. Britain, however, could use its sheep not just for mutton but for wool with which to develop a textile industry. Over time, Britain would become much wealthier than Portugal because its range of industries and the wealth they produced was greater.

Neoclassical economists base their arguments on provocative theories. Yet, a theory's worth lies not in its cleverness but in its applicability. Is the neoclassical belief that the less government the more economic growth true? Not in the real world. Neoclassical economists cannot conceive of the idea that nations can benefit when they promote their industries to give them greater domestic or foreign market shares. The real-life practice and the frequent success of that practice discredits all the ideal assumptions that neoclassical economists hold so dear.

From America's independence to the Great Depression, the economy has expanded at an average rate of 1 percent a year. Throughout that period, depressions were deep, prolonged, and frequent. Since Roosevelt's New Deal, business cycles have been less erratic and recessions less frequent or severe. Washington's ever more sophisticated macroeconomic and industrial policies have clearly accelerated the nation's economic development and alleviated the duration and severity of its depressions. From 1854 to 1945, America experienced 58.3 percent (636 months) of economic expansion and 41.7 percent of contraction. From 1945 to 1991, the economy expanded for 470 months (82.9 percent) and contracted 97 months (17.1 percent).[9] Political economist Robert Reich states very clearly the reality:

> Every major industry in America is deeply involved with and dependent on government. The competitive position of every American firm is affected by government policy. No sharp distinction can validly be drawn between private and public sectors within this or any other industrialized country; the economic effects of public policies and corporate decisions are completely intertwined.[10]

The Political Economic Argument

To neoclassical economists, free markets are the economic ends and means for which we should all strive. Political economists have a completely different value system. Their goal is the national creation and distribution of wealth. The means to that end depend on circumstances, but always include rational policies that benefit the entire economy and those that target the most important sectors for development. More specifically, the government may provide or allow a targeted industry protection from foreign imports, export promotion, cartels, subsidies, tax relief, infrastructure, and other favors.

In his explanation, Chalmers Johnson focuses on industrial policy as a comprehensive, strategic plan for national development:

> Industrial policy means the initiation and coordination of governmental activities to leverage upward the productivity and competitiveness of the whole economy and of particular industries in it. Above all, positive industrial policy means the infusion of goal-oriented, strategic choices into public economic policy. It is the attempt by government to move beyond the broad aggregate and environmental concerns of monetary and fiscal policy. . . . At the very least it involves the understanding that in advanced industrial democracies, in which economies of scale alone dictate huge investments and the employment of thousands of individuals, changes of industrial structure are only poorly accomplished through the market mechanism. Equally to the point, in democracies the workings of the market are commonly preempted by political action. Rather than leaving such political interventions solely to pressure groups and other well-organized interests, industrial policy seeks to solve problems before they arise.[11]

Macroeconomic and industrial policies differ more in scope than kind. Every macroeconomic policy will benefit some economic groups and hurt others. For example, devaluing the nation's currency may help exporters while harming importers; a revaluation has the opposite effect. A tax system in which all contribute equally – however defined – has yet to be devised by any country. Every tax system has its relative winners and losers. Government spending aids those industries from which it buys. A rise in interest rates may boost bank profits but hit everyone else.

The justification for industrial policies is that they can develop a nation's economy far more rapidly than would otherwise have occurred. Government can provide the strategic outlook so often lacking in businesses. Few have explained this better or more succinctly than Sadanori Yamanaka, who headed Japan's Ministry of International Trade and Industry (MITI): "One of the most important functions of the state is to facilitate economic development and to enhance the popular welfare. Since industrial activity is the cornerstone of national economic development, all states practice a wide variety of industrial policies, albeit under different names and in different forms."[12]

At the industrial policy debate's heart lie conflicting conceptions of national security. Neoclassical economists take a narrow view of national security as resting on military forces. The government's proper role is to maintain a strong military force while leaving virtually everything else to marketplace magic. During the 1980s, by nearly tripling military spending and cutting back virtually all other government programs, the Reagan administration exemplified this ideal.

Political economists deride the neoclassical notion of national security as hopelessly naive. Instead, they assert that a military can only be as strong as the economy which feeds it. If the United States practices free trade while its competitors carefully manage their industrialization and trade, then America's national economic development will be shaped by foreign governments and corporations. In their book *Selling Our Security*, Martin and Susan Tolchin argue that Washington's unreciprocated free trade policies literally sell out American security in the form of technologies, firms, natural resources, laboratories, endowed university chairs, and even entire industries to the highest foreign bidders. The Tolchins write: "The ease of acquiring assets in a nation that refuses to differentiate between potato chips and computer chips virtually invites the rest of the world to snap up its choice industries."[13]

Societies are no longer condemned solely to exploit what nature provides them. The global trade system allows governments and entrepreneurs to create comparative advantage by buying raw materials from around the world and refining them into products. Under "strategic trade theory," a nation's goal is not freer trade but greater wealth. If trade barriers, industrial policies, and export promotion contribute to greater wealth, then governments are justified in using those means to that end.[14]

Strategic trade theory was inspired partly by the neomercantilist means Japan's political, bureaucratic, and corporate leaders used to transform their nation from a war-devastated, poverty-stricken country into an economic superpower. No country's industrial policies have been more successful than Japan's. Tokyo has nurtured an ever more technologically sophisticated set of industries into global champions. During the 1950s and 1960s, Tokyo concentrated on developing such heavy industries as steel, shipbuilding, and automobiles, and from the 1970s through today, high technology industries like microelectronics, aerospace, supercomputers, biotechnology, superconductors, to name the more prominent.

Neomercantilist policies provide domestic firms with scale economies of production which reduce prices and provide windfall profits which can be reinvested in research, development, and marketing, thus making their products ever more competitive. This simultaneously weakens and sometimes devastates foreign rivals which do not enjoy such protection. Profits that foreign firms could have realized in free trade accrue to those firms supported by neomercantilist policies.

The more expensive an industry's start-up costs, the more essential it is for that industry's survival quickly to achieve economies of scale and advance along the learning curve. For example, a plant producing the most advanced computer chips now costs $1 billion. An enormous and growing volume of semiconductors must be sold to begin to pay back such a huge investment. In such an industry with high start-up costs, steep learning curves, and rapid technological innovation, any firm that falls behind is doomed. Government protection is essential for investors to build and operate such factories. If the domestic market is not large enough to provide a satisfactory return, then capturing foreign markets is essential. Dumping is the best way to seize both domestic and foreign market share.

Do industrial policies work? As Laura Tyson puts it, "Industrial policy by itself is never a guarantee of an industry's success. Nor is the success of an industrial policy – with success defined as sustaining local production – any guarantee that the policy was economically rational or welfare improving."[15] For example, among the democratic industrial nations, none wield more systematic sets of industrial policies than Japan and France. Both Tokyo and Paris guide their economies with indicative five-year plans, promote strategic industries and technologies with the full range of possible measures, and forge close ties between bureaucratic, political, and corporate leaders. There are differences between Japanese and French industrial policies. Tokyo's policies have been far more successful than those of Paris in promoting and distributing wealth, and nurturing global corporate and industrial champions. While Japan has at least several huge, privately owned corporations in an industry, France usually has only one, and it is often government owned and a money loser.

While political economists evaluate an industrial policy on whether or not it works, neoclassical economists criticize America's industrial policies on ideological grounds. During the heady Reagan years, the Republican Party blasted any industrial policy advocates. For example, a Senate Republican task force on international trade in March 1984 bluntly concluded that "American industrial competitiveness will not be enhanced by additional government guidance or control."[16] Two months later, a House Republican technology committee issued a report which concluded that: "We believe that the proper role of government in promoting U.S. technological and industrial competitiveness is to 'target' the process by which new ideas and products are developed – the process of innovation. That is, our government should focus on creating an environment in which innovation, new ideas, and new companies are likely to flourish and in which firms in mature industries can modernize." In other words, government should stick to macroeconomics and avoid industrial policies. The report did concede that "every administration, including this one, has developed and implemented a vast and expensive array of specific, targeted aids to industry... [which] lie jumbled in an untidy and expensive heap for want of a strategy to harmonize them." Rather than provide that strategy, the Republicans instead called for sweeping away that untidy heap of policies.[17]

Setting aside such ideological assertions, political economists concede that industrial policies have two potential downsides. Protectionism may cause domestic prices to rise, which may hurt not only consumers but producers as well, whose high-priced components may make finished goods uncompetitive overseas. Another possibility, however unlikely, is that states may retaliate and a trade war could erupt as happened in the 1930s, which devastated everyone.

THIS BOOK'S THEMES

So what should be the government's role in the economy? Do free or managed markets best promote economic development? Who can best pick industrial winners and losers, the government or private sector?

This book attempts to answer those and related questions by exploring the evolution and results of federal policies toward a half-dozen economic sectors. Those policies are largely determined by the representatives of the targeted industry, bureaucrats from agencies and departments that administer that industry, and politicians who have firms from that industry in their districts. These "iron triangles" capture a "virtuous" political economic cycle in which they use their united power to grant themselves favorable policies, which in turn enhances their power. As will be seen, the results of such a politicized industrial policy process vary considerably from one industry to the next. Hamiltonians and Jeffersonians alike will find examples of industrial policies that fortify or besiege their assertions.

1 Steel and Automobiles: The Heavy Industrial Complex

No businessman in his or her right mind would favor a free market. For businessmen, the Darwinian "war of all against all" world of the genuinely free market can be "nasty, brutish, and short." The struggle to survive is incessant; business life expectancies are fleeting. The average small business in the United States has merely a one in ten chance of struggling beyond its fifth year.

Instead, businessmen savor monopolies in which they can sell exorbitantly priced products to captive consumers. The public be damned if they find the goods shoddy or inadequate for their needs. Or, if not a monopoly, a cozy oligopoly might do just as well. Oligopolies with price leaders provide the stability that allows production and prices to rise gradually over time.

More than most industries, steel and automobiles eschew free markets. Entry and maintenance costs are enormous. The roller-coaster business cycles of expansions followed by depressions that hurt nearly everyone in society, are particularly harsh for large-scale heavy industries like steel and automobiles with huge fixed costs in equipment, workers, and components. By mutual unspoken agreement, America's steel and automobile industries have been oligopolies for most of their respective histories. Ever since J. P. Morgan formed it in 1901, US Steel has been the industry's price leader. By the 1910s, Ford had turned its low-priced Model T into the industry standard, in the process bankrupting hundreds of small-scale car makers and forcing the survivors to match its prices. In the 1920s, General Motors surpassed Ford to become the industry's price leader, a position it has held ever since.

Few question the strategic importance of steel and automobiles to the American economy. Together they directly account for about 5 percent of the nation's jobs and wealth. More so, those two industrial giants are the dynamic hubs for scores of related raw material, intermediate, and finished products employing tens of millions of Americans and foreigners alike. Steel's strategic importance to the economy was evident as the nation began to industrialize in the early nineteenth century. Then, by the 1920s, steel's economic weight was eclipsed by that of the automobile industry. The saying "as steel goes, so goes the nation" could well have given way to, "as GM goes, so goes the nation," that was actually coined a generation later.

Both the steel and automobile industries have experienced similar cycles of catch-up to foreign rivals, global dominance, decline, and renaissance. Although steel and autos remain powerhouses of America's economy, in global terms both industries reached their summit around mid-century. American steel production was 36.8 percent, or more than one-third of global production in 1900, a percentage which peaked at 63.7 percent in 1945. That percentage steadily declined to 11.1 percent of global production by 1985, a percentage that had held consistent into the mid-1990s. Likewise, America's automobile industry was the world leader for several decades straddling the mid-century. In the early 1950s, Detroit produced 80 percent of the world's automobiles. But foreign rivals caught up in the 1970s. In 1980, Japan surpassed the United States in total automobile production. By the mid-1990s, Japan accounted for about half of the world's automobile production and the United States around one-quarter.[1]

How has Washington abetted or inhibited the development of America's steel and automobile industries? Despite those industries' strategic importance, Washington has mostly been hostile. Over the years, Washington has not hesitated to rattle its antitrust saber at both industries, particularly its price leaders US Steel and General Motors. Protective tariffs did shield steel and automobiles during their early decades. But after each industry had achieved global power, Washington lowered tariffs and allowed foreign firms the unreciprocated freedom to battle against America's steel and automobile giants in their home market. It was only when foreign dumping and trade barriers had battered both industries to the verge of collapse that Washington belatedly rode to the rescue of steel in the 1970s and automobiles in the 1980s.

As with most other American industries, Washington has no comprehensive development policies toward either steel or automobiles. Free market ideals and the government's role as referee rather than coach largely govern public policies toward those industries, regardless of their importance to the national economy or the devastating effects of foreign rivals nurtured by their own sets of rational industrial policies. Yet, at times, those industries have managed to wring benefits from Congress and the White House that tide them over bleak and prosperous times alike.

STEEL

America's iron and steel producers have sought protection from foreign competition and cooperation on prices, markets, and production among themselves ever since the nation's independence. For the most part, they have gotten what they have demanded.[2] When Congress first met under the new Constitution in 1789, iron and steel lobbyists were able to push through protective tariffs. Throughout the following decades of tariff tug-of-war between northern manufacturing and southern plantation interests, the budding iron and steel industry managed to retain high enough walls to avoid extinction by lower-cost foreign products. In 1855, producers formed the American Iron and Steel Association (AISA) to present an organized, united front in Washington to lobby for higher tariffs on iron and steel imports. The Union victory in the Civil War tipped the tariff balance toward the industry. Tariffs remained high for the rest of the nineteenth century and well into the next.

Despite these advantages, the iron and steel industry was not immune to the business cycle. In 1893, the economy plunged into a depression that lasted much of the decade. Industrialists responded by cutting prices and squeezing out more production, which in turn further depressed prices. Virtually all of the nation's production, from the largest corporation to the smallest farm, sold at a loss. Free markets were ruining the economy.

America's corporate elite tried various remedies to overcome the free market, combining in trusts, mergers, and cartels of various kinds to divvy up markets and maintain prices. During this era, no man had a more powerful hold over America's economy than J. P. Morgan who owned directly or indirectly hundreds of interlocking corporations and managed scores of industries. As he had for other troubled industries, Morgan addressed the structural depression in the steel industry by creating an oligopoly, led by his creation, the US Steel Corporation. Morgan established US Steel, America's first billion-dollar corporation, by welding together two-thirds of the nation's steel capacity and imposing financial and managerial wizard Elbert Gary on its throne.

Not only did Gary rule the corporation and lead the industry until his death in 1927, but his successors implemented his "managed competition" philosophy for another half-century. Few have spoken out as eloquently against free markets as Gary, who maintained that, "destructive competition is not reasonable, not desirable, and never beneficial in the long run to anyone."[3]

Despite its size, it took US Steel several years to assert its power as price leader. Gary first tried systematizing a base-point pricing scheme that had been used unsuccessfully over the previous decade. He made it work; gradually the other steel firms conformed to US Steel's guidance. Perhaps even more importantly, he encouraged exports. US Steel's exports tripled from $100 million in 1903 to $305 million in 1913, underwritten by yearly investments which averaged 16.5 percent of the firm's total revenue.[4] Exports disposed of excess production and relieved downward price pressures at home. But they also made America's steel-makers dependent on unstable foreign markets for an increasing share of their income and sometimes muscled onto turf jealously guarded by foreign steel-makers. Unfettered by a free market ideology, foreign governments had no compunction about subsidizing the exports of their steel industries or encasing domestic markets within tariff walls. But those development policies were not vital to the prosperity let alone survival of foreign steel-makers. America's steel workers enjoyed the highest wages of any steel industry anywhere, a price factor unrelieved by the industry's greater economies of scale. In all, American steel was more expensive than foreign steel.

Although, by the early twentieth century, America's steel industry had become the world's greatest producer, its supremacy rested on shaky foundations. In 1916, an industry spokesman admitted that "whether we retain this surpremacy will depend largely upon the efficiency of our merchandising and industrial organization and the cooperation of our Government with business."[5]

But the hoped-for government aid was not only lacking – the more rigidly the steel industry fell into line behind its leader, the more Washington opposed the oligopoly. Democratic and Republican administrations alike favored using antitrust laws to break up US Steel. This threat caused Gary to try a less overt means of managing markets than the base-price system. In 1908, he founded the American Iron and Steel Institute (AISI), thus superseding the AISA, which expired in 1912. Yet this move provoked rather than quelled those clamoring for an antitrust suit. In October 1911, President Taft authorized a Justice Department antitrust suit against US Steel in hopes of breaking up the behemoth into its original units. The suit dragged on until 1920 when the Supreme Court dismissed it in *United States* v. *United States Steel Corporation et al.* In 1924, a Federal Trade Commission suit did succeed in forcing the steel industry to abandon its base-point price-fixing system. The victory, however, was fleeting as the industry adopted a multiple-point based price-fixing system that seemed to evade antitrust laws.

American policy makers faced a terrible dilemma during the 1920s. The Senate's rejection of participation in the League of Nations revealed the strength of isolationism within the United States. Yet American prosperity depended on European prosperity. Not only did an increasing range of American industries depend on European markets for many of their sales, but the Europeans owed Americans billions of dollars. If Europe's economy did not revive, it could not afford to buy American products or remit interest on its debt to American financiers. The United States was locked in a debt circle in which the German inability to pay reparations to France and Britain meant that none of the three could pay back all they owed to the United States.

The Harding White House responded with the Dawes Plan of 1924 whereby the United States would loan Germany more money, with which it would repay its debts while France and Britain reduced the reparations burden on Germany. The plan overcame a repayments crisis that threatened to sink the sputtering global economy. But part of the American payments was invested in Europe's steel industry. In the short-run, Washington saved the global economy from collapse but at the expense of American steel producers.

In 1926, French, Belgian, and German steel-makers joined the International Steel Cartel, which divvied up global markets and tried to maintain price and production levels. Other European steel-makers joined over the next few years. Although the Great Depression broke up the cartel, it was revived in 1933 and by 1935 included France, Belgium, Germany, South Africa, Britain, Poland, Czechoslovakia, and steel-makers from several other nations.

In 1928, US Steel reacted to the International Steel Cartel by trying to build one of its own, the Steel Export Association (SEA), which was allowed under the 1918 Webb–Pomerene Act. But the American cartel simply could not compete with the international cartel in terms of industrial power. The Americans would eventually join the foreign cartel.

As if the foreign threat were not trouble enough, steel executives were confronted by an increasingly assertive workforce throughout the 1920s. The workers had lost a bitter strike in 1919, and were quiescent during the short depression of 1921 to 1922 when steel production plummeted to 35 percent of capacity. The steel industry responded to the depression with mass layoffs and twelve-hour, seven-day workweeks for the survivors. Work conditions got so bad that the laissez-faire Harding White House intervened on labor's behalf in 1922. By 1923, to keep peace in the industry during an expanding market, first US Steel and then most of the other firms agreed to an eight-hour day.

The 1929 stock market crash and subsequent Great Depression devastated the steel industry. The depression was compounded by the 1930 Smoot-Hawley Act whose tariff walls saved a diminishing domestic market for domestic steel producers, but at the price of prompting foreign governments to retaliate by locking American steel-makers out of those markets.

Aspects of President Roosevelt's New Deal helped revive the steel industry. The National Industrial Recovery Act (NIRA) allowed the steel industry, like all other sectors, to maintain an overt price and production cartel, overseen by the National Recovery Administration (NRA). Although the Supreme Court ruled the NIRA and NRA unconstitutional in 1935, the cartel unofficially continued. The Reciprocal Trade Act of 1934 authorized the President to negotiate trade treaties with other countries that included up to 50 percent reciprocal tariff reductions. The subsequent treaties helped American steel and other products back into foreign markets.

While steel executives lauded these policies, they condemned the 1935 passage of the National Labor Relations Act (NLRA), which ensured the right of workers to organize into unions and bargain collectively with management. In June 1936, John Lewis, the president of the United Mine Workers of America (UMWA), set up a Steel Workers Organizing Committee (SWOC) to unionize the industry. At first only US Steel recognized SWOC. In 1937, the Supreme Court upheld the NLRA in *United States* v. *Jones and Laughlin Steel Corporation.*

Meanwhile, assailed at home and abroad, in 1937, US Steel and Bethlehem Steel tried to convince the rest of America's steel-makers to adopt an "if you can't beat 'em, join 'em" stance toward the International Steel Cartel. America's industry was split over whether to join or not. Several smaller producers like Armco Steel and National Steel had invested in advanced production techniques and concentrated on speciality steels, which gave them a comparative advantage over foreign producers. Most of the industry, however, remained locked into high labor prices and inefficient open-hearth production techniques which made their prices uncompetitive. Most of America's steel-makers eventually joined the International Steel Cartel under an agreement which superficially appeared to be in accordance with the Webb–Pomerene Act but in fact violated it by allowing participants to set import and price levels.

In 1938, Congress set up a committee called the Temporary National Economic Committee to investigate abuses in the steel and other industries. Nothing came of it, however, as World War II broke out in Europe and threatened to engulf the United States. With threats looming across the Atlantic and Pacific, more than ever, the United States needed a powerful industrial base of which steel was the foundation. Instead of trying to break it up, Washington increased its subsidies to the industry and further loosened any remaining restrictions over the steel cartel. By 1940, US Steel enjoyed 40 percent of government subsidies to the industry, which allowed it to expand its market share that year from 34.1 percent to 41.3 percent.

As German blitzkriegs conquered western Europe in the summer of 1940 and Japan took over northern Indochina, Washington realized that encouraging domestic steel expansion through cartels, subsidies, and tax depreciation allowances would not be enough to meet the demands of global war. In late 1940, Washington embarked on a $1.07 billion program to build 15.2 million tons of steel capacity to be owned by the government's Defense Plant Corporation for the war's duration.[6]

When the Japanese attacked Pearl Harbor in December 1941, America's economy was largely prepared to wage war across both the Pacific and the Atlantic. A mere two years later in 1943, with victory clearly on the horizon, Washington began planning for reconversion. America's total steel capacity had risen from 81.6 million tons with 82.1 percent capacity in 1940 to 90.5 million with 98.1 percent capacity in 1943. Although capacity rose even higher to peak at 95.5 million tons in 1945, that year's utilization was only 72.5 percent as government orders sharply declined. Steel ingot production peaked in 1943 at 88.8 million tons, having risen from 66.9 million in 1940. It then dropped to 79.7 million in 1945. By 1945, the Allied powers alone had 138 million tons of steel capacity. Global demand in 1937 had been only 133.5 million tons. So even if all other steel-makers went bankrupt and global demand reverted to its former level, the former Allies would still have 4 million tons of overcapacity. Most observers forecast that the overcapacity would cause a devastating postwar depression.[7] Not just the steel sector was at risk. Depression haunted every economic sector, particularly the small businesses that lacked the capital and markets to survive a prolonged downturn.

The feared steel depression did not materialize. Pent up consumer demand exploded when the wartime wage, price, and rationing controls were lifted. In 1946 and 1947, while total steel capacity contracted slightly from 91.8 million tons to 91.2 million tons, utilization soared from 72.5 percent to 93.0 percent as the domestic economy expanded robustly and foreign orders poured in. The production of ingots soared from 66.6 million to 84.8 million tons.[8]

There were economic troubles. In late 1945 and throughout 1946, over 5,000 strikes affecting 4.5 million workers cost the economy over 116 million hours of lost work and untold wealth.[9] The most debilitating of these strikes hit the steel industry. With 750,000 members, the United Steel Workers of America was the nation's largest union. In November 1945, they voted to strike in January if management did not grant their demands for higher wages and benefits. Management was tempted to negotiate but first had to receive permission from the Office of Price Administration (OPA) for an increase in steel prices to pay for the concessions. The OPA rejected the steel industry's request for a $7 a ton increase in steel prices. Management then rejected the union's demands. The steel workers walked out in January 1946 in what became the worst strike until then in American history. In February, the OPA reluctantly agreed to a $5 per ton increase. Management then granted the union an eighteen and one-half cent an hour wage increase. By February 18, the workers were back in the mills.

But the damage had been done. That year's steel production dropped by 16 million tons at a time when demand had soared. And the White House's haste in giving in to the price hike encouraged workers in other industries to strike for higher wages. Although the OPA would close shop in November 1946, the yearly pattern in the steel industry would persist of union demands, management stonewalling, a strike, the president's jawboning for a deal, an eventual compromise increase in wages and benefits, and finally a steel price hike.

Convinced that the steel industry's collusion, strikes, and price increases were the core of the nation's economic problems, President Truman targeted it for reform. In August 1947, the Justice Department filed antitrust suits against the

AISI and 101 steel firms because of their continued practice of allocating precalculated steel freight charges. In 1948, the Supreme Court ruled against a base-point price system for the cement industry and prepared to hear the case of the Federal Trade Commission (FTC) against the steel industry. Faced with an inevitable defeat, the steel industry announced it would abandon the practice. That same year, the Commerce Department's Office of Industry Cooperation created a special steel committee with fifteen steel executives as members to investigate the industry and propose reforms. The committee eventually struck nineteen deals for the allocation of steel and pig iron production.

Meanwhile, as after World War I, Washington aided foreign steel-makers in Europe and Japan following World War II for the same reasons. American and global economic prosperity were interdependent; they rose and fell together. In 1945, American steel's productivity was so powerful that it could have wiped out the remnant of the steel industries in Europe and Japan, thus endangering those nations' recovery. If that was allowed to happen, while America's steel industry would reap more profits in the short-term, America's economy would inevitably suffer without robust overseas counterparts with growing demands for American goods and services.

America's industrial policy toward the European and Japanese economies and their steel industries was highly successful. The Marshall Plan eventually pumped into Western Europe's economy over $14 billion, of which hundreds of millions of dollars were invested directly into the steel industry. The $2.2 billion in American aid to Japan similarly rebuilt that nation's steel industry along with the rest of the economy. Although only a trickle of American steel had surmounted the import barriers protecting Europe and Japan before the war, Washington now encouraged rather than assailed those tariff and nontariff walls.

The European steel-makers soon reestablished their cartel and used it to capture markets around the world. In May 1951, representatives of France, Italy, Germany, Belgium, the Netherlands, and Luxembourg signed the Treaty of Paris, which established the European Coal and Steel Community (ECSC). Japan's steel industry also quickly revived.

About 82 percent of its open-hearth capacity and 87 percent of its rolling capacity survived the war. Japan's Ministry of International Trade and Industry (MITI) used American money and technical assistance, trade barriers, and cartels to nurture its steel industry into the world's most competitive by the 1960s. Altogether, between 1947 through 1960, Washington dispensed $1.411 billion in aid to steel industries in twenty-seven countries and the ECSC, of which the ECSC received $100 million and Japan $203.8 million. The actual aid to foreign steel-makers may have been closer to $2 billion.[10]

Washington's policy of building up rival foreign steel industries quickly damaged America's. The huge export markets the steel industry captured during the late 1930s through 1945 withered steadily after the war. And increasingly, foreign steel devoured larger shares within America itself. But that policy's self-destructiveness would not be evident until the late 1960s when foreign steel seriously threatened the domestic industry.

Throughout the late 1940s, the Truman Administration and the steel industry harshly debated how much steel production capacity the country needed, with the former advocating expansion and the latter reduction. The steel industry feared that investing in more production would lead to overcapacity, lost profits, and, for many, eventual bankruptcy.

The Korean War resolved this stand-off. In June 1950, communist North Korea invaded South Korea. President Truman forged an American-led alliance to defend South Korea. By November, China had joined North Korea. A bloody stalemate ensued. Washington provided the economic support for its forces through the Revenue and Defense Production Acts of November 1950, which allowed defense industries accelerated depreciation allowances for new investments in capacity. In addition, the Reconstruction Finance Corporation (RFC) provided low-interest loans for those investments. In December, Truman created an Office of Defense Mobilization to coordinate industrial production for the war.

The steel industry responded to these incentives. From its early postwar nadir of 91.2 million tons in 1947, America's steel capacity expanded steadily every year to peak at

148.5 million tons in 1960. Utilization, however, varied considerably during those years, from a peak of 100.9 percent in 1951 during the Korean War's height to a mere 60.6 percent in 1958 during that year's recession, strikes, and influx of foreign steel.[11]

In early 1952, as an armistice for the Korean War seemed more likely and price controls were eased, steel workers again demanded higher wages and benefits. When management refused to accept those demands, the workers struck. The strike threatened America's economy at a delicate time amidst the Korean War negotiations. On April 8, Truman ordered the government's seizure of the steel industry. The owners sued. On June 2, the Supreme Court ruled in the owners' favor. Truman reluctantly released the mills. On June 24, the steel strike was settled with higher wages and prices.

During the 1950s, American steel priced itself out of both foreign and domestic markets. Each year, the steel unions negotiated higher wages and benefits with management, whereupon, shortly thereafter management would announce higher steel prices. By 1959, steel wages were 28 percent higher than the manufacturing average. These steel price hikes contributed to 40 percent of the nation's inflation between 1947 and 1958.[12] Walter Adams asserts that the "persistent price escalation of steel prices during the 1950s was the primary cause for the industry's lackluster performance during the 1960s – resulting in the erosion of domestic markets by substitute materials and imports, the loss of export markets . . . and the decline in return of investment."[13]

Instead of increasing prices, the industry could have lowered costs by investing in more efficient steel-making methods that raised productivity. Unfortunately, they refused to do so. American steel-makers delayed modernization for decades, thus steadily undermining their international competitiveness. As late as 1946, 88.4 percent of American steel was produced with open-hearth casting, a century-old method. During the 1950s, while European and Japanese steel-makers invested heavily in the process, very few American investments were made in the continuous casting method in which steel was immediately cut into useful shapes, as opposed to the prevailing open casting method in which the steel was first molded into ingots, billets, and slabs, and only then, after cooling, reheating and processing, cut. Continuous casting saved enormous energy and labor costs. A related innovation was to use a basic oxygen furnace (BOF) in casting, which cut installation costs by 50 percent and operating costs by 10 percent over that of open-hearth furnaces. Despite these advantages, only two American steel firms invested in small BOF plants during the 1950s. By 1955, 87.8 percent of American steel still flowed from open-hearth furnaces.[14]

The steel industry offers several excuses for its failure to innovate. The cost advantages of continuous casting and BOF did not become apparent until the late 1950s; before then the risk seemed to exceed the potential benefits. Unlike its foreign rivals, which were heavily subsidized by both their own governments and the United States, America's steel industry lacked sufficient investment funds. Fearing that to acquire too much debt would make the industry vulnerable to downturns, the steel firms financed most of their investments from retained earnings – from 1946 through 1956, the steel industry borrowed only $1.5 billion of its $8.5 billion of investments. Furthermore, there seemed little reason to invest in any method – the industry already suffered from overcapacity, an evil which would have been worsened by new investments. When it did invest, it simply added to existing capacity (rounding out), which cost an average $100 per ton, rather than develop a greenfield site at anywhere from $300 to $400 a ton.[15]

To deepen the industry's troubles, diminishing domestic supplies and expanded global demand raised prices for all minerals involved in steel production. The price index for iron ore rose from 88.6 in 1947 to peak at 181.7 in 1957 before dropping slightly to 171.0 in 1960. That for coke rose steadily from 84.2 in 1947 to 170.4 in 1960. Ferro-manganese doubled from 90.6 to 189.4 in 1957 before dropping to 166.6 in 1960. Pig iron merely doubled from 83.6 in 1947 to level off at 163.0 from 1957 to 1960. The only constant was iron and steel scrap, whose price index fluctuated from 96.9 in 1947 to 82.9 in 1960 with a peak of 132.5 in 1956.[16]

America's iron-ore and other mineral fields became a liability rather than an asset to the steel industry. While sources of iron ore, coal, and limestone elsewhere in the world became relatively cheaper, most American steel producers remained dependent on domestic sources transported by rail to the smelters. Unfortunately, American ports were not equipped to handle the huge bulk carriers that helped bring down foreign iron-ore prices.[17] This raw-material price problem was particularly acute for midwestern steel-makers who suffered the diminishing supply and thus rising cost of Mesabi iron ore from the Great Lakes region. The St Lawrence Seaway would not open until 1958. Then, when it did open, ships conveyed not just cheaper foreign iron ore but cheaper foreign steel as well.

The industry was well aware of these problems but felt inhibited by antitrust laws from doing anything about them. Instead, it turned to Washington for help. In 1953, the AISI proposed a plan by which Washington and the industry could continue the coordination of investments, production, wages, prices, and markets that worked so well during the Korean War. The Eisenhower Administration spurned the plan. Historian Paul Tiffany explains why:

> Given the acknowledged significance of the steel industry to national security, one might well have believed that this sector would receive more favorable treatment at home. But just as a statist containment (i.e., the encouragement and underwriting of allied industrial policies) of international communism shaped Eisenhower's foreign policy, its antithesis – the protection and expansion of free-enterprise capitalism – sparked much of his domestic agenda. Under this contradictory regime, government could not step in to aid home industry no matter how vital (or how international) the industry's activities. Market forces were presumed to define domestic outcomes. Yet, at the same time, the benevolent hand of America's government was deemed justified in assisting foreign industry in such cooperative (and quasi-socialist) programs as the Schuman Plan. Eisenhower's adminstration remained strongly committed to this inconsistent ideology throughout his eight years in office. As such, the president must bear ultimate responsibility for the serious long-term dysfunctions he created for many industries, steel included.[18]

Instead of protecting industry, after taking office the Eisenhower Administration eliminated the industrial advisory committees, and wage and price controls, and reduced the depreciation allowances that had encouraged the industry's expansion. If the White House was merely indifferent, Congress was openly hostile to the steel industry. The Joint Economic Committee (JEC) began an investigation of steel price hikes in 1955. From 1957 through 1961, Tennessee Senator Estes Kefauver targeted steel for the first of a series of Antitrust and Monopoly Subcommittee investigations into price hikes and corruption in American industries. Kefauver's spotlight on corrupt industrial practices may have been magnified by the fact that he was the Democratic Party leader and aspirant for party presidential nominee in 1952, 1956, and 1960. The Subcommittee's report in 1958 castigated the industry for its price policies and recommended that the Justice Department launch its own investigation. The White House did not take the advice.

A 1959 steel strike challenged Eisenhower's laissez-faire policy toward the industry. In July, 511,000 steel workers walked out and would stay away for 116 days. In September, Eisenhower did meet separately at the White House with labor and management, to no avail. On October 19, he asked the Justice Department to file for an end to the strike under the provision of the Taft-Hartley Act, which allowed the president to call for an 80-day cooling off period. On November 5, the Supreme Court upheld Eisenhower's injunction and ordered the steel workers back to the mills. On January 4, 1960, labor and management agreed to a new round of wage and price increases.

The year 1959 was a watershed in the steel industry's history. That year, steel imports exceeded exports for the first time in the twentieth century. While the United States exported 1.677 million tons of steel, it imported 4.396 million tons, thus causing a 2.719 million ton deficit. The 116-day strike was primarily responsible for the trade deficit. American steel consumers were forced to buy from foreign rather than domestic producers. The previous year the United States had exported 2.823 million tons and imported only 1.707 million tons, for a 1.116 million ton surplus. Ever since 1959, the United States has suffered a trade deficit in steel. America's steel industry was clearly in decline. By 1960, America's percentage of global steel production had plummeted to 26.1 percent, from 46.6 percent in 1950 and 63.7 percent in 1945.[19]

Although American steel prices remained among the world's lowest, imports took an ever larger share of the domestic market from the 1960s through the 1980s. The reason was foreign dumping and Washington's failure to respond adequately to that assault. Foreign steel-makers were protected in their own markets, which allowed them to charge high prices to their own consumers. They used these windfall profits at home to subsidize their dumping of steel in America's vast, largely unprotected market. American steel producers could not afford to match the foreign steel prices and thus lost ever more market share.

Although the AISI had been pleading for protection for years, it was not until 1968 that Washington finally stepped in to help. By that year, the sustained dumping of Japanese and European steel in the United States had seized 12.2 percent of the market. President Johnson negotiated a "voluntary export restraint" (VER) that curtailed the Japanese and Europeans to specific quotas through 1974. The foreign steel-makers grudgingly followed the quotas for two years. Then, in 1970, the Japanese burst their quota by 13 percent and the Europeans by 9 percent, leading to a new round of negotiations and another VER. The quotas were critical for preventing a free fall in American steel production. By 1970, the United States produced only 20.1 percent, or one-fifth of global steel production.[20]

The rise in oil prices from $2.75 a barrel in 1973 to $34 a barrel by 1981 launched a succession of tidal waves through the global economy. The decade of low growth and high inflation particularly damaged steel and other natural resource-hungry industries. President Nixon's imposition of wage and price controls in 1974 simply postponed the inevitable time when the steel industry would suffer from higher raw materials prices and falling demand. By 1975, the global steel market had plunged into recession. Foreign steel-makers responded by dumping their steel to retain market share and reduce stockpiles. Japan's market share in the United States rose from 5 percent to 8 percent from 1976 to 1977 while Europe's share rose from 3 percent to 6 percent. Other foreign steel-makers from Romania, India, Brazil, South Africa, and elsewhere captured another 4 percent of the market. By 1977, the total foreign penetration of America's steel market was 18.1 percent.

America's beleaguered steel-makers had no recourse but to sue. In October 1976, the AISI responded to the influx of foreign steel with an anti-dumping petition against Japan and the European Community. Then in February 1977, Gilmore Steel filed its own petition against five Japanese producers. In September 1977, US Steel joined the fray with its own petition. In October the International Trade Commission (ITC) ruled in favor of the Gilmore petition after finding that the Japanese had dumped their steel at an average 32 percent below production costs. Meanwhile, five highly protectionist bills worked their way through Congress. Given all this pressure, the Carter administration finally established a task force in September 1977, led by Treasury Under-Secretary Anthony Solomon, to determine what should be done. In December, Solomon issued his task force's report, which criticized the anti-dumping procedures as too ponderous to be effective. Instead, Solomon recommended a trigger-price-mechanism (TPM) in which tariffs would be imposed when imported prices fell below a certain level. In April 1978, President Carter imposed the TPM in return for a steel industry agreement not to file any more anti-dumping petitions. The system worked. By the first quarter of 1979, the foreign share had dropped to 12.5 percent of America's steel market.

The respite from foreign dumping did not last long. In March 1980, US Steel filed a broad anti-dumping petition. The very same day US Steel filed its petition, the White House revoked TPM. As usual, Washington put America's geopolitical commitments ahead of its geoeconomic needs. US Steel's filing had followed a series of worsening international crises in 1979 which included the communist Sandinista revolution in Nicaragua, the Islamic revolution in Iran, and the Soviet invasion of Afghanistan. To manage these crises, the White House needed the full support of its European and Japanese allies. As it did throughout the Cold War, Washington bought its allies' tepid support at the expense of American industries.

Without TPM, foreign steel-market shares widened within the United States. Congress threatened to pass protectionist bills. In October 1980, on the national election's eve, Carter decided to reimpose the TPM. Once again, TPM reduced the foreign market share and deterred dumping. By April 1981, foreign shares had dropped from 18.5 to 15.2 percent while American steel firms were operating at 88.6 percent of capacity, the highest in a decade.

Unfortunately for America's steel industry, this revival was short-lived. Reagan's policy of a strong dollar and high interest rate policies devastated America's steel industry, along with scores of other industries. The high interest rates inhibited American firms from borrowing money for badly needed investments while the overvalued dollar gave foreign firms an enormous cost advantage. By December 1981, foreign steel had soared to capture a 23.7 percent market share. That fall, American steel firms closed 23 mills and laid off 50,000 workers.[21]

In November 1981, after months of intensive AISI lobbying, the Reagan White House reluctantly agreed to file anti-dumping petitions against foreign steel-makers. In January 1982, US Steel went much further, filing 132 countervailing duty and anti-dumping petitions. The White House responded by dropping TPM. In June 1982, the ITC found that foreign firms had been dumping in the United States. Rather than impose higher tariffs, the White House negotiated a VER which limited foreign steel to a 20 percent share in return for an abandonment of the dumping cases. In the short-term, Reagan's decisions to abandon TPM and its anti-dumping suits in return for a limited VER was a disaster for America's steel industry. As a result, from 1982 through 1986, the steel industry lost $12 billion, over twenty-five firms filed for bankruptcy, capacity dropped from 154 million tons to 112 million tons, employment dropped from 399,000 to 163,000, and capacity utilization averaged 65 percent (it plummeted to 48.4 percent in 1982, the lowest level since the Great Depression).[22]

After crippling the steel and other American industries through inane macroeconomic policies and the refusal to impose rational industrial policies, the Reagan White House inadvertently saved it through a reversal of its high dollar and interest rate policies. In 1985, the pragmatist Jim Baker took ideologue Don Regan's place as Treasury Department Chair. Baker negotiated the September 1985 Plaza Accord among the United States, Japan, Germany, France, and Britain (Group of Five) to devalue the dollar. In the two years between 1985 and 1987 the dollar's value against the yen was cut in half from 256 yen to 125 yen. Although the yen remained overvalued and Japan's trade surplus with the United States intractable, the Plaza Accord diminished significantly the huge price advantage Reaganomics had given Japanese and other foreign producers. American industries began their long road to recovery.

After two decades of bashing by Japanese and other foreign rivals, America's steel-makers scored an enormous comeback by the mid-1990s. In 1994, the industry earned $1 billion after suffering losses of $350 million the previous year. The industry operated at an extraordinary 97 percent of capacity in 1994 and 98 percent in 1995.[23]

Several long- and short-term factors contributed to American steel's turnaround. Had not Washington imposed import barriers and tough anti-dumping laws in the 1970s, the industry would not have survived the foreign steel onslaught. The Carter administration's TPM and VER deterred foreign dumping and restricted foreign market shares. Unfortunately, Reagan's TPM and 1984 VER were relatively ineffective because they were set at levels which did not deter or restrict foreign steel-makers. No administration to date has been successful in pressuring foreign governments to stop subsidizing their steel industries. American steel-makers remain handicapped because they lacked this key advantage that their foreign rivals enjoyed. Macroeconomic policies, particularly those affecting the dollar's value, have been quite as influential in helping or harming the steel industry along with the entire American economy. Just as the strong dollar of the early 1980s nearly wiped out America's steel industry, the weak dollar since then has been the most important reason for the industry's revival. Finally, international factors largely beyond Washington's control also helped the steel industry. The global oil glut from the mid-1980s combined with conservation measures steadily to reduce electricity costs. Between 1981 and 1993, the energy consumed by American steel mills for each ton shipped dropped from 30 million British Thermal Units (BTUs) to 19 million BTUs.

Although these policies saved the industry from destruction, only the steel producers themselves could recapture their past dynamism and competitiveness. The industry did so by ruthlessly cutting excess capacity and workers, and investing in the most advanced technologies. Between 1977 and 1987, 45 million tons of steel production capacity – the more inefficient, undercapitalized, and unimaginative steelmakers – went out of business, easing the competition somewhat for the remainder. During the 1980s, the survivors invested over $23 billion in the most modern equipment, all the while cutting costs. In 1980, only 20 percent of American steel plants employed the highly efficient continuous casting method; by 1994, 86 percent did. The industry has become increasingly specialized. Non-union mini-mills turn out speciality steel to fill market niches and pressure the larger unionized mills to further cut costs. Between 1953 and 1992, the number of steel-workers dropped from 650,000 to 175,000, reaping enormous savings for producers.

When the import restraints expired in 1992, America's producers were competitive enough to survive without them. Government protection for steel has not allowed the industry to reap windfall profits; in fact, since the mid-1980s, steel price increases have lagged about 20 percent below the consumer price index. The investments and cost-cutting resulted in steady productivity rises whereby the Americans eventually surpassed the Japanese and European manufacturers. In the early 1980s, it took about ten hours per worker to produce a ton of steel; by the early 1990s, a ton of steel took only half of that. In 1995, it took an American worker 4.42 hours to produce a ton of steel compared with 4.49 hours for a Japanese, 4.61 for a French worker, 4.69 hours for a German, or 4.71 for a British worker. As a result of all these factors, the cost of producing a ton of steel dropped from $650 in 1982 to $525 by 1992. In 1980, a ton of sheet metal used for cars cost $504; in 1989, it costs $440, a price that would have looked even cheaper if adjusted for inflation. Within a few years, a new generation of steel technology promises to plummet prices to as low as $250 a ton. Lower steel prices have helped stimulate demand in the 1990s, from 90 million tons in 1991 to 106 million in 1994. In the housing industry, steel has become competitive with lumber, whose costs have recently risen with logging restrictions. These cost savings, in turn, are enjoyed by any American industry that uses steel, making it more competitive in global markets.

A steel-maker from the 1950s would have trouble recognizing the steel industry today. Most workers operate computers in air-conditioned offices; only a fraction work in the blast furnaces. Steel plants are no longer located near coal and iron-ore deposits. Northern Indiana along Lake Michigan, however, remains a popular site for steel industry given its rail, trucking, and shipping transportation links, educated and skilled workforce, and relatively low state taxes. The bitter antagonism between management and labor that characterized the industry for decades have given way to cooperative, cordial relations. Labor has been more flexible in job classifications, hours, and benefits. They have had little choice; the steel industry's employment dropped from 550,000 in 1980 to 171,000 in 1994. Production has increasingly shifted away from the huge steel corporations to the mini-mills. In 1980, the five largest firms produced 60 percent of all domestic steel; in 1990, only 40 percent. Imports, meanwhile, peaked at 27 percent of the market in 1984 but have since dropped to about 17 percent. Exports reached their nadir in 1985 at around $1 billion but rose to 7.0 million tons in 1995. Despite the industry's newfound health, America still imported 24.4 million tons of steel that year. In all, American steel production was a $30 billion industry.[24]

Despite its recent dazzling comeback, America's steel industry still has some problems. Although it has laid off hundreds of thousands of redundant workers, the steel industry still has to pay pensions and health benefits. US Steel, for example, supports five retired workers for every one at its mills. Without a national health care system like those of other industrial countries, American industries must pay directly for their workers' health needs. This imposes an enormous competitive disadvantage. The average wages and benefits package for the industry in 1994 was $29.57 an hour. And, unfortunately, even though the United States is the low-cost steel producer, it still suffers a trade deficit with

Japan and the European Union. Nonetheless, the steel industry remains dynamic and fully prepared for the competitive battles of the twenty-first century.

AUTOMOBILES

What product is more intimately entwined with contemporary American culture than the automobile? For twentieth-century Americans, the automobile provides mobility and often status for a restless, largely rootless population. No nation anywhere has as high a proportion of car owners and as developed a road system as the United States.

It therefore comes as some surprise to Americans to learn that some past illustrious and ingenious citizen was not the first to invent the automobile. The concept is not new. Leonardo da Vinci and Roger Bacon predicted its coming. The Frenchman Nicholas Joseph Cugnot unveiled a steam-powered, three-wheeled vehicle in 1769. The Englishman Richard Trevithick produced his own version in 1801. It was only in 1805 that the American Oliver Evans ran a steam-powered, wheeled dredge through Philadephia's clogged streets. Between 1859 and 1895, Sylvester Roper built ten steam cars in Massachusetts. None of these inventions caught on. Nor did the Belgian Etienne Lenoir's two-cycle coal gas car in 1862 or German Nicholas Otto's four-cycle machine result in mass production. It was the Germans Karl Benz and Gottlieb Daimler who in 1885 produced the first successful internal combustion, gasoline-powered vehicle. But it was the Frenchman Armand Peugeot who marketed such a machine in 1889 and called it an "automobile." The name stuck.

During the 1890s, scores of tinkerers in Europe and eventually the United States began making automobiles. In 1893, Charles and Frank Duryea built the first American automobile in Springfield, Massachusetts. By the decade's end at least 30 entrepreneurs across the United States were turning out automobiles; during the twentieth century's first decade the number of automobile producers had risen to hundreds and perhaps thousands. By one account, in the century after 1893, over 1,900 firms have produced over 3,200 different models of internal combustion-driven vehicles.[25]

Early manufacturers were frequently wagon or bicycle makers (and at least one piano maker and another of sewing machines) who hooked up an engine, gears, and crankshaft to their contraptions. Engines often came from steamboat or locomotive manufacturers. Producers usually bought the parts on credit and sold the completed automobile for cash. Most of these businesses turned out a few expensive prototypes before going bankrupt. Henry Ford, for example, failed in his first two automobile enterprises before he firmly established Ford Motor Company in 1903.

What role did Washington play in the automobile's early history? At first, nothing of importance. In 1893, Washington created within the Agriculture Department the Office of Road Inquiry, the predecessor of today's Federal Highway Administration. The new agency's purpose was to improve rural roads, not for the new-fangled machines that most people had never heard of let alone seen, but for wagons hauling produce to market. That same year in a completely unrelated event, Bellefontaine, Ohio, laid America's first concrete street. Other towns and cities began paving their own streets.

Despite these efforts, the nation's road system remained primitive – only 200 miles of paved rural roads by 1900. Nonetheless, three years later, not one but three enterprising and adventurous entrepreneurs drove their cars from San Francisco to New York. The automobile was becoming a rich man's toy not merely for in-town jaunts but for bone-jarring cross-country journeys.

By World War I, the nation's most important manufacturers were concentrated in Detroit. Several factors combined to make Detroit the capital of automobile making. The hardwood forests of Michigan and iron-ore fields of Minnesota were nearby. Rail networks linked Detroit within a day of the midwest and northeast markets and days from the rest of the country. The city was filled with small manufacturers which could tool automobile parts. The banking system was sound and eager to invest in the promising new industry. And finally, fortuitously, Detroit produced a half-dozen tough, far-sighted entrepreneurs who quickly established their products, cooperated with each other, and bought out rivals across the country.

It was Henry Ford who converted a luxury plaything for the rich into an affordable means of transportation for the middle class. He did so by churning out thousands and then tens of thousands of automobiles via assembly-line production. The assembly line revolutionized production by bringing together product standardization, part interchangeability, speed, process synchronization, and scale economies for buying parts and producing the final product. Until Ford's innovation, automobiles were built in place with assembled parts. The process was slow and expensive. Before Ford marketed his Model T in 1908 with a sticker price of $600, the cheapest automobile cost around $1,000 and often rattled apart not long after hitting the road. Unlike most other automobiles, the Model T was dependable and its parts were readily available. Ford cranked out 12,292 Model Ts for $600 each in 1909, the first full year of production, and 260,720 for $490 each in 1914. In 1914, with millions of dollars pouring in, Ford could justify paying his workers five dollars a day, twice the average automobile wage.[26]

Washington regulated the early industry through existing patent and antitrust laws. The first official automobile association – the Association of Licensed Automobile Manufacturers (ALAM) – was formed in 1900 to administer a patent for a two-cycle engine. In 1909, Henry Ford sued ALAM for access to the patent, arguing that the association represented a technology cartel. He lost the first round but in 1911 won in the Circuit Court of Appeals, which granted him access to the patent. In 1915, the National Automobile Chamber of Commerce (NACC, today the Motor Vehicle Manufacturers Association) formed to manage patent cross-licensings and lobby Washington to change its laws to prevent ALAM-like patent cartels.

Ironically, while the foreign threat was a shadow of what it is today, Washington in those days did not hesitate to impose tariffs which reduced auto imports to no more than a trickle. During the industry's first five decades, America's auto makers enjoyed freedom from foreign competition by sheltering behind tariff walls of 30 to 45 percent from 1913 to 1922, 25 to 50 percent from 1922 to 1934, and 10 percent from 1934 to 1950.[27]

American participation in World War I temporarily stalled

the industry. In 1918, the War Industries Board ordered the automobile industry to cut production in half to free up raw materials for war production. But many producers received lucrative government contracts for producing trucks, aircraft engines, and other supplies.

During the 1920s, the industry shook out the over 160 automobile makers which had existed as recently as 1919. The 1920–21 depression bankrupted scores of those small companies as orders plummeted. By the mid-decade, there were a mere two score of producers, of which General Motors, Ford, and Chrysler dominated. Under Alfred Sloan's leadership, General Motors had leapfrogged Ford to become the nation's largest producer by innovating the multiple-division corporation which produced an array of prices and styles of automobiles. General Motors was essentially a coalition of five autonomous manufacturers, each of which was responsible for designing, producing, and marketing its own automobiles. Ford responded by dropping the Model T's price to $290. By the time Ford turned out its last Model T in 1927, it had produced 15,007,003 of them. But a more affluent and discriminating public increasingly preferred enhanced style and power in an automobile, even if it meant paying more. "Planned obsolescence" in quality and style ensured a steady stream of buyers. Throughout the 1920s, Ford simply got a smaller share of an expanding market. The industry turned out 1,116,119 automobiles in 1921 and 5,337,087 or nearly five times more in 1929. The year of the New York stock market crash, one of every six American families owned an automobile. An increasing percentage of these were bought on credit. During the 1920s, American car makers began building automobiles in Canada, Europe, and Japan. By 1929, foreign car sales contributed 11 percent to the American car makers' total revenues.[28]

The Federal Highway Act of 1921 attempted to facilitate the automobile industry by constructing cross-country two-lane highways. After Washington designated a route, it negotiated with the states for right-of-way and construction costs in which they split the bill fifty–fifty. States began imposing a one or two cent tax on gasoline and used the revenues to pay for highway construction. The system fed itself – the more traffic, the more revenues, the more roads, the more traffic, and so on. During the 1920s, the federal, state, and local governments together spent about $2 billion annually on road construction.

The 1929 stock market crash and subsequent Great Depression devastated America's automobile industry as it did all other economic sectors. By the mid-1930s, the twenty-three automobile makers of 1929 had withered to a dozen, of which the "Big Three" controlled 85 to 90 percent of the market. From 1929 through 1933, vehicle production dropped from 5.0 million to 1.3 million, employment from 447,448 to 243,614, and weekly wages from $35.14 to $20.[29]

Elements of President Franklin Roosevelt's New Deal helped maintain the survivors in the automobile industry. The National Industrial Recovery Act (NIRA) of 1933 allowed manufacturers in all industries to form price cartels and allowed workers a minimal wage, set work hours and conditions, and the right to bargain collectively. The NACC administered the automobile cartel. Ever the maverick, Henry Ford refused to join his corporation with the cartel. Although the government could have prosecuted Ford for noncompliance, it turned a blind eye to his defiance, not wishing to make him a political martyr when so much of the New Deal remained controversial and tenuous. In any event, Ford would have had little to fear – in 1935, the Supreme Court ruled the NIRA illegal.

The most successful manufacturers had nation-wide chains of dealers. In 1938, the Federal Trade Commission investigated a complaint by the National Automobile Dealers Association that manufacturers restrained trade by requiring them to sell automobiles at fixed prices. Nothing came of the investigation. A similar investigation in 1942, however, resulted in the FTC ordering General Motors to stop requiring its dealers to sell only its products. Dealers were more successful in getting states to pass laws preventing auto makers from arbitrarily locating and terminating dealerships.

Perhaps the most important federal impact on the automobile industry was the National Labor Relations or Wagner-Connery Act of 1936, which legalized trade unions, reinforced by the Fair Labor Standards Act of 1938. In the decades until then, the American Federation of Labor (AFL) had made several unsuccessful attempts to organize the industry, but company thugs had literally beaten down the efforts. In 1936, the AFL chartered the United Auto Workers (UAW), which then went to the Council for Industrial Organizations (CIO) when the latter split off that year. Under the leadership of Homer Martin, and Walter and Victor Reuther, the UAW scored rapid gains by instituting "sit down" strikes whereby the workers simply stepped away from their tools and machines within the factory. In 1937, General Motors was the first to accept the UAW; all other companies soon followed except, predictably, Ford. Over the next few years, the widely publicized beatings of UAW representatives, including Walter Reuther, by Ford assailants cost the company sales and prestige. In 1941, the National Labor Relations Board intervened in a bitter strike at Ford, which not long after grudgingly accepted the UAW.

Under federal guidance, the automobile industry made an enormous contribution to winning World War II. In 1940 and 1941, Roosevelt established the National Defense Advisory Council (NDAC) and Office of Production Management (OPM), respectively, to coordinate war production. In 1941, the OPM asked the automobile industry to reduce production by 20 percent to free those resources for military goods. In December 1941, the OPM organized the Automobile Manufacturers Association into the Automotive Council for War Production, which was in turn composed of twelve divisions: (1) machine and tool equipment; (2) tooling information; (3) contracts; (4) aircraft engines; (5) airframes; (6) ammunition; (7) artillery; (8) small arms; (9) marine equipment; (10) military vehicles; (11) propellers; (12) tanks and tank parts. By the war's end, Washington had invested $29.986 billion in the automobile industry to build products in all twelve areas, including 2.5 million trucks, 660,000 jeeps, 450,000 aircraft engines, and 170,000 marine engines. These automobile industry contributions, however, were only fractions of the total. For example, the $11.216 billion worth of aircraft, aircraft subassemblies, and parts produced by the automobile industry was only 38.7 percent of the total produced by the United States. Even more surprisingly, the $3.808 billion worth of tanks and parts turned out by the automobile industry was only 13.1 percent of the total.[30]

In October 1944, the Office of War Mobilization and Reconversion was created to ease the economy's transition from war to peace. The Automotive Council for War Production set up a Contract Termination Committee to manage the industry's transformation. In May 1945, the War Production Board authorized the production of 100,000 automobiles, in contrast to the mere 139 made in 1943 and 610 made in 1944.[31]

The autoworkers launched a strike in 1945–46 that lasted 113 days. Although General Motors stonewalled the UAW until its strike funds expired, it was clear that it would eventually have to concede on union demands. Two years later in 1948, the industry did give in to UAW demands for wage increases tied to inflation or cost of living adjustment (COLA) and a forty-hour week. In 1949, Ford agreed to a minimum retirement income, a standard which was soon accepted throughout the industry. In 1955, Ford led the way again with a deal to contribute to federal unemployment benefits. Each year between 1948 and 1982, the unions received greater wages and benefits.

By 1955, the Big Three held 90 percent of the domestic market, which represented 80 percent of global automobile sales. In America's market, General Motors took about 50 percent, Ford 27 percent, and Chrysler 17 percent, while American Motors, Studebaker-Packard, and foreign imports fought over the remaining 6 percent. The pattern would hold for another decade. General Motors had the manufacturing clout to bankrupt its competitors. Antitrust laws, however, checked the behemoth's power. The Justice Department harassed General Motors throughout the 1950s, forcing it to divest itself of such partly or wholly owned subsidiaries as Euclid, Bendix, Greyhound, Hertz, North American Aviation, and National City lines. In 1957, the Supreme Court issued an antitrust ruling against Dupont and ordered it to divest itself of its 23 percent share of General Motors stock. (The FTC did not just pick on General Motors; in 1968 it ordered that Ford divest itself of the Electric Autolite Company it had purchased in 1961, a ruling upheld by the Supreme Court in 1973.) Unable to enjoy true monopoly power, General Motors instead served as the oligopoly's price leader. It was Charles Wilson, the former

General Motors president, who in 1953 at his Senate confirmation hearings to become Defense Secretary declared, "I have always believed that what's good for the country is good for General Motors, and vice versa."

Washington did more than occasionally rattle its antitrust saber to maintain a healthy, competitive industry. In 1956, Congress passed the Interstate Highway Act, which created a Highway Trust Fund to finance construction. As with similar legislation after World War I, the new act boosted not just the automobile industry but the national economy by uniting markets with interstate highways and stimulating local employment.

During the 1960s and early 1970s, the Big Three's hegemony over America's automobile market was slowly eaten away by imports, first by Germany's Volkswagen and then by Japanese corporations which specialized in small cars. The Big Three tried to compete by introducing their own small cars, but none of them established the cachet that imports enjoyed. By 1973, foreign imports had seized 15 percent of the market.

Ironically, as in steel and a host of other industries, Washington had helped develop the Japanese and other foreign firms as rivals to America's automobile industry.[31] Ford and General Motors first established assembly plants in Japan in 1925 and 1927, respectively, and quickly captured 90 percent of the market and threatened to wipe out Japan's manufacturers. Tokyo, however, was determined to create a competitive domestic automobile industry. It subsidized Japanese corporations, discriminated against American auto makers, and eventually nationalized them outright in 1939. During America's Occupation of Japan (1945–52), Washington conspired with Tokyo to build up Japan's automobile industry with subsidies, cartels, import barriers, and export incentives. If America's auto makers had been allowed to sell freely in Japan after the war, they would have succeeded in wiping out Japan's weak automobile industry and enjoying that vast and growing market for themselves forever after. The subsequent history of American and Japanese economic development, and their trade and investment relationship, would be completely different. Unfortunately for American wealth and power, that did not happen.

Other policies hobbled America's automobile industry in international competition. Starting in the 1950s and continuing through the 1970s, Washington issued sets of regulations which eventually encompassed all aspects of the automobile industry. The Dealers' Day in Court Act of 1956 allowed sellers to negotiate their own deals with buyers. Previously, dealers had had to accept the manufacturers' prices. Henceforth, prices had to be clearly posted, broken down, and suggested rather than mandatory.

As America's cities sprawled across the landscape and hundreds of millions of vehicles clogged the nation's roads, smog became an increasingly severe problem. California was the first state to address the issue seriously. In 1960, Sacramento required all automobiles sold in the state to maintain minimal emission standards. In 1963, Congress responded to growing public support for anti-pollution laws with the Motor Vehicle Air Pollution Control Act, followed up in 1965 with emission standards based on California's of no more than 275 parts per million (ppm) of hydrocarbons and 1.5 ppm of carbon monoxide. Washington then asserted a national responsibility for fighting pollution under the Air Quality Act of 1967, although it allowed states like California to impose even tougher standards. The new standards were 220 ppm for hydrocarbons and 2.3 ppm for carbon monoxide. In 1970, Washington not only passed the Clean Air Act, which set even stricter air quality controls, it created the Environmental Protection Agency (EPA) to enforce anti-pollution laws.

During the 1960s, growing numbers of Americans became concerned about safety issues. In 1962, in the face of fierce Big Three lobbying, New York passed a law requiring cars sold in the state to install seatbelts. Ralph Nadar's 1965 book *Unsafe at Any Speed*, documenting the danger of driving General Motors' Corvair, galvanized national support for more stringent automobile safety regulations. Congress responded in 1966 with the National Traffic and Motor Vehicle Safety Act, which set national standards for the first time. The Transportation Department and National Highway Safety Administration administered the law. The regulations yearly saved thousands of lives and billions of dollars in related costs.

The industry responded to these anti-pollution and safety challenges in a predictable pattern: "First, industry spokesmen denied that the problem existed; they then conceded that it did exist but asserted that it had no solution; finally, they conceded that it could be solved but that the solution would be very expensive, difficult to apply, and require a long time to develop."[33] Reviled as those regulations were by the industry and free market ideologues, they worked wonders in reducing the damage, costs, deaths and injuries from automobile pollution and crashes. Thus the economy developed and more wealth was created than would have occurred without those regulations.

The quadrupling of oil prices by the Organization of Petroleum Exporting Countries (OPEC) in 1973–74, and further doubling in 1979–80, set off a decade of stagflation in the United States and around the world. Congress responded to the oil crisis with several laws. In 1974, it set the interstate highway speed limit at 55 miles per hour, an action that saved lives as well as fuel. The Energy Policy and Conservation Act of 1975 set a company average fuel economy (CAFE) standard which required every car manufacturer to achieve a minimum average of 27.5 miles per gallon for its automobile fleet by 1985. The EPA was charged with enforcing it.

The rise in oil prices devastated America's automobile industry. The popularity of big "gas guzzling" American cars plunged. Unable to produce a small, fuel-efficient car which could compete with Japanese imports, the Big Three saw their share drop from 84.6 percent to 73.1 between 1973 and 1980 while the share of mostly Japanese imports soared from 15.4 percent in 1973 to 26.9. In 1980, the Big Three lost $4.3 billion; Chrysler teetered at bankruptcy's brink. Auto makers closed a score of plants in that and preceding years; hundreds of thousands of American autoworkers found themselves on the streets. That same year Japan surpassed the United States as the world's largest auto maker.

In an unprecedented action, Chrysler asked Washington for a bail-out. The request set off a bitter debate, with most economists denouncing any government guarantee of loans to Chrysler as a "socialistic" sullying of markets, while most political economists argued for such a guarantee to a strategic firm in a strategic industry. The Carter administration was as split as Congress over the issue. In 1979, Congress finally passed and Carter signed the Chrysler Loan Guarantee Act, which enabled Chrysler to raise $1.5 billion in desperately needed loans. The decision may have violated economic theory, but it helped develop America's economy and create more wealth. Chrysler used the guarantee to borrow enough money to overcome its difficulties. Today, Chrysler is a model of corporate dynamism and success.

That same year, Ford and the UAW asked the International Trade Commission (ITC) for a different kind of relief, a relief from the tidal wave of Japanese imports that threatened to destroy America's automobile industry. The plaintiffs filed for import relief under Section 201 of the 1974 Trade Act. The ITC investigated the petition and rejected their plea, ruling that "although the U.S. automobile industry had suffered severe injury, foreign automobile imports were not a substantial cause of this injury."[34]

Although unable to secure protection for their home market, American car and car-part manufacturers pressed Washington to open Japan's markets, arguing that the Japanese subsidized their sales in the United States by closed markets at home within which they gouged Japanese consumers. In 1979, the Carter White House took up the cause. After months of bitter negotiations, Tokyo finally agreed in 1980 to eliminate tariffs on 38 automobile-part categories. But the promise was meaningless since the Japanese simply excluded imports by informal cartels. Meanwhile, the Carter Administration rejected automobile industry requests for special tax reductions to spur investments.[35]

Throughout 1980 and into 1981, pressure was building within Congress to retaliate against Japanese automobile dumping and import barriers. Senators Lloyd Bensten (D-Texas) and John Danforth (R-Missouri) introduced a bill that would have imposed tariffs on foreign manufacturers which annually sold over 100,000 automobiles in the United States.

To head off this threat to foreign imports, the Reagan White House began negotiations with Tokyo over a voluntary import restraint (VER) on automobiles. On May 1, 1981, Tokyo agreed to limit its exports to the United States at 1.68 million vehicles for each of the next three years. In

1984, Tokyo raised the level to 1.8 million. In agreeing to the deal, the Reagan Administration naively played into Japanese hands.

As in other industries, Japan's strategy in automobiles has been simple yet devastatingly effective. First, develop the industry through cartels, import barriers, and government-provided subsidies, infrastructure, and tax allowances. Then, begin exporting low-cost autos to the United States and elsewhere to increase economies of scale and market power. When foreign auto makers and their governments protest, stonewall for as long as possible before making symbolic concessions. Fourthly, begin building auto assembly and parts factories overseas to jump any quota and tariff walls and counter complaints about unemployment, and build a powerful lobby group in Washington and the state capitals. Finally, march upscale through midsize, luxury, and sport models to dominate the industry.

Ironically, the United Auto Workers encouraged the Japanese to invest in the United States. The Japanese happily complied. A strengthening yen and wage increases had raised the cost of automobile production in Japan. Opening plants in the United States would finesse the existing quota and the threat of higher tariffs on imports. Greenfield sites with non-union labor would keep down costs. American workers would simply assemble parts made in Japan. Throughout the 1980s, Japan's automobile makers all opened or expanded assembly plants in the United States. Although Japanese vehicles built in the United States have captured about 10 percent of the market, only 3 percent of the United Auto Workers' 900,000 members are from Japanese owned factories.

Desperate for jobs and revenues, the states also played Japan's game as they competed with each other to attract new investments. In doing so, they often ended up giving away a wealth of public assets to Japanese automobile corporations in return for opening plants in their state. Tax holidays that can last a decade and infrastructure are among the benefits states can shower on investors. These give-aways can hurt national interests in several ways. Foreign investors have benefited enormously from state investment policies. Foreign free trade zones in the United States number over 200. Most of them are used by automobile assembly and parts plants. The foreign car manufacturers that set up factories in those zones enjoy advantages denied to their American rivals.

Nonetheless, the Japanese import quota gave the Big Three a vital breathing space which they used to revitalize themselves. In 1982, management and the UAW struck a historic deal whereby the latter agreed to a two-and-a-half-year wage freeze, the postponement of COLAs, and the elimination of paid days off. In return, management promised to guarantee the pensions of workers with fifteen or more years' service and shelved plans to eliminate some obsolete factories. In 1984, in return for a $1 billion employment security fund, the UAW moderated its wage and benefit demands despite massive industry profits, recognizing the need for management to retool the industry. These settlements saved the industry tens of billions of dollars, much of which was invested into productivity.[36]

The Big Three have redoubled their production and marketing efforts overseas. Ford and General Motors had first ventured into foreign markets in the 1920s; Chrysler did not do so until the 1950s. They also strengthened their joint ventures and investments with Japanese and other foreign auto makers: General Motors with Toyota, Isuzu, and Suzuki, Ford with Mazda, and Chrysler with Mitsubishi. Each of the Big Three imports Japanese-made cars under a Detroit label. Most of these are small cars that the Big Three cannot profitably make themselves. Thus by importing rather than fighting them, they get a small take of Japan's profits in return for a minimal investment.

The most controversial tie-up between an American and a Japanese firm occurred in 1984 when General Motors and Toyota announced plans to create a joint venture called New United Motors Manufacturing, Inc. (NUMMI), which would build and operate an assembly plant in Fremont, California. Chrysler protested that the joint venture violated antitrust laws. After investigating, the FTC negotiated an agreement whereby NUMMI could produce no more than 240,000 automobiles annually and would dissolve after twelve years. Ironically, the FTC has outlawed any similar joint ventures between American firms.

Despite its joint ventures with Japanese firms, the industry remains bitterly opposed to Japanese protectionism and dumping, none more so than Chrysler and the UAW. In the early 1980s, Chrysler lobbied the White House and Congress for a tax on Japanese imports equal to the $1,750 in tax revenues that American-made autos contributed in employees' and manufacturers' taxes to federal, state, and local taxes. It also touted consumer tax credits for automobiles made in the United States. Finally, Chrysler called for the creation of a US Trade Policy Council composed of corporate and union executives to rally against foreign rivals. Neither Congress nor the White House took up any of Chrysler's proposals. Meanwhile, the UAW advocated a Fair Practices in Automotive Products Act, which would have required all domestic and foreign manufacturers annually selling more than 100,000 vehicles in the United States to buy or build at least 10 percent of the car's value there, with an additional 10 percent added for every additional 100,000 units sold, up to 90 percent for manufacturers selling 900,000 or more vehicles. Although the House approved versions of this bill in 1982 and 1983, the efforts died in the Senate. Even if the bill had passed, Reagan would most likely have vetoed it.

Meanwhile, the Reagan Administration followed other policies that at best had a mixed effect on America's automobile industry. The corporate average fuel efficiency (CAFE) standard is currently 27.5 miles per gallon. The CAFE inadvertently helps America's car industry by requiring that any car included in the fleet have 75 percent domestic content. The Big Three, thus, must produce small cars in the United States that they would otherwise have conceded to foreign producers. The penalty for noncompliance is calculated by multiplying each tenth of a mile per gallon over the standard by the number of automobiles in the fleet, then multiplying that by $5. In 1985, the Reagan White House allowed Ford and General Motors a one-year reprieve from the requirement when the companies complained that they could not comply. Chrysler protested that the Reagan decision penalized it for complying with the law, while promoting Ford and General Motors for violating it. The White House ignored Chrysler's arguments.

The Reagan White House's strong-dollar policy from 1981 to 1985 devastated the automobile industry as it did so many other American businesses. It was not until Treasury Secretary Jim Baker abandoned the strong dollar policy in 1985 that America's automobile and other industries experienced some relief. The yen doubled in value in the late 1980s, easing the pounding of American car makers by Japanese producers.

Unfortunately, the high dollar's devastation had been wrought. Since 1980, Japan has remained the world's largest auto maker. From 1970 to 1980, the share of Japanese cars sold overseas rose from 20 percent to 55 percent, and has since risen to 65 percent. Today, about one in three cars sold in the United States is made in Japan or by an affiliate in the United States. Japan's automobile lobby in Washington has enormous and growing clout – more than enough to derail any significant retaliatory measures proposed in the White House or Congress.

Despite these dazzling successes, Japan's auto makers must struggle with some problems. As the yen has tripled in value over a decade, from 265 in 1985 to 85 in 1995, before receding to 110 in 1996, automobiles made in Japan have lost their competitive advantage. Japan's auto makers seem to be locked politically into no more than one-third of America's market, while their domestic market has been stagnant for years. The Big Three have revitalized themselves, and have recently enjoyed record profits and slowly growing market shares.

Despite the persistent vehicle and parts trade deficit with Japan, by the early 1990s, America's automobile makers had restored their profitability and dynamism. In 1992, America's automobile producers became more cost effective than their Japanese rivals. The direct costs of producing a small car were $5,415 for Ford, $5,841 for Chrysler, and $7,205 for GM, compared with $6,216 for Toyota, $6,618 for Honda, $6,782 for Nissan, and $6,826 for Mazda. Despite the plunge among the Big Three's workforce from 623,133 in 1985 to 442,708 in 1995, wages made up a greater and parts a lesser cost for American producers. This was a remarkable turnaround from the early 1980s when the Japanese could produce a small car for $1,500 to $2,500 less than the

Americans.[37] In 1994, Ford surpassed all its rivals to produce five of the eight most popular models in the United States.

Did the cost advantage affect trade between the two countries? Unfortunately for the United States, no. In 1994, Japan's trade surplus with the United States reached $65.7 billion, of which automobiles and auto parts made up $45 billion! That year, 15,086,637 new vehicles were sold in the United States, of which 8,993,679 were automobiles and 6,909,958 were light trucks. Almost a quarter of these were Japanese – Japan's share edged upward to 23.3 percent of America's car and light-truck market while the Big Three dipped to 73.2 percent. General Motors accounted for 33.3 percent of the 15.1 million vehicles sold in the United States, followed by Ford's 25.2 percent share, Chrysler's 14.6 percent, Toyota's 7.2 percent, Honda's 5.2 percent, Nissan's 5.1 percent, Mazda's 2.5 percent, Mitsubishi's 1.5 percent, Hyundai's 0.8 percent, and Isuzu's 0.8 percent. The European automakers had a 2.6 percent sliver, up slightly, and the South Koreans a minute 0.9 percent. Every tenth of a point represented 15,000 sales. When the number of Japanese cars sold under American label is included, Japan's actual share of the market soars to over 30 percent. As much as 9.5 percent of Chrysler's sales, 2.7 percent of GM's, and 2.2 percent of Ford's are vehicles made by foreign producers.[38]

In stark contrast, in 1993, the Big Three sold only 19,335 vehicles in Japan, less than 1 percent of the market, compared with the 1.5 million vehicles Japan's producers either exported to or produced in the United States, accounting for a 30 percent overall market share. As with other Japanese industries, Tokyo protects the automobile industry in a variety of ways. Tokyo itself imposes severe barriers in the form of taxes and strict unit inspections of each vehicle, which holds up mass sales and thus increases each vehicle's cost. Customs officials in the United States and elsewhere approve automobiles by the shipload. Tokyo encourages its automobile makers to squeeze out any foreign competition through distribution cartels. While Tokyo claims that dealers are free to sell whatever cars they want, in reality, the dealers are locked into exclusive distributorships with Japan's producers.[39]

Nonetheless, decades of American and European pressure have caused Tokyo to allow a greater foreign automobile market share. Of 2,000 Japanese automobile dealers, the number selling foreign vehicles rose from 85 in 1988 to 530 in 1994. Most of these dealers simply displayed a token foreign car or two while continuing to vigorously sell the Japanese makes. In 1993, foreign-produced models took an 8.6 percent sliver of the market. However, many of those "imports" were produced by Japanese automakers in the United States and elsewhere and hardly qualify as foreign.

Neither Presidents Bush nor Clinton succeeded in their respective well-publicized and strenuous attempts to open Japan's automobile market. In February 1992, after months of negotiations, Tokyo promised to double its import of American-made auto parts from $10 billion in 1990 to $19 billion in 1994, and raise the domestic content of Japanese vehicles built in the United States to 70 percent from what it claimed was then 50 percent. Those knowledgeable about Japan scoffed at the promise. In 1992, there were over 300 Japanese parts makers operating in the United States with new plants opening weekly. It is the Japanese producers who will enjoy the greater "exports" to Japan. Those Japanese producers would have probably sold more anyway. Since the yen has more than doubled in value since the mid 1980s, the United States has become a relatively low-cost manufacturing country.

In 1992, bills were introduced in committee that would have required the President to negotiate a deal limiting not only Japanese exports but sales of Japanese vehicles built in the United States. Ford, Chrysler, and the United Auto Workers supported the law; GM opposed it, fearing it would encourage other countries to close their own markets. The bill died.

From 1993 through 1994, the Clinton Administration engaged Tokyo in a series of negotiations designed to break down Japan's automobile cartels. These negotiations fanned animosities among Americans and Japanese alike, but failed to open Japan's markets. As in other negotiations, Tokyo stonewalled the negotiations with repeated claims that its markets were the world's most open and that the Americans did not sell more because their products were inferior and they did not try hard enough. It was only after the White House threatened sanctions that Tokyo promised to open its "open" markets. But the Japanese never fulfilled any of their promises.

Those who favored reciprocal trade relations and government support for the nation's economic development were encouraged when Bill Clinton won the presidency in November 1992. On April 28, 1993, the Big Three's presidents asked the Clinton White House for the government's help in regaining global preeminence, including measures on trade, technology, health costs, and regulations. In addition to the President, the heads of virtually every department and agency dealing with industry were present. Clinton promised to study the issue and put together a policy.

A half-year later, on September 29, 1993, President Clinton, Vice President Al Gore, and the presidents of the Big Three automobile makers announced that they would jointly develop a five-person automobile that will get 65 miles to the gallon, accelerate from zero to 55 miles an hour within twelve seconds, cause minimal pollution, and will be affordably priced, within a decade. The details have yet to be worked out. It remains unclear whether the Big Three are to develop the model together or each their own prototype. Regardless, they will share information and technology to minimize any costly research and development duplications.

The joint venture was part of an overall Clinton policy of converting government laboratories from developing weapons to consumer goods. Under the supervision of the Advanced Research Projects Agency (ARPA), the laboratories can contribute super-strong light-weight materials, super-efficient motors, virtual design and prototyping, and advanced capacitators which store electricity, a spin-off of Reagan's Star Wars program.

The realization of such an automobile could be an enormous boost not just to the Big Three but to consumers. The average car burns 500 gallons of gasoline a year. Gasoline prices are currently cheap but will inevitably go up as global supplies dwindle. A car that burns two-thirds less gasoline would give its owner significant savings, along with lessening America's dependence on imported oil and alleviating pollution problems.

The Clinton policy represented a profound break with Washington's past practices of propping up the automobile industry with one hand and slapping it down with the other. Democratic Representative Sander Levin explained that for the automobile industry, "We've never had any kind of Government strategy. We're now moving toward a comprehensive plan rather than a piecemeal approach."[40] In words inimical to classical economists, Vice President Gore justified the Clinton Administration's breakthrough policy in terms usually reserved for the space program or nuclear weapons: "We have a strategic interest as a nation in meeting the goal we've set in this program. It's an act of patriotism but also an act of good business sense because I predict this will result in breakthroughs that are likely to position our American auto industry to dominate the growing world market in the next century."[41]

LEGACY

Few industries match the strategic importance of steel and automobiles. Washington's policies have helped and hindered both industries. Despite two centuries of steel making and a century of automobile making in the United States, neither industry yet enjoys a comprehensive government policy which nurtures its development. Politics rather than grand strategy continues to plague federal policies toward steel and automobiles.

What more could Washington have done for either industry? In the case of steel, Paul Tiffany argues, nothing, given the ideological and political constraints of all policy making:

> from 1910 onward there is no question of the significance of the steel industry to national economic welfare; this was clearly and consistently recognized by public officials, company leaders, and spokespersons for other concerned constituencies. Yet . . . nothing of substance ever developed to improve matters. . . . Proponents for an industrial policy in steel do not sufficiently address the historical framework of institutional relations in this area nor do they

appear to appreciate the deeply embedded culture of distrust that has long animated the involved parties.[42]

The same is true of Washington's failure to address systematically problems with the automobile industry. UAW head Doug Fraser could have been speaking for nearly any American industry when he declared:

> Government involvement is essential to help the industry become competitive. Contrast our auto industry with those of Germany and Japan. Governments there plan what will happen to their industries. We don't and we are hurt by it. . . . We have had inadequate fiscal actions and disastrous monetary policies, the wrong energy program, and an international trade posture which increasingly leaves our industries at the mercy of other governmental designs.[43]

The reason for this policy disarray was nicely captured by Reagan White House Office of Management and Budget (OMB) head Bob Bedell: "We see no more reason for the government to be involved with the auto industry, than for it to be involved with the grocery industry."[44]

For the steel, automobile, and other industries bashed by foreign imports and shut out of foreign markets, the most significant legal weapon has been to file anti-dumping petitions with the International Trade Commission (ITC). The process is ponderously slow; the ITC takes an average thirteen months to decide a case. Then, in 95 percent of cases, the ITC throws out the petition. According to the ITC criteria, selling goods below production costs is not enough to evoke penalties; victims of dumping must prove they have suffered "material injury." The investigators must base their findings on production and price information provided by the foreign firms. Needless to say, foreign governments and industries are less than forthcoming in providing incriminating evidence of their aggression. While the investigation is proceeding, dumped imports continue to batter the American industry. In the rare event that the ITC rules in the industry's favor, the case then goes to the Commerce Department for final approval. And then, even if the Commerce Department gives its blessing, the penalties imposed on the predatory foreign firms are rarely more than a financial slap on the wrist. The rare and meager retaliation hardly seems worth the enormous time and cost invested in a petition.

Washington has refused to use tariffs in retaliation against Japanese neomercantilism except in one area, light trucks. Light truck imports to the United States suffer a 25 percent tariff. Ironically, the tariff was originally imposed in retaliation for European rather than Japanese neomercantilism. In 1962, the Kennedy Administration raised the rate when the European Community refused to import more American chickens – the so-called "chicken war." Chickens are hardly a strategic industry, but their growers are a powerful lobby. Though unexpected at the time, the tariff's effect since then has been at once to save America's light truck production and to raise federal revenues. Such are the rather bizarre quirks of American industrial policy.

The antitrust laws which govern today's economy were written over a century ago when the United States was relatively free from the adverse effects of foreign trade. Perversely, the same antitrust laws which prevent domestic steel or automobile producers from working together allow them to form alliances with foreign producers to compete against other American firms. This gives foreign producers an enormous competitive advantage. Japanese automobile firms, for example, can play one American firm off against the others by offering joint production, marketing, or technology deals. Antitrust laws even prevent American producers from pooling their resources to comply with federal safety and environmental regulations. Instead, enormous resources are wasted in regulatory compliance through duplicated efforts.

At times, Washington has actually conducted industrial policies for foreign steel and automobile producers which it denied American industries. Following both world wars, Washington actually subsidized the reconstruction of foreign steel and automobile industries. It was in America's broad national interests to do so. The steel and automobile industries were the backbone of Europe's and Japan's economies. World trade could not revive if America's competitors did not revive. Thus in the short-run it made sense for Washington to help its competitors with subsidies and the toleration of trade and investment barriers in those countries – essentially an industrial policy which favored foreign rather than American producers. Unfortunately for the latter, Washington failed to insist that a level industrial and trade-policy playing field prevail once those foreign industries had revived.

Washington's macroeconomic policies have had just as diverse effects on the two industries. Both industries are sensitive to interest rate shifts and the dollar's value. Those industries are hurt when interest rates and the dollar rise, and helped when they fall. Likewise, shifting tax policies over depreciation allowances, investment credits, and "loss-carry-forwards" have also lightened or worsened those industries' woes. No administration's macroeconomic policies have been more destructive to the steel and automobile industries than the Reagan Administration's high interest rate and strong-dollar policies. Those policies devastated domestic steel and automobile producers by giving their foreign rivals an enormous cost advantage all around the world while discouraging domestic industry investments.

Overall, Washington's contradictory and inconsistent macroeconomic, industrial, and trade policies have helped more than they have hurt America's steel and automobile industries. And today, those two industries have recovered from the devastation wrought on them by Reaganomics to become global leaders in quality and price. Unfortunately, the recent comparative advantage of steel and automobiles has not regained for them the global market dominance they once enjoyed. But perhaps the Clinton White House or some future administration will insist on world-wide level market playing fields for those two industries. If so, American steel and automobiles will once again become global leaders.

2 Banks and Stocks: The Financial Industrial Complex

Money is the lubricant of any modern economy – too little, and the economy stalls, too much, and its prices overflow. A lack of money characterized America's first three centuries. Coin was always scarce. Tobacco leaves and wampum during the early colonial era and banknotes during the early republican era were the primary mediums of exchange. Although "greenbacks" appeared briefly during the Civil War, the United States did not even have a standard national currency until the early twentieth century. All along, neither the government nor the banks could raise enough money to feed entrepreneurial demands. Uncertainty over unregulated financial markets undoubtedly led millions of Americans to squirrel away their savings in cookie jars rather than bank vaults. The scarce supply of finance kept interest rates high and borrowers limited. Entrepreneurs who hoped to build canals, railroads, or factories had to look abroad for much of their capital. Foreign investors tended to spirit their profits overseas rather than spend or save it within the United States, leaving America all the poorer.

The reason for this lack of hard money and resulting economic stagnation was quite simple. For most of American history until the early twentieth century, banking was a free-for-all in which fraud, corruption, and bankruptcies were frequent. The federal government sporadically attempted to impose some degree of order on the financial world. Americans tried and rejected the First (1802–11) and Second (1816–36) National Banks. Politics and ideology rather than economic reason killed off both. It was largely the states which chartered and, to varying degrees, regulated banks. Regulations varied from none to reserve requirements against deposits. States demanded the right to control or free their own banks, then often whined for relief from Washington

57

when bankruptcies wiped out their finance. If banks were at best lightly regulated, the federal and state governments largely left stock markets and insurance to market whims.

It was only after the third and longest-lasting national bank, the Federal Reserve, was created in 1914 that the supply of currency began to meet the demand, and order began to be imposed on the market chaos. Even then, the Federal Reserve was unable to prevent the 1929 stock market crash and subsequent depression. Most banks were not a safe place to deposit money until the 1934 Glass-Steagall Act and 1935 Securities and Exchange Act asserted government oversight and regulations on the system. Then, after two generations of relative stability and steady growth, in the late 1970s and 1980s Washington caved in to deregulation demands. The result was the savings and loan and banking crises of the late 1980s, which may eventually exact from the economy a half-trillion dollars in direct and indirect costs.

From the earliest days to the present, laissez-faire attitudes toward finance have retarded America's economic development. The myth that "free markets" cure all ills and satisfy all needs has afflicted the financial industry just as severely as any other sector. In reality, there were never purely "free" financial markets. Government and private finance have always been symbiotically linked; as one developed so did the other. Government regulation has expanded in response to industry demands as well as market failures. Most of the very regulations that many business leaders so deplore were enacted to protect not just consumers but also the managers of capital. This chapter analyzes the development of that relationship between government and private institutions and policies which has shaped the financial system.

THE FINANCIAL SYSTEM'S DEVELOPMENT

During the seventeenth century, wampum, or strings of tiny purple and white beads made of shells, was the standard currency for New England and most of the mid-Atlantic colonies. Wampum's value depended on the local supply. The rarer purple shells were generally worth two of the more common white ones. From America's earliest days, governments regulated wampum and other currencies. Connecticut, for example, in 1645 set a penny's value at three purple, and six white shells. Scoundrels abounded even in those simpler times. White and Indian counterfeiters alike dyed white shells purple and passed them off. By the early eighteenth century, wampum had been largely replaced by more abundant coins, but it had served its purpose.

Other materials served as money when coin was scarce. The average deerskin, or buck, was worth about a dollar. Beaver pelts varied considerably in value but were solid currencies. Tobacco of varying weights and qualities also served as legal tender. What circulated was not tobacco itself but the receipts for what its owners stored in another's warehouse. Corn receipts served the same purpose on a smaller scale.

These "currencies" served their immediate purpose, but the lack of coin inhibited colonial development. The scarcity of currency was one reason that only six business corporations were formed before the Revolution. Of the six, one was an insurance company and the others were trading firms. Two nonprofit organizations were also incorporated, of which one was an insurance company and the other the New York Chamber of Commerce.

In 1652, Massachusetts opened what would be the only colonial mint. The mint melted down silver bullion or plate into shillings and three- and six-cent pennies, all stamped with the image of a pine tree. King James II revoked Massachusetts' charter in 1684 and the mint was forced to close. Although Virginia's original charter also allowed it to coin money, for lack of silver no mint was ever opened.

Not just English pounds, shillings, and pence, but a wide range of currencies circulated through the colonial economy including most commonly Spanish, Portuguese, and Dutch coins. Starved for currency, the colonies attracted coins by offering more of their goods in exchange for them. The competitive devaluation of their products simultaneously depressed the value of their goods for British investors and tax revenues for Parliament. Neither a Royal Proclamation nor subsequent Act of 1708 setting a maximum rate for Spanish dollars at six shillings, however, was effective in curbing the devaluations.

Another important reason for the scarce coinage was the persistent trade deficits of the thirteen colonies with Britain and most other realms. Each colony, of course, had its own shifting trade account. The northern and middle colonies generally suffered deficits while the southern colonies mostly enjoyed surpluses or at least balances. Parliament annulled various colonial attempts to nurture infant industries behind high tariff walls. Likewise, the navigation and enumeration laws restricted the colonists' ability to trade freely. By the Revolution, the colonies owed Britain over $28 million.[1]

The financial astuteness of the colonial governments varied considerably. As today, the colonial governments competed with businesses for scarce funds to finance their duties and ambitions. Taxes on imports and land were common, and some governments for a while taxed exports and even income. But these sources were often not enough to meet expenditures. Government debt rose sharply when colonial legislatures attempted to fulfill their military obligations to the Crown during the various wars against the French and Indians.

One way to pay off their debts was to print money. For example, in 1690, during the King William's War, Massachusetts printed 7,000 pounds sterling worth of certificates and gave them to various creditors; it issued an additional 33,000 pounds sterling of certificates the following year. Other legislatures issued their own certificates.

"Land banks" were another source of income for colonial legislatures. The government would issue notes to towns and counties, which in turn loaned them to entrepreneurs against their land's value. The typical issue was valued from 50 to 500 pounds sterling and had to be repaid at 4 percent interest within five years. The governments tended to overissue these notes, which in turn depreciated them. In 1730, London ruled that no colonial legislature could issue more than 30,000 pounds worth of notes a year.

Boston and Philadelphia merchants also experimented with paper money. After all, it was only a small step from the corn or tobacco receipts circulating to printing paper money. In 1733, a group of Boston entrepreneurs pooled enough coin, land, and other commodities upon which to issue 110,000 pounds sterling worth of notes, to be redeemable after a decade, in silver, at 19 shillings to the ounce. The notes disappeared from circulation after silver rose to 27 shillings per ounce. In 1741, another group of Boston investors raised enough resources to issue 150,000 pounds sterling worth of notes. The bank was successful until, in 1751, Parliament extended the 1719 Bubble Act forbidding issues of credit to New England and thus forced it to close. Similar schemes elsewhere failed for a variety of reasons. In 1764, Parliament extended the credit ban to governments and merchants alike in all thirteen colonies. By this time, paper certificates composed as much as about 60 percent of the $12 million worth of currency then circulating.[2]

During the late seventeenth and early eighteenth centuries, some entrepreneurs raised money with lotteries. Although the legislatures eventually banned the private lotteries, some issued their own lotteries to fund special projects, particularly colleges. Yale, King's College (Columbia), Harvard, Academy and Charitable School of Philadelphia (University of Pennsylvania), Princeton, and Dartmouth all owe their origins to lotteries.

None of the financial demands of the French and Indian wars prepared the colonial governments or Continental Congress for the War of Independence. Congress had no power to levy taxes, but could simply request that the states donate necessary funds in proportion to their populations. Overwhelmed by their own financial needs and sometimes British occupation, the states contributed little or nothing.

Congress tried raising funds by opening loan offices in the states, but received only about $11 million in return for the certificates. Congress was more successful in securing foreign loans, mostly from France, Holland, and Spain. Most of these loans and occasional grants came either directly from or through Paris. But these funds were not enough.

By necessity, Congress created America's banking system. Financing the government and war had proved overwhelming to Congress's Board of Treasury. In 1780, Congress established the Bank of Pennsylvania to handle the foreign loans. In May 1781, Congress chartered America's first full-fledged commercial bank, the Bank of North America, or National Bank as it came to be known, and contributed $254,000 to its initial $400,000 subscription. The National

Bank proved a good investment for Congress; eventually private investors bought out the government's shares at a premium. Yet even these banks could raise no more than a pittance toward the war effort.

The only recourse was to print money. In 1775, Congress's Board of Treasury issued $6 million of non-interest bearing notes to be redeemed between 1779 and 1786. Expenses soared along with inflation. Congress issued another $19 million of notes in 1776 but expenses rose ever faster. An issue of $13 million in 1777 was followed by one of $63 million in 1778. Meanwhile, the states issued their own notes, an amount which would eventually exceed $200 million. The result was hyperinflation. By 1780, notes had fallen to less than 2 percent of their printed value, inspiring the expression, "not worth a Continental."

The states and Congress tried to dampen the hyperinflation by several means. The New England states held a convention at Providence in December 1776 in which they agreed to impose price controls over a list of goods and wages, higher taxes, and limited issues of paper money. A second price convention was held at Hartford in January 1778. In September 1779, Congress declared that no more than $200 million could circulate. Congress called for a price convention of all the states, at Philadelphia in 1780. None of these conventions or declarations successfully reined in the hyperinflation. Congress would not heed its own limit; by the time of the Treaty of Paris in 1783, it had issued $240 million!

The Articles of Confederation adopted in 1781 granted the new government little more power to raise revenue than that of the Continental Congress. A common treasury would be funded by levies imposed on the states according to their respective populations. Only Congress was allowed to coin money and regulate its value. Congress could also borrow money, provided at least nine states agreed.

Yet the coinage shortage continued long after independence. In 1786, Congress set the silver dollar's value at 375.64 grains of fine silver and the gold dollar's value at 15.253, for a ratio of gold to silver of 1 to 15.253. Unable to afford the metals, the Confederation never actually minted any silver or gold coins, but confined its issues to several tons of copper cents and half cents.

The issue of state debts and tariff power inspired the Constitutional Convention. Neither the Continental Congress nor Articles of Confederation had granted Congress the power to levy tariffs. Each state determined its own tariff rates. In 1785, the states agreed to a Congressional request that they allow Congress the power to levy a 5 percent duty on certain imports. But that amount was simply not enough to finance the government. In September 1786, delegates from Virginia, New York, New Jersey, Pennsylvania, and Delaware met at Annapolis to discuss the tariff, trade, and debt issues. Realizing that delegates from every state were necessary for any reform proposals to be accepted, they agreed to convene a general convention at Philadelphia the following year.

For four hot, contentious months from May to September 1787, as many as fifty-five delegates from twelve states debated what kind of government to give the United States. The result was a series of ingenious compromises that have governed the United States for over two centuries. Among the most important duties of the federal government was that concerning economic policy. The United States Constitution empowers Congress to "lay and collect taxes, duties, imposts, and excises, and to pay the debts . . . of the United States . . . all duties, imposts, and excises shall be uniform throughout the United States." In addition, only Congress could "coin Money, regulate the Value thereof, and of foreign Coin," while the states were forbidden to "coin Money; emit Bills of Credit; make any Thing but gold and silver Coin a Tender in Payment of Debts." But it limited federal direct taxation in proportion to the population rather than income. One could argue that a financial policy allowed the Constitution's ratification. Those favoring a federal government essentially bought out those who preferred the confederation by promising that the central government would take over all the states' debts.

When George Washington took office in April 1789 the nation was ill-equipped to raise enough money to finance the government's operations, let alone pay off the national debt. Eventually, the government employed a variety of means to finance itself. Tariffs became an increasingly vital source of revenue. On July 4, 1789, Congress passed its first tariff law, which established varying levies on different imports to balance northern manufacturing demands for protection, the agrarian south's demands for free trade, and the government's need for revenue. In 1792, Hamilton issued his "Report on Manufacturers," which called for higher protective tariffs to nurture a range of infant industries. Congress responded with higher tariffs. Sales of public lands also contributed to federal revenues. The Land Ordinance of 1785 and Northwest Ordinance of 1787 established the prices and conditions for public land sales. Excise taxes were the most controversial source of revenue. In 1791, Congress levied a 25 cent per gallon tax on whiskey made from foreign goods and 18 cents per gallon from domestic goods. The tax sparked the Whiskey Rebellion in western Pennsylvania in 1793–94, which was only crushed with a federal army led by George Washington. The hated tax was repealed in 1802 after tariff revenues rose high enough to cover it.

In 1790, the United States had only four banks, which collectively could not begin to meet the need for public and private finance. In addition to the National Bank and Bank of Pennsylvania founded by Congress, were the Bank of New York and Bank of Massachusetts established by state charters. Private banks proliferated from the four of 1790 to peak at 90 in 1811 on the eve of the 1812 War as most states had either no or few restrictions on banks, loans, or reserves. In addition to chartering banks, states could encourage the pooling of capital by chartering business corporations. Most early corporations were organized to build toll bridges, roads, and canals.

In December 1790, Treasury Secretary Hamilton issued his "Report on a National Bank," in which he argued that a genuine central bank was vital for reducing the national debt and stimulating economic development. The issue split the nation's political leaders between "federalists" like Hamilton, John Adams, and George Washington, who favored the bank, and "republicans" like Thomas Jefferson and James Madison who feared it would give the national government too much power and was unconstitutional.

After a bitter and prolonged debate, Congress approved a bill creating the First National Bank; Washington signed it into law on February 25, 1791. The First Bank was capital-

ized at $10 million, of which the government would sub-
scribe one-fifth. Stockholders would vote in proportion to
their shares to elect twenty-five directors. Nonresident share-
holders could not vote. Interest was limited to 6 percent,
the Bank could not buy any public debt nor lend the federal or any one state government more than $100,000 un-
less Congress authorized it to do otherwise. The Bank's public
stock was offered in July 1791 and sold out within an hour.
Its headquarters were in Philadelphia while branches were
eventually opened in eight other cities.

The First Bank's most important duty was to service the
national debt. The total national debt in 1793 was about
$75 million, which amounted to less than $20 for each of
the country's 4 million citizens. Of the total, $18.3 million
was in state debts that the federal government assumed in
1793 in return for federal certificates, which received interest
rates of 6 to 3 percent. Of the $10 million foreign debt,
about $6.4 million was owed to France, $3.3 million to
Holland, and $174,000 to Spain.

Although, between 1790 and 1800, 20 percent of all federal government revenue went to paying off the debt, because of accumulating interest the total debt had actually
risen to $83 million. When Albert Gallatin became Treasury
Secretary in 1800, he submitted a plan to reduce the debt
by $38 million over eight years by cutting government ex-
penses, reducing excise taxes on whiskey and salt, and raising tariffs. Gallatin succeeded in reducing the national debt
to $57 million in 1808 despite the $15 million Louisiana
purchase and 1807 embargo.

The new nation also needed a national currency. In 1791,
Congress accepted a Hamilton proposal that the bimetallic
currency standard of 15 to 1 ratio between silver and gold
be maintained, and that no foreign coins be used as legal
tender three years after the first coins were minted. The
coins began to be produced in 1794, but never in a quantity that supplied the nation's financial needs. Persistent trade
deficits and interest on foreign debts steadily drained money
from the United States. To help relieve the shortage, in
1797, Washington allowed Spanish dollars to continue to
be used as legal tender. Coins remained in short supply;
most loans were made with notes rather than coins.

Despite the higher tariff rates, trade and revenues expanded steadily between 1790 and 1807. Then, in 1807, President Jefferson imposed a trade embargo in retaliation for the continued British search and seizure of American sailors and even ships which were supplying France during the Napoleonic wars. By the end of 1808, exports had dropped by 80 percent and imports by 50 percent. By 1814, imports were only 10 percent of their 1807 peak. Tariff revenues plunged accordingly, to the nadir of $6 million in 1814.

As if the embargo's blow to American trade and government revenues was not bad enough, opposition grew against the First Bank. Although Jefferson had eventually seen the wisdom in having a National Bank, other prominent politicians such as Henry Clay and George Clinton, and businessmen like John Jacob Astor, vociferously opposed the bank. When the Bank's charter came up for renewal in 1811, Congress voted it down by one vote in each house. Many who had voted against the bank soon saw the folly of their decision. The result was a financial disaster. With the First Bank's restraining hand on the nation's financial markets lifted, the number of banks shot up from 90 in 1811 to 250 in 1816. Fraud and bankruptcy rose even higher. The Treasury had to deposit its money in private banks. The Banks' stocks and deposits were redeemed. Branches were sold off. All told, the country suffered a severe self-inflicted financial wound on the eve of war with Britain.

When Congress boldly declared war on Britain in June 1812, its financial resources for fulfilling its commitment were meager indeed. The 1807 embargo had deprived the government of enormous revenue. The 1811 decision to destroy the First Bank tossed away what little influence Washington had over the nation's budding financial markets. Higher excise taxes contributed little to the Treasury, and were vastly unpopular, particularly in New England, which had already suffered enormous losses from the embargo. A proposed income tax was deemed unconstitutional; Congress could only levy a national tax by assessing the states on their relative populations. To finance its unpopular war, Washington reverted to borrowing. The Treasury Department worked with a group of prominent New York and Philadelphia bankers to sell $93 million of bonds through 1815, thus boosting the national debt to $132 million.

By 1816, with the war over, the nation's leaders could address a problem that had become increasingly obvious over the previous five years – the nation's need for a central bank. Ironically, the Jeffersonian Republicans championed the Second Bank while the Hamiltonian Federalists resisted. Politics explains the reversal. The Federalist minority feared a Second Bank could solidify the power of the Republican president, James Monroe, and a majority for his party in Congress.

The Second Bank was much stronger than the First Bank. The charter allowed the Second Bank to operate for twenty years and capitalized it with $35 million; Washington would again own 20 percent of its stock. With its headquarters in Philadelphia, twenty-five branches were eventually opened. As with the First Bank, the Second Bank was subscribed shortly after its stock was publicly offered. Although foreigners were allowed to own shares – they would eventually own one-fourth of the total – they could not vote.

Within two years of its birth, the Second Bank successfully resisted a severe challenge to its authority. When Maryland tried to impose a $25,000 tax on any bank operating without a state charter, the Second Bank sued. In *McCulloch* v. *Maryland*, the Supreme Court struck down Maryland's tax law. In explaining the Court's unanimous opinion, Supreme Court Justice John Marshall maintained that "the power to tax was the power to destroy," and no state could destroy a federal institution. The decision was a significant shift in the power balance between Washington and the states.

Until Nicholas Biddle became its president in 1823, the Second Bank's operations were modest. Biddle aggressively used the bank to pay down the national debt and limit state banks by sending home their notes for redemption once a week. The Second Bank's fiscal responsibility strengthened the nation's financial system by weeding out its speculative banks and raising the survivors' credibility. By 1835, the Second Bank had paid off the national debt – the United States was debt free for the first and probably last time in its history.

But the Second Bank's vigor spawned enemies. The weaker banks resented the federal crimp on their transactions. New York bankers were jealous that the Second Bank's headquarters were in Philadelphia, and thus diverted considerable business from their own coffers. But the worst enemies were among some prominent politicians who opposed the Second Bank on purely ideological grounds. One of Andrew Jackson's most fervent goals when he entered the White House in March 1829 was to destroy the Second Bank, or "monster" as he and his powerful supporters called it. Like most Second Bank opponents, Jackson lacked even a rudimentary understanding of banking. He simply believed that all banks were bad, and the Second Bank, as the nation's largest, was the worst of the lot.

Jackson vowed not to renew the Second Bank's charter when it would expire in 1836. Meanwhile, in 1833, he ordered that government funds no longer be deposited in the Second Bank and its branches, but in state banks instead. Jackson's supporters among bankers received the lion's share of the thirty-three depositories. In 1835, Congress renewed the Second Bank's charter by votes of 167 to 85 in the House, and 28 to 20 in the Senate. Nonplussed by the Second Bank's overwhelming support, Jackson vetoed the bill.

The consequences of the Second Bank's demise were severe. The Second Bank's destruction contributed to the Panic of 1837 whose collapse of financial markets and bankruptcies depressed the economy until 1843. Many of the states used the Treasury deposits as gifts and never repaid them, thus weakening the federal government's financial base. The loss to the Treasury, however, was not necessarily a loss to the nation. Whether the states repaid the funds or not, they mostly invested the money in building infrastructure such as roads, canals, and railroads, which stimulated economic development.

With the Second Bank's restraint on the money market and note issues destroyed, the United States entered an era of "free banking" in which the number of banks and circulating notes mushroomed, and with it problems of corruption, fraud, and inflation. Starting with New York in 1838, states competed fiercely with each other for scarce capital by enacting free banking laws in which virtually anyone could hang out a banking shingle. Until that time, state legislatures granted licenses only after carefully considering the investors' assets, character, and plans; most states had strict reserve requirements. In the free banking era, scarce cur-

rency tended to be frittered away in "get rich quick" speculative schemes rather than invested in the infrastructure and
manufacturing projects that would develop the economy.
Fly-by-night frauds were common. By 1860, there were over
1,600 banks across the country, with a total capital of $400
million and bank note circulation of $200 million.[3]

Jackson compounded the blow his destruction of the Second Bank had dealt America's economy with several other
financially irresponsible measures. In May 1830, the President vetoed a bill which would have continued financing
the Maysville and Washington Turnpike Road. In justifying
his decision, he argued that infrastructure was solely the
concern of state and local governments – any federal contribution was unconstitutional! Lacking federal funds, the
states and private investors instead turned to foreign governments and corporations. In 1838, foreigners held $80 million
of state bonds and $30 million of bank and railroad bonds.[4]

Jackson's assault on the nation's economic development
continued. In 1833, he signed a Compromise Tariff that
reduced the average duty from 33 percent to 20 percent by
1842, giving no consideration to the needs of infant industries nurtured by the tariff protection. In June 1836, he
succeeded in pushing through a law forbidding the Treasury Department from depositing any funds in any bank to
sustain its credit, no matter how important that bank was to
its regional economy. As a result, many otherwise respect-
able banks went under, dragging down their local economies
with them. The following month, in July 1836, Jackson issued
the Specie Circular, in which the federal government would
no longer accept paper money for land sales. Public land
sales plunged and never again reached their 1836 height of
$25 million, a figure larger than that year's customs duties.
As a White House tenure in which ideology superseded
common sense to the economy's detriment, Jackson's must
rank with those of Herbert Hoover and Ronald Reagan.

In trying to get government off people's backs and to free
markets, Jackson retarded rather than expanded the nation's
economic development. Yet, the economy eventually did shake
off the depression and expand, albeit at a slower rate than
might otherwise have occurred. Fortunately, the tariff reduction from 33 percent in 1833 to a uniform 20 percent

in 1846 did not cripple most nascent industries. However, the complaints among manufacturers led Congress in 1846 to pass a sophisticated tariff schedule with four different rates ranging from 100 percent to 25 percent depending on how the import adversely affected America's economy; some goods not produced in the United States, like tea and coffee, were admitted with no tariff. America's industrialization proceeded steadily as an increasing amount of money earned by trade merchants was invested in factories, railroads and canals that created a national market for manufacturers, and inventors and entrepreneurs joined hands.

In refusing to develop the institutions vital for raising enough money to satisfy their demands at home, America's governments and business made themselves dependent on foreign money. As with the 1812 War, Washington's abandonment of its central bank left it financially crippled in paying for the Mexican War (1846–48). To help finance its invasion and conquest of Mexico, the Treasury Department resorted to floating loans in foreign markets. By 1849, foreigners owned one-third of the $75 million federal debt.

And all along, the states and private businesses also had to look abroad for a large share of their investment capital. By 1853, foreigners owned $222 million worth of America's outstanding state and business securities, or 18 percent of all outstanding shares, of which about 50 percent were state bonds, 25 percent were bank, insurance firm, and canal bonds, and the other 25 percent rairoad bonds. Thus 18 percent of state and business loan repayments flowed overseas that could have been recycled within America's economy had the nation enjoyed a sophisticated enough financial system. By 1860, the foreign holdings of American securities had risen to $400 million![5]

Gradually, private entrepreneurs began to develop the financial instruments that Washington refused to provide. As early as 1792, a group of New York security dealers tried to regulate fees among themselves, but it was not until 1817 that they organized themselves into a formal stock exchange. In 1800, a group of Philadelphia brokers formed their own tentative exchange. Stock exchanges eventually emerged in other cities. New York's exchange did not trade 1,000 shares a day until 1830. However, thereafter the proliferation of railroad stocks caused the New York Stock Exchange to boom. Industrialization changed the types as well as amounts of listed shares. In 1835, the exchange listed shares for 26 banks, 32 insurance firms, and 21 railroads; by 1856, there were 42 railroads, 35 banks, 9 insurance firms, and 20 industrials in manufacturing, mining, and real estate.[6] The development of the telegraph in the 1850s caused a further explosion of share listings and sales, and the further consolidation of financial power in New York's Stock Exchange and its banks.

Washington refused to regulate the burgeoning stock and bank markets, arguing that it was the states' responsibility to do so. The states in turn refused to regulate financial markets, fearing that to do so would drive business elsewhere. As a result, the volatility of financial markets grew with their size and unification into one huge national market. There was no central bank to provide order and regulate the money supply. Speculative bubbles would burst and unleash tidal waves that swamped investors across the country. The Panic of 1857 was particularly severe, financially depressing the country just as the Civil War was about to tear it apart. Government revenues dropped and the national debt doubled from $30 million in 1857 to $60 million in 1860.

Every administration before Lincoln's must be faulted for failing to develop a national currency. The bimetallic standard established in 1792 was a terrible idea because the values of gold and silver constantly shifted. Rather than try to mint a coin that reflected the relative value of gold and silver, it was easier not to try. And those few bimetallic coins that did roll off the press became toys for speculators rather than tools for investors. Even if Washington had settled on an exclusively silver or gold dollar, the effort to mint it would have been stymied by the lack of either metal. Ironically, the 1849 gold strike in California did little to solve this dilemma. Most of the gold was exported to finance America's swelling national debt rather than coined or invested in the United States. It was not until 1853 that Congress passed a law which abandoned the bimetallic currency. Then, in 1857, Congress passed a law outlawing foreign coins as legal tender. Unfortunately, Washington failed to fill the void left by the loss of the bimetallic and foreign currencies. Coin was as scarce as ever.

America's dependence on foreign money never became more crippling than on the Civil War's eve. During the 1860 presidential campaign, the differences among the four candidates over states' rights and slavery were so stark that many observers believed that secession and Civil War were inevitable. As a result, foreign and domestic investors alike began recalling their loans.

Considering Washington's financial straitjacket, it is astonishing that it was eventually able to mobilize the vast armies, navies, arms, munitions, transportations, uniforms, and foodstuffs vital for victory in the Civil War. Washington financed the war with long-term bonds, short-term treasury notes, higher excise taxes, an income tax, higher tariffs, and the printing of greenbacks – all authorized by acts of Congress. These efforts required unprecedented cooperation between Washington and the banks. The Treasury Secretaries periodically met with representatives from the leading New York, Boston, and Philadelphia banks. Without confidence in the White House's financial leadership, the banks would not have financed the government's debt and all the innovative bills passed by Congress would have been meaningless.

The National Banking Act of 1863 and its 1864 revision helped shift the regulatory power balance from the states to Washington. Under the Act, Washington established a national bank system whose members had to maintain certain reserve requirements and use uniform national bank notes. The Act simultaneously taxed the notes issued by state-chartered banks, at a rate which reached 10 percent by 1866 and rendered the notes unprofitable. Thus only national bank notes remained in circulation, although the notes were not legal tender. By 1865, there were 1,601 national banks with 171 million notes backed by federal bonds. Meanwhile, state banks declined from 1,466 with $239 million in outstanding notes in 1863 to only 349 banks in 1865.[7] The Bank Act at once strengthened and centralized the banking system.

Unfortunately, the 1863 and 1864 Banking Acts had two flaws which eventually enabled the state banks to reassert a power balance with the national bank system by the late nineteenth century. The Acts did not allow the national banks to have branches or deal in real estate, nor did they prevent state banks from using national notes. The states took advantage of the federal restriction and attracted banks by allowing them to open branches and deal in real estate, thus offsetting the tax penalty on issuing their own notes. Those advantages plus the minimal and often non-existent reserve requirements explain the resurgence of the state-chartered banks.

Washington also failed to diminish America's dependence on foreign capital. After initially selling off their investments as the crisis burst into Civil War between 1860 and 1861, foreigners surged back into the nation's financial markets thereafter. By 1866, foreigners owned $350 millon, or one-eighth of the federal debt, $150 million of state and city debt, and $100 million of railroad and other industrial stock. By 1869, this amount more than doubled to $1.5 billion as reconstruction in the south and new factories and railroads elsewhere across the country demanded more money than the nation's financial system could provide.[8]

The federal government's attempts to create a national banking system were unable to regulate the oceans of money sloshing through the nation's financial markets. The system encouraged speculation. One of the most notorious occurred in September 1869. Financiers Jay Gould and Jim Fisk tried to corner the gold market by persuading President Grant and Treasury Secretary Boutwell not to sell any gold during the harvest period since the influx of greenbacks to the Treasury would lower prices for farmers. The President and Secretary agreed to this seemingly altruistic request on behalf of the nation's farmers. Then, while President Grant was on vacation, the conspirators tried to buy up as much gold as possible. Prices rose as the supply decreased and other speculators jumped in to take advantage of the situation. By the time Grant agreed to sell gold, Gould and Fiske had made a vast fortune. Not long afterward, a speculative binge in railroad stocks pushed fifty-five companies into default by 1873, thus provoking that year's Panic and subsequent depression. Speculator and free banking interests paid off enough Congressmen to pass the Resumption Act of 1875, which further stimulated speculation by removing all limitations on national bank-note issues.

Throughout the late nineteenth century, the most controversial financial issue in American politics was not speculation but the price of silver, which had dropped steadily for several reasons. The world was turning away from silver toward gold. In 1821, Britain was the first country to adopt the gold standard. A half-century later, in 1871, Germany cemented its currency in gold, followed by the Scandinavian countries in 1873, and the Latin Monetary Union of France, Belgium, Italy, Switzerland, Greece, and Romania in 1874. As European countries embraced gold they dumped silver on global markets. While Europe turned to gold, the United States experienced a silver boom as production doubled between 1870 and 1873, then doubled again by 1893. Not surprisingly, all the silver on global markets caused the price to decline from $1.29 in 1870 to $0.78 in 1893, thus threatening the fortunes of all those new western silver barons.

For political rather than economic reasons, the United States bucked the gold trend. Although, having abandoned the bimetallic currency in 1857, Washington could have minted silver coins, it annually produced only $160,000 before 1870. The American dollar's value dropped with that of silver. Although most businessmen and congressmen favored switching to a gold-backed currency, silver interests prevailed. They did so with a classical political swap of a silver purchasing act for higher tariffs to protect eastern industrialists. The Bland-Allison Silver Purchase Act of 1878 required the government to mint up to $4 million of silver each month. Arguing that it would devalue the dollar, President Hayes vetoed the bill. Congress overrode his veto. The controversy did not die there. The issue split the nation for another generation, with the Populist and Democratic parties favoring silver and the Republicans opposed to it.

In 1890, silver backers pushed another bill through Congress which would have provided for the unlimited coinage of silver. Instead, those opposed succeeded in watering down the Sherman Silver Purchase Act to a compromise whereby the government would buy about 50 million ounces of silver a year, but did not even have to mint them into coins. This industrial policy sop for the silver barons did serve their interests – the price of silver rose from $0.93 to $1.21 over the next three months. Ironically, the relatively few silver coins that emerged from the 1878 and 1890 Acts would not remain in circulation; the coins were so big and unwieldy that people preferred to exchange them for notes, which accounted for 90 percent of purchases as late as 1890; coins were used only for small retail transactions.[9] The Treasury sat on an ever larger mountain of silver coins. And after an initial surge, the value of silver plummeted to $0.63 an ounce by late 1893 amidst the global silver glut, a chain reaction of bankruptcies among railroads and banks, and the subsequent New York Stock Market Panic.

During the remaining 1890s, silver peaked as a political issue. Citing silver's continuing erosion of the dollar's value, a majority in Congress repealed the Silver Purchase Act in 1895. Yet these political and economic realities left silver advocates ideologically unbowed. Western populist William Jennings Bryan made silver the centerpiece of his unsuccessful runs as Democratic Party candidate for president in 1896 and 1900. But by 1900, silver advocates had spent their political capital. A majority in Congress realized that American economic interests were best served by the gold standard. On March 14, 1900, President McKinley signed the Gold Standard Act, marking the decisive defeat of silver interests.

The silver price decline affected only a small percentage of America's workforce. The controversy deflected attention from a range of far more serious problems gnawing away at America's economy. Industrial "robber barons" ruled America's economy and gouged consumers through a web of trusts, cartels, and mergers. By 1901, over 200 industrial conglomerates worth over $10 billion dominated virtually every industry in the United States. Meanwhile, agricultural prices plummeted as mechanization and the opening of the Great Plains to crops flooded markets with foodstuffs and bankrupted tens of thousands of farmers who could not make their mortgage payments. Industrial workers in the railroads and mines increasingly staged strikes and fought bloody battles with owners and police over higher wages and better conditions. Immigration surged, particularly from eastern Europe; many carried along socialist and anarchist ideas.

Meanwhile, throughout the late nineteenth and early twentieth centuries, as the United States became ever more deeply involved in international trade and investment, foreign opportunities and problems alike increasingly became American ones. The European embrace of the gold standard had contributed to the silver controversy in the United States. European imperialism in Africa and Asia threatened the access of American merchants to those markets, and thus jobs and wealth at home. European depressions weakened the demand for American goods and dried up foreign capital for American investors.

Washington seemed increasingly unable to affect any of these problems. Gridlock largely prevailed as those who favored the status quo blocked proposed reforms. But eventually progressive forces were able to push through laws which boosted Washington's ability to manage financial markets. The 1887 Interstate Commerce Act, 1890 Sherman Antitrust Act, and 1914 Clayton Act were designed to arrest the concentration of capital which had proved so economically and politically destabilizing. Two Surpreme Court rulings – *United States* v. *Knight* (1895) and *United States* v. *Swift* (1902) – strengthened these laws. Nonetheless, the antitrust acts packed greater symbolic than legal power; the government broke up very few conglomerates.

Independent banks supported these antitrust laws since the cartels had become financial powerhouses which elbowed aside banks in loan markets. As if the conglomerates did not erode banking power enough, insurance firms became ever bigger players in the nation's financial markets. The big three insurance corporations, New York Life, Equitable, and Mutual, acquired a reputation for risky investments and questionable business practices that rattled financial markets. In 1905, the New York Assembly authorized Senators William Armstrong and Charles Evans Hughes to lead an investigation of the insurance industry. The committee recommendations for limiting insurance investments in common stock and real estate, and forbidding their underwriting of security issues or joining syndicates, became law, and eventually served as legal models for other states and even Washington.

After Hughes became New York governor he continued his attempts to reform the financial system. A 1909 report recommending that no stock be listed without its firm revealing its financial position and limiting stock trading to margins of at least 20 percent cash did not become law. The New York Stock Exchange did voluntarily strengthen its listing requirements although it rejected any setting of margins as market interference. Inspired by New York's efforts, in 1912 the House Committee on Banking and Currency, led by Louisiana Representative Arsene Pujo, began its own investigations of stock markets. Pujo's recommendations then formed the basis for New York Assembly laws forbidding "bucket shops" or taking bets on stock prices, a broker's continued operation after bankruptcy, and fictitious sales. In all, the laws and reforms limited some abuses and tolerated others. The New York Stock Exchange had became a pillar of America's financial system. By 1913, the number of industrial shares listed was 191, or thirteen times greater than in 1865 at the Civil War's end, while the 147 railroad issues had doubled during the same time.

Support for banking reform also rose in Congress. The 1908 Aldrich-Vreeland Act allowed national banks to form "national currency associations" or pools to maintain liquidity during financial panics, and also created a National Monetary Commission of nine members from each House to recommend further reforms. In 1911 Congress created a postal savings system whose deposits were guaranteed, although the banking lobby forced it to keep interest rates low. Even more extraordinary was the passage in 1913 of the Constitution's 16th Amendment, which allowed an income tax.

The National Monetary Commission's final report in 1912 called for a central bank. In 1913, when Democrats swept the presidency and Congress, the recommendation resulted in that year's bill creating a Federal Reserve system in which all national banks were required and all state banks and insurance firms permitted to join, and supervised by a five-member Board. Members were required to keep reserves proportionate to their demand and time deposits. The country was divided into twelve districts, each presided over by a reserve bank. The Board could regulate the nation's money supply by raising or lowering interest rates and reserve requirements, or buying or selling government securities.

These reforms fortuitously preceded World War I, and gave Washington the financial tools to underwrite America's participation in the war from April 1917 to November 1918. The outbreak of war in August 1914 caused stock markets to plummet and a minor depression to ensue as European investors repatriated their money. The New York Stock Exchange closed from July 31 until December 15, 1914. But the European demand for American goods, services, and capital soon caused the economy to surge and converted the United States into the world's creditor nation.

Washington had financed previous wars through borrowing. It raised most of the money for World War I through higher income, excise, and inheritance taxes, along with borrowing through bonds. It mobilized the economy for war with unprecedented controls over industrial production, wages, and prices, asserted through eight different existing or specially created institutions.

Recession accompanied the postwar demobilization. Although Washington still clung to a largely hands-off policy, the Federal Reserve Bank of New York did cut its discount rate from 7 to 4.5 percent between May and November 1921. Other reserve banks did not follow suit, and the New York Reserve's action proved too little too late. The economy struggled out of recession largely on its own, stimulated by a pent-up demand for new houses, automobiles, and consumer electronics. That consumer demand largely fueled an unprecedented decade of expansion. The only depressed sector was agriculture, whose continued overproduction kept prices low and foreclosures high. The government tried to pump money into agriculture through its Farm Loan Board inaugurated in 1916, but to little avail.

The worst problem threatening American prosperity came from overseas. Because of a combination of the overwhelming desire among Americans to return to "normalcy," the traditional American isolation from European entanglements, and President Wilson's ineptness, the Senate rejected the Versailles Treaty by which the United States would have joined the League of Nations. Yet, the rejection of the League did not immunize the United States from global problems. The European belligerents all owed huge debts to the United States. Britain and France were the largest debtors, and serviced their debts with German reparations. Unfortunately, Germany's economy was wracked by depression and hyperinflation and thus Berlin had trouble paying its reparations. In 1923, Paris sent troops into the Ruhr industrial region when Berlin suspended payments, an action that only compounded Germany's depression. Britain, meanwhile, succeeded in negotiating a debt reduction agreement with Washington. France demanded and received a similar deal.

The reduction of Europe's debt burden simultaneously strained America's financial system. Like it or not, the United States had to emerge from its isolationism and accept leadership over the global financial system by pumping it with enough money to keep it afloat. In 1924, Washington financially floated Germany with the Dawes Loan to help it pay its reparation bill. The Young Loan of 1928 was a similar American plan to maintain the financial flow from reparation and debt. Meanwhile, Latin American countries increased their borrowing from the United States and many ran into problems repaying their loans. Washington ended up rescheduling their debts and loaning them additional money.

Washington did an exemplary job of managing the global financial system during the 1920s. It turned a blind eye, however, to problems festering within its own financial system. When New York's stock market crashed in October 1929, domestic rather than international factors were largely to blame. Speculators had bid up the market until its collapse was imminent. Perhaps as late as spring 1929, the Federal Reserve could have dampened the ever burgeoning speculative bubble with tighter interest rates. Yet, it stood by and did nothing until August when it raised the rate. An action that could have gently squeezed some air from the bubble a half-year earlier, popped it as investors panicked and frenziedly sold their stocks.

Perhaps the most important reason for the Federal Reserve's reticence before August 1929 was the fear that higher interest rates would attract overseas funds, which would weaken those economies and thus their ability to service their debt to the United States. The outflow of funds would also have undermined the efforts of those countries which had resumed the gold standard. In 1925, Britain was the first to do so; by 1927 Italy, Denmark, Poland, India, Argentina, and Estonia had also accepted the gold standard. If those countries abandoned the gold standard, gold's value would drop, thus hurting the United States, which held half the world's total by 1927.

The stock market did not cause the depression. Saturated markets for homes, automobiles, and consumer electronics were pushing the economy into recession by fall 1929. Like the stock market, much of the 1920s' consumer binge was financed by credit. When the economic pillars of the stock market and mass consumption collapsed, they cracked a third pillar, the banking system, thus converting what could have been a relatively short recession into the Great Depression.

The Hoover administration did little to assuage and much to worsen the Great Depression. Revenues dropped with the depression. Hoover tried to balance the budget by cutting back spending and increasing taxes, thus causing more unemployment and less consumption. In 1930, Hoover signed into law the Smoot-Hawley Act, which raised tariffs to 50 percent of the value of imports. In trying to save American jobs from foreign competition, the law actually worsened the depression as foreign governments raised their own barriers and world trade collapsed. The Federal Reserve refused to supply enough liquidity to the banking system to prevent its downfall. Despite these negative actions, the White House did create the Reconstruction Finance Corporation (RFC), which made loans to banks and industries.

By the time Franklin Roosevelt entered the White House in March 1933, the economy was at half its 1929 level, one of four in the workforce were jobless, and the wholesale price level had plunged from 93 to 64. Within days of taking office, Roosevelt declared a bank holiday, an action made into law by Congress on March 9. The Treasury Department then investigated every bank, allowing only those which were financially viable to open. Roosevelt reinforced the banking system by signing in July 1933 the Glass–Steagall Act, which created the Federal Deposit Insurance Corporation (FDIC). Banks and savings and loans companies could join the FDIC, which in turn insured deposits below a certain amount (initially $2,500 and then $3,500 after 1935). The 1934 Securities and Exchange Act established the Security and Exchange Commission (SEC) to police stock markets and empowered the Federal Reserve Board to regulate the credit of any registered security. The SEC's powers were reinforced by the 1935 Public Utility Holding Companies Act, which rationalized that industry, and the 1940 Investment Company Act whereby all investment firms and advisors except banks had to register with the SEC. The 1934 Gold Reserve Act set gold's value at $35 an ounce and made government the sole legal holder, buyer, and seller of gold. The Silver Purchase Act of 1934 was one last gesture to the silver industry; by 1938 the Treasury had bought up 40,000 tons of silver. The Banking Act of 1935 strengthened the Federal Reserve by allowing it to increase reserve requirements, and reducing the board to seven members and extending their term to 14 years. Meanwhile, the Federal Reserve tried to pump money into the economy by lowering the discount rate to 1.5 percent by 1934 and keeping it around that level throughout the Great Depression.

Bailing out the financial system was simply not enough to restore the United States to prosperity. Roosevelt's New Deal included not just bank reforms but a range of initiatives which attempted to transform virtually every economic sector and confront every socioeconomic problem. The bottom line of all of these policies and programs was to do what the existing financial system had failed to do, putting enough money into the pockets of consumers and businesses so that they could buy their way back to prosperity. By 1940, the RFC alone had disbursed over $10 billion either directly or via other programs, of which one-third went to banks, one-third to other industries, and the final third to farms and relief. The Farm Credit Corporation, Farm Security Administration, and Electric Home and Farm Authority were the largest programs which targeted agriculture. The Federal National Mortgage Association ("Fanny May") provided low-interest mortgages to home buyers. The Export Import Bank provided loans to those involved in international trade. The Public Works Administration, Works Progress Administration, Civilian Conservation Corps, National Youth Administration, and National Recovery Administration employed millions to build infrastructure across the country, while the Tennessee Valley Authority transformed an entire region from entrenched poverty into growing prosperity with dams, roads, electricity, and factories. The Social Security Act at once provided pensions for those 65 years or older and unemployment insurance. The Fair Standards Act set a minimum wage and forbade the use of child labor in interstate commerce.

Finally, the New Deal included attempts to rebuild the global economy. The 1934 Reciprocal Trade Act empowered the President to negotiate trade treaties, which included mutual tariff reductions. The Act marked a remarkable shift in trade policy initiative from Congress to the White House. By 1939, the White House had concluded twenty-one bilateral and multilateral treaties. Like other New Deal initiatives, these treaties helped arrest and reverse the Great Depression, but were unable to end it.

The Great Depression only ended with American participation in World War II as GNP grew from $126 billion to $214 billion between 1941 and 1945 while unemployment dropped from 14 percent to 1.5 percent. Washington was never better prepared to fight a war than it was in December 1941. In June 1940, Congress had granted the RFC almost unlimited powers to mobilize industry for war. The RFC created an array of public companies such as the Defense Plant Corporation, Metals Reserve Company, Defense Supplies Corporation, Rubber Reserve Company, War Damage Corporation, and United States Commercial Company to organize and finance specific defense-industrial sectors. In 1942, the White House established the War Production Board to coordinate investment, production, and supply. Throughout the war, the federal government invested $9 billion in 2,300 industrial projects in 46 states.[10] A free financial market could never have won World War II, and no one with any credibility has ever suggested that it could have.

Washington financed the war with a mix of higher income, inheritance, and excise taxes and bonds. The only significant tax-free investments were municipal and state securities. Income tax revenues alone increased twenty times from 1941 to 1945, while total tax receipts rose from $8 billion to $48 billion. Expenditures, however, soared from $13 billion to $100 billion. About half of the economy was devoted to war. In 1946, the accumulated national debt was $269 billion, up from $49 billion when the war started.

The Federal Reserve kept interest rates low to reduce the government's borrowing burden. The Office of Economic Stabilization maintained strict wage, price, rationing, and credit controls to contain inflationary pressures. Under government pressure, the New York Stock Exchange raised margin requirements several times to a height of 100 percent by 1945 to curb speculation. Anticipating a period of inevitable postwar inflation and unemployment, Washington drew up and implemented demobilization plans. The military industrial output peaked in 1943. After this, in anticipation that the war would be won in a couple of years, the government gradually reduced output to meet current demand. Industries began retooling from defense to consumer goods.

Washington also anticipated the need to restore the global economy. In June 1944, representatives of 44 countries met at Bretton Woods, New Hampshire, to establish two international organizations which could revive the global economy by pumping it with money. Both the International Monetary Fund (IMF) and the International Bank for Reconstruction and Development (IRBD) were banks. IMF members experiencing balance-of-payment problems could borrow from a common pool composed of membership dues. As the organization's name suggests, IRBD members could borrow to finance reconstruction and development projects. The dollar was tied to gold, which was valued at $35 an ounce. At Bretton Woods, representatives also laid the groundwork for what became the General Agreement on Tariffs and Trade (GATT), which was based on most favored nation (MFN) relations and periodic negotiation rounds to lower trade barriers. Twenty-three nations created GATT in 1947. By leading the creation and funding of these international organizations, Washington accepted full responsibility for managing and serving as banker for the global economy. Since then every administration has recognized that domestic prosperity, depends on global prosperity, which in turn flows from American leadership.

In 1946, when Washington lifted its array of economic controls, axed spending, and demobilized 8 million soldiers, inflation and unemployment did temporarily explode. However, industry quickly met the pent up demand for goods and services. Meanwhile, the 1944 GI Bill of Rights provided each demobilized soldier with $300, $20 of weekly unemployment insurance for up to a year, cheap housing and small business loans, and college tuition. By 1947, the economy leapt 5.7 percent while unemployment dropped to 2.4 percent.

While overall the economy performed splendidly, the political parties were torn over how to reduce the national debt. The Republicans favored tax and spending cuts to reduce the debt over time. President Truman wanted to maintain higher taxes to finance the debt as well as curb inflation. In 1948, Republicans overrode Truman's veto of a tax cut package of which 40 percent went to the wealthiest 5 percent of the population, state and municipal securities remained exempt, and the oil, gas, and mining industries enjoyed high depletion allowances. The tax cuts did boost the economy but did not pay for themselves as the Republicans promised; the national debt rose ever higher.

Then, in 1950, the United States aided South Korea against North Korean and Chinese aggression. Washington raised taxes to pay for what would be a three-year effort. In 1954, President Dwight Eisenhower cut spending and taxes. The economy expanded vigorously. A decade later, in 1964, President Lyndon Johnson pushed through an even sharper set of tax cuts that had originally been proposed by his predecessor, John Kennedy. During the 1960s, the economy reached unprecedented levels of expansion and prosperity, at the expense of a soaring national debt. All along, the Federal Reserve attempted to balance inflation with growth by manipulating interest rates, margin requirements, and reserve levels.

The Glass–Steagall and Securities and Exchange Acts of the 1930s, along with responsible Federal Reserve guidance, helped keep the financial system just as prosperous as the rest of the economy. Overall, the number of commercial banks contracted by 2 percent to 13,804 between 1945 and 1965, while branch offices of banks rose from 3,723 to 15,486. Banking laws in 1952 and 1965 encouraged the growth of branch banking. A 1956 law required bank holding companies to divest themselves of nonbanking investments. By 1965, 53 bank holding companies operated 468 banks with 1,486 branches and $27.6 billion of deposits. The 1960 Bank Merger Act, amended in 1966, empowered the Federal Reserve to oversee all bank mergers. The most powerful banks increasingly looked overseas for new markets. By 1965, 13 banks had over 200 branches in over 50 countries. All national banks were required to be Federal Reserve members; together they accounted for 35 percent of all commercial banks in numbers and 58 percent in deposits. Of the state banks, 60 percent of their total deposits and 16 percent of their numbers were members of the Federal Reserve system. Of the nearly 14,000 banks, only 263 were not FDIC members. Yet another reason for the unprecedented health and concentration of the banking industry was the introduction of new ways to make money such as certificates of deposits (CDs), commercial paper, money markets, and credit cards. Credit cards alone rose from 5 percent to 20 percent of personal consumption in the two decades after 1965; this easy consumer credit was a vital spur to the nation's economic development.[11]

The savings and loan industry expanded just as robustly during these two decades, from $10 billion to $129 billion in deposits. Although legally inhibited from employing the diverse range of investment opportunities that banks enjoyed, the savings and loan industry attracted deposits with slightly higher interest rates and profits from mortgages in an ever growing housing market.

Despite this expansion of the financial system, the market did not satisfy all credit and investment needs. Financial institutions refused many loans because they were too risky, or would grant them only after charging exorbitant interest rates. Washington filled the gap by establishing different government credit agencies, which numbered 74 with over $100 billion in outstanding loans by the mid-1960s. Many of these loans were targeted on small-scale entrepreneurs as provided for by the 1953 Small Business Act and 1958 Small Business Investment Act. The first government credit institution dates to 1917 when federal land banks to farmers were created. Loans from the Federal Farm Mortgage Corporation meant economic life or death for an increasing number of the nation's farmers. The Home Owners Loan Corporation loaned money to home buyers who could not get an affordable loan from the market system. In addition to loans, virtually all businesses from the smallest "mom and pop" store to the largest corporation received government aid through various tax shelters and reductions, protection from competitive imports, export assistance, and outright grants. Ironically, many of the recipients of these business welfare handouts deplore "big government" aid to jobless or homeless individuals. And it was the market's failure to provide such funds to those businesses that prompted government to fill the gap.

By the late 1960s, government spending, the deficit, and inflation surged because of the ever rising costs of President Johnson's Great Society welfare programs and the Vietnam War. Meanwhile, for several interrelated reasons, the United States suffered an ever worsening balance-of-payments problem. The United States annually sent tens of billions of dollars overseas to meet foreign aid and military commitments. Washington had tolerated trade barriers in Japan and western Europe to help them develop. The downside was that Japanese and European firms became ever more competitive in the United States as well as overseas. The fixed currency system could not be adjusted to reflect these shifts in geoeconomic power, thus contributing to Japanese and European economic dynamism.

Richard Nixon took office in March 1969 determined to revive American geoeconomic power. He tried to reduce foreign trade and investment barriers, and stem foreign dumping, especially by Japan. In August 1971, he imposed wage and price controls, set a 10 percent surcharge on tariffs, and took the United States off the gold standard, all in an attempt to reverse a worsening trade deficit and higher inflation. In December 1971, he negotiated the Smithsonian Agreement among the leading industrial countries to devalue the dollar by 10 percent. In March 1973, he allowed the dollar to float against other currencies.

These positive measures were swamped in November 1973 when the Organization of Petroleum Exporting Countries (OPEC) chose to raise oil prices and nationalize foreign oil companies. The result was a quadrupling of oil prices in 1973 and 1974. OPEC further doubled oil prices in 1979 and 1980. Between 1973 and 1980, oil prices rose from $2.50 to $34 a barrel, prompting a decade of global economic stagnation and inflation which American presidents acting alone or in concert with the leaders of other democratic industrial nations were powerless to counter. Over the long-term, however, the high oil prices encouraged new oil exploration, production and conservation which led to an oil glut by the mid-1980s. By 1985, oil prices had dropped to about $15 a barrel.

The oil crisis led directly to a global debt crisis. The OPEC nations had trouble investing their windfall profits at home so they redeposited many of them in American and other western banks. With the United States and other western economies mired in slow growth and high interest rates, bankers could not find enough demand for loans at home. Instead they lent much of the money to Third World countries to help them cover their growing debts from higher oil costs. Over time, the Third World debts grew as these countries proved incapable of generating enough business to service their debts and instead had to borrow more from hard-pressed American and other western bankers.

The swelling debt exploded into crisis in 1982 when Mexico suspended its debt servicing, encouraging similar actions by other heavily indebted Latin America governments. Eventually, the United States and other creditor countries rescheduled each defaulter's debts, but at the expense of American banks, which had to write off tens of billions of dollars in bad loans. As a result, American banks reduced their loans and deposits throughout the region. Foreign rivals eagerly filled the void. Between 1983 and 1988, the foreign assets of American banks fell by 12 percent.[12]

Meanwhile, American banks, savings and loans companies, insurance firms, and other financial institutions devised new ways of making money. According to economist Joseph Nocera, three innovations during the late 1970s democratized financial markets – the credit card, mutual funds, and discount brokers. Entrepreneurs devised the latter two: Edward Crosby invented money market funds and Charles Schwab discount brokerage. Like many economists, Nocera sees the vast expansion of private debt which those three innovations helped stimulate, as a "force for good" because investors now "have tools and resources at our disposal that were formerly unavailable to us, and we have been handed possibilities for making money that had always been out of our reach."[13]

Entrepreneurs also benefited from financial innovations during the late 1970s. Another source of money for financial institutions was in venture capital, which rose in value from about $10 million in 1975 to $31 billion in 1989. Where once a handful of firms managed venture capital, by the late 1980s over 650 firms competed in what had become a fiercely competitive market.[14] What transformed the industry? In 1978, the Carter White House and Congress agreed to cut capital gains taxes and relax regulations that prevented pension funds from investing in venture capital.

During the 1980s, junk bonds proved to be a much more controversial financial instrument. Junk bonds are the securities of firms which lack investment-grade ratings. At a huge loss to the Treasury, the federal government stimulates the junk bond industry by allowing tax breaks for interest fees and dividend payments. Meanwhile, it penalizes corporate dividends twice, once on profits and again when earnings are distributed to investors. Although the US tax code has offered these borrowing incentives since 1909, it was not until the 1980s that the potential to borrow virtually unlimited amounts of money with very little collateral rocketed off into the financial stratosphere.

Called the J. P. Morgan of the 1980s, Michael Miliken revolutionized the use of junk bonds to finance huge multibillion dollar deals. Miliken was the first to understand the potential of junk bonds to revolutionize financial markets. Working out of the investment bank Drexel Burnham Lambert, he organized networks of buyers to purchase, restructure, and then sell corporations. In doing so, he first became a billionaire and then went to prison for violating insider-trading laws. Inspired by his example, scores of other financial firms and hundreds of other traders got involved in the junk bond market. Throughout the 1980s, junk bond deals mushroomed, leading to ever more expensive buy-outs and an ever growing debt mountain. Leveraged buy-outs (LBOs) financed with junk bonds rose from $3 billion in 1980 to $39 billion in 1988.

Junk bonds are highly controversial. Proponents argue that junk bonds can allow capital-starved industries, and particularly the small and medium-sized firms in them, to prosper, thus developing rather than distorting the economy. Junk debt allows managers to become part owners, thus making them more rather than less responsible for the company's fate. Leveraged debt allows for the complete restructuring of corporations, the firing of entire ranks of unnecessary workers and managers alike, and the selling off of money-losing divisions and enterprises. When they rather than the public own the company, managers can work toward long-term growth rather than short-term financial juggling to satisfy quarterly profits. Stockholders, meanwhile, can sell out to the junk bond buyers at premium rates.

Critics counter that all the junk debt weakens rather than strengthens the economy. Having purchased a corporation with junk bonds, the temptation is to pay down the debt and reap an enormous personal fortune by selling off its crown jewels rather than the dead wood. Research and development is often one of the first areas to be cut back, thus hurting the corporation's long-term prospects. The demand for borrowing the billions of dollars to finance the buy-outs causes interest rates to rise and the economy to slow. The new owners are often unfamiliar with the business and can make inappropriate investments and other decisions. If a recession or interest-rate jump strikes, the owners become desperate to keep the money flowing, and the temptation to speculate soars. Thus do once-dynamic corporations such as Revco, Fruehauf, and Southland enter Chapter-11 bankruptcy (a legal means of financially and administratively reorganizing a company while remaining free from creditors). The herd mentality for junk-bond-financed purchases can not only inflate prices for corporations but collapse them when the psychology shifts and investors run elsewhere. Junk bonds helped sink the savings and loan industry.

While government policies encouraged financial innovation in some areas, they discouraged it in others. During the late 1970s, American banks increasingly lost out to their foreign rivals in Euromarkets while foreign banks captured greater shares of America's domestic market. Federal regulations crimped the American banks' expansion into Euromarkets by setting high reserve floors and low interest rate ceilings. Thus American banks often lacked the capital to invest or competitive rates to attract capital. Although the reserve requirements did not apply to overseas branches, they still had trouble competing in volume and price. Throughout the 1980s unprofitable foreign branches were closed and the Euromarkets conceded to foreigners.

As if the overseas problems of American banks were not bad enough, their domestic hobbles allowed foreign banks to take an ever larger share of the market during the 1970s. In response to the banking industry's complaints about the unfair advantages foreign banks had in the United States, in 1978, Congress passed the International Banking Act, which leveled the playing field at home. In 1981, the Federal Reserve Board allowed the creation of International Banking Facilities (IBFs) whereby American and foreign banks could run international financial instruments within the United States. The IBFs were not subject to the reserve or interest rate restrictions that crippled America's overseas banking.

Unfortunately, the IBFs proved to be too little too late. Burned in the Euromarkets during the 1970s, American banks hung back from the IBFs and allowed them to be dominated by foreign banks. By March 1990, of 522 IBFs, 329 were controlled by foreign banks. Americans own only 10 of the 57 IBFs with $2 billion or more in assets. Japanese financial giants control about 65 percent of all IBFs. In effect, the Federal Reserve created a type of institution by which the Japanese increased their growing domination over international financial markets.[15]

Overall, American banks declined at home and abroad during the 1980s. By 1990, foreign banks accounted for 21 percent of all lending in the United States, and nearly one-third of the $600 billion commercial and industrial loan (C&I) market. About 75 percent of all American firms deal with foreign banks. As if these foreign inroads into America's domestic financial markets were not alarming enough, in 1990, the Internal Revenue Service reported that many foreign banks systematically exaggerated their operating expenses in the United States in order to reduce their tax burden. With its Reaganomics personnel and budget cutbacks, the IRS found it increasingly difficult to regulate domestic and foreign taxpayers. Meanwhile, the foreign market shares for American banks continued to decline. By 1991, none of the world's twenty largest banks, and only two of the top fifty, were American.[16]

As with the banking system, federal policies made and then broke the savings and loan industry. Traditionally, commercial banks made little profit from mortgages so they did not offer them. During the late nineteenth century, the government established the savings and loan industry to provide cheap mortgages for those who wanted their own home. During the Great Depression, 40 percent of the nation's banks failed, while only 5 percent of the more conservatively run savings and loans companies went under. Although President Roosevelt opposed federal deposit insurance, fearing it would encourage unsound banking, a majority in Congress favored it to protect depositors and encourage savings. Roosevelt signed into law a promise that Washington would guarantee $5,000 in deposits. In the same bill, to encourage deposits, the interest rate for savings and loans was allowed to be a quarter percentage point above that of banks. Throughout its history, the savings and loan system has succeeded in providing affordable homes to Americans. Today America's 60 percent home-ownership to population ratio is the world's highest. Yet, by the late 1980s, the savings and loan industry teetered on the brink of total collapse. What went wrong?

During the 1970s, the savings and loan industry faced a crisis as inflation surged beyond their interest-rate ceilings and they could not compete with other financial institutions for loans or investments because their money was tied up in long-term mortgages. The savings and loan industry faced insolvency as depositors withdrew billions of dollars and invested that money in higher-yielding accounts elsewhere, including treasury bills and money-market accounts.

In 1980, with broad bipartisan support, Congress deregulated the industry's interest rates, allowed it to invest in real estate and make commercial loans, and raised the value of deposits covered by the FDIC from $40,000 to $100,000. President Carter signed the bill. Savings and loans were soon offering depositors interest rates of 13 percent! Despite these measures, the outflow of money from the industry persisted. In 1982, Congress passed and President Reagan signed a bill allowing savings and loans companies to make an even greater range of unsecured commercial loans, including junk bonds, and depositors to open an unlimited number of insured $100,000 accounts.

Although the money began pouring in, most savings and loans soon became trapped in a vicious financial circle. To survive in the deregulated market, they had to offer high interest rates to depositors. To pay those rates, they increasingly invested in highly speculative ventures like real estate and junk bonds. As long as the speculative bubble expanded, they survived. But the collapse of those markets was inevitable because they were artificially pumped up by a herd psychology rather than by solid assets. These problems were compounded by widespread bad management and sometimes outright fraud. Few managers or depositors worried about the mounting debts because they were confident that the FDIC would bail them out if disaster struck.

Throughout the 1980s, the industry's problems worsened. Reaganomics tripled the national debt. To finance that debt, the Reagan White House borrowed the money rather than increase taxes. Real interest rates rose and the savings and loans companies invested in ever more risky schemes to pay back depositors. Many of these investments were in the southwest where the oil industry's expansion provided the funds and demands for a real estate boom. By 1986, a global oil glut had cut oil prices in half, dragging down the interrelated real estate, junk bond, and building industries. The financial woes of savings and loans firms which had invested in the region worsened; many collapsed. This problem was compounded by yet another. Although deposit insurance was designed to help the middle class, the nation's wealthiest also could benefit, particularly after the ceiling was raised to $100,000. A millionaire could divide his money into $100,000 accounts, each of which was insured by the federal government and ultimately by taxpayers. As the system became insolvent in the late 1980s, the fleeing of these large accounts compounded the crisis. Then the October 1987 stock market crash cut into the cash flow that kept the industry alive.

By the late 1980s, the problem had become a crisis. The saving and loan industry lost $8 billion in 1987, $14 billion in 1988, and $19 billion in 1989. All along, the White House and Congress ignored signs that the savings and loans firms were speculating ever more money in ever more dubious schemes, and in so doing piling up ever greater mountains of debt. If President Reagan had even the foggiest notion of the budding crisis, he certainly did not want to acknowledge the ever worsening problem on his watch, and then have to mount an expensive buy-out. As if Reagan's neglect were not damaging enough, his administration's officials exacerbated the crisis. Treasury Secretary Don Regan not only repeatedly denied requests by federal regulators for more money, personnel, and powers to deal with the crisis; he and others in the Reagan White House tried to gut existing regulatory institutions and laws. In the name of "market magic," half of the S&L (Savings and Loans) regulators were fired in the early 1980s. Most in Congress did not want to risk losing the often ample campaign funds from the savings and loan industry by pointing to the problem and demanding reforms. The most outrageous reported example of the corruption involved the so-called "Keating five" – Senators John McCain, Alan Cranston, John Glenn, Donald Reigle, and Dennis Deconcini – who had taken $1.3 million in contributions from savings and loan tycoon Charles Keating and then intervened with federal regulators on his behalf. Although those senators stayed in office, two representatives, House speaker Jim Wright and Tony Coelho, were forced from office for similar machinations that would eventually cost taxpayers hundreds of billions of dollars. And what of government's "watchdogs"? The mass media mostly ignored the crisis, which seemed too technical and complicated to sell to a largely ignorant and indifferent public.

By the late 1980s, the ever swelling savings and loan debt had become so threatening that responsible congressional leaders could no longer ignore it. In August 1989, President Bush signed a bill which represented the largest government bail-out of an industry in American history. The bill created the Resolution Trust Corporation (RTC), with powers to nationalize the troubled savings and loans industry, pay off depositors, and sell off assets to repay some of the debts. The RTC was under the supervision of four bureaucracies – the Treasury Department; the FDIC, which actually runs it; the Resolution Trust Corporation Board, which sets broad policies and dispenses funds; and the Office of Thrift Supervision, which seizes the insolvent institutions and gives them to the RTC to administer and sell off. The bill also required savings and loans firms to raise their mortgage-related loans from 60 percent to 70 percent of their business, barred them from trading in junk bonds, and restricted their ability to invest in real estate. The restrictions made survival even more problematic for many of the savings and loans companies. Mortgages are not very profitable unless an institution is large enough to enjoy economies of scale. William Seidman, already FDIC head, was named to also lead the RTC.

The RTC became the world's largest owner of financial assets, junk bonds, and real estate. By May 1990, it had taken over 423 institutions with $220 billion in assets, of which it had sold off only $93 billion.[17] The RTC faced a dilemma. It was pressured to sell off the junk bonds, real estate, and other assets as quickly as possible. But the more assets it dumped on already depressed markets, the lower those markets would sink and the losses to taxpayers would soar even higher. Then in 1991, to make matters worse, the FDIC, the RTC's sugar-daddy, lost about $11 billion, giving it a deficit of $7 billion. To make up the deficit, it had to borrow money from the Treasury. Future losses were expected. The FDIC's fund, which protects $2 trillion in financial assets, was essentially bankrupt.

The bail-out directly cost American taxpayers about $200 billion, or $1,300 per person in the short-term, and may eventually cost about $500 billion, or $5,000 per person, over forty years as interest is paid and inflation takes its toll. However, the real cost of the financial crisis is hundreds of billions of dollars more in lost economic opportunities and wealth, caused by the diversion of hundreds of billions of dollars from taxpayers to depositors. Washington's borrowing of billions of dollars caused interest rates to rise, thus dampening the economy. And even if there had never been a crisis, deregulation encouraged speculation in real estate and buildings, which largely redistributes existing wealth, rather than in manufacturing and research and development, which actually creates new wealth. Warwick McKibbin of the Brookings Institute and Jeffrey Sachs of Harvard created a computer to encompass the indirect costs of the savings and loan debacle. They estimate that the misallocation of capital will cost the United States $500 billion in cumulative GNP by 2000.[18]

Few mourned or were outraged by the loss of a half-trillion dollars of American wealth. If most Americans are "mad as hell" about "big government," corruption, and waste, why then did they not mass in the streets to protest such an outrageous loss of their own money? No depositors lost any money. The money to pay depositors was largely borrowed – taxpayers did not pay higher taxes. Most of the savings and loan failures were concentrated in the southwest. The issue barely caused a ripple in the mass media or governments elsewhere. Since both political parties were responsible for the disaster, neither wanted to make it an issue. And no one can feel the loss of potential earnings – even a half-trillion dollars. In fact, the greater the losses, the more abstract they become. Much more tangible and thus politically targetable is, say, the existence of welfare mothers.

America's financial system survived the savings and loan crisis. In 1991, there were 14,370 banks and savings and loans firms across the country. Banks numbered 12,300, of which the FDIC judged 8,900 or 72 percent as being well capitalized, 3,000 or 24 percent as adequately capitalized, and 400 or 3 percent as undercapitalized. Savings and loans numbered 2,070, of which 1,150 or 56 percent were well capitalized, 580 or 28 percent were adequately capitalized, and 330 or 16 percent were undercapitalized. Foreigners own 20 percent of America's banking industry and 30 percent of its loans.

The federal government guarantees most of the financial system. In other words, taxpayers pay if a government-backed institution goes belly up. In 1990, Washington had guaranteed $1.7 trillion in insured savings accounts and credit unions, $1.3 trillion in disaster insurance for pensions, floods, war risk, and overseas investment, $800 billion for home and farm mortgages, $600 billion for Federal Housing Administration and Veteran's Administration housing loans, student loans, and small business loans, and a mere $200 billion for agriculture.[20]

In February 1991, the Bush White House submitted a bill to Congress that would have radically reformed the industry. The bill allowed banks to operate in two or more states, trade in securities and insurance, and own businesses, and would also allow corporations to own banks, pump $70 billion into the FDIC, and merge the four financial regulatory agencies into two. Over the next six months, the House and Senate banking committees took apart the bill, abandoned most of its parts, and finally passed different versions. The two bills then went to a conference where a compromise was finally hammered out by late October. On November 4, the House rejected the compromise. New bills were introduced and passed in each House.

The bill that Congress finally passed on November 26 was a ghost of Bush's initial proposal. The bill was stripped of such tenets as abolishing the 1933 Glass-Steagall Act, which prevented banks from investing in securities and insurance, allowing corporations to own banks, granting regulators greater powers to shut down bad banks, and consolidating the financial regulatory agencies. All that remained were a $70 billion grant to the FDIC and an ease on interstate banking.

Why did Bush's bill fail? All along, opponents argued that bankers make enough mistakes within their present limits – allowing them to dabble in stocks, bonds, and insurance would just compound potential financial disasters. They pointed to the savings and loan industry, which was allowed to expand its operations and ended up bankrupting itself. These arguments eventually convinced a majority. But the most important reason for the failure rests on George Bush's shoulders. After his initial plug, the President became curiously indifferent to his bill's fate. If he had thrown all his political weight behind the bill, it might well have passed. Perhaps he was just tired after having earlier that year succeeded in getting Congress to allow him to declare war against Iraq, approve Clarence Thomas's appointment to the Supreme Court, and block a civil rights law.

On May 12, 1992, the FDIC voted to increase premiums by an average of 22 percent, with weaker institutions paying a higher increase than stronger ones. The decision shored up the system at the cost of higher interest rates to borrowers and 4 percent lower earnings to bank stockholders. The new rate would yield additional revenues of $1.25 billion. The FDIC then followed up this action a week later, on May 20, when it capped the interest rates which the weaker banks and savings and loans firms could offer consumers, thus discouraging the sort of free market and resulting speculation that had nearly destroyed the financial system a decade earlier.[21]

The reforms continued under the Clinton administration. In 1993, Congress finally passed an interstate banking law. The law removed most of the restrictions preventing banks in one state from having branches or owning banks in another. The national banking market will allow economies of scale and weed out many inefficient banks. American banks will stand on equal footing with their foreign rivals, which have long enjoyed national markets. Glass–Steagall, however, remains on the books. Unlike their foreign rivals, American banks cannot enter the securities industry. Nor do American banks enjoy the protection of investment barriers and government subsidies that most of their rivals take for granted. Congress has long considered but not acted on a bill empowering the president to retaliate against the unfair banking policies of other governments.

One of the biggest obstacles to small businesses is securing enough credit at affordable prices. In 1993, Congress considered bills which would establish a secondary market for small business loans to be traded like mortgage-backed securities. Thus, a bank could sell its loan to a small business to another investor, and with the cash make additional loans. Proponents argued that the bill would allow small businesses access to inexpensive, abundant credit. Critics claimed the market would be too unregulated and thus open to fraud. Neither of the bills passed.

Washington's student loan program has been a hefty indirect subsidy to the banking industry. Rather than loan students federal money directly, Washington lent it through the banking system. As a result, students had to borrow from one or more of 8,000 lenders, 47 guarantee agencies, or 26 financial dealers such as Sallie Mae, the Student Loan Marketing Association which trades student loans on the secondary market. Students might finish college with a dozen loans from as many lenders, each of which took at least a 3 percent cut. Origination and insurance fees cost students up to 8 percent of their loans. When students failed to repay their loans, Washington rather than the banks picked up the tab. By the late 1980s, students defaulted on about 30 percent of their loans. The system is one in which banks garner all the profits, students pay high prices for their debt, and taxpayers bear the system's high financial burdens, including the high default rate. Although tighter requirements after Clinton took office cut the student default rate in half to 15 percent, the cost to taxpayers remains exorbitant.

In 1994, President Clinton proposed a new loan program which would allow students to borrow directly from the government rather than from banks, give them five repayment options, and halve origination and insurance rates. Students could repay their loans by paying the Internal Revenue Service a fixed percentage of their income for twenty years or until the loan was repaid, whichever came first. The direct loan portion of the $23 billion program will increase from $825 million of $15 billion in 1994 to $8.4 billion in the 1995–96 academic year. By cutting red-tape and the fixed 3.1 percent profit that the government gives banks, Clinton's program could save taxpayers $4.3 billion over five years alone. Students too would benefit from less bureaucracy and lower fees. A student borrowing $5,000 now has to pay a $400 insurance and origination fee. With that fee cut in half, students would save more than $2.4 billion over five years.

Banks and secondary lenders bombarded Capitol Hill with protests and threats. Clinton's proposal ran into obstacles in the Senate where Republicans set aside rhetoric about smaller government and spending cuts, and instead continued to support the bank handouts. The final bill limited direct government loans to 50 percent of the total and would phase in the reforms through the 1997–98 academic year. The subsidized interest rate to banks was cut to 2.5 percent above the rate on three-month Treasury bills. The loan limit remained unchanged at $23,000 for undergraduate and $65,500 for graduate students. As Representative Robert E. Andrews, a New Jersey Democrat, put it, "We are shifting from an entitlement to banks to an entitlement for students."[22]

LEGACY

Despite the Clinton Administration's limited reforms, America's banking laws remain obsolete, an overreaction against the bank failures of the Great Depression that happened 60 years ago. Those laws were written long before the emergence of a range of sophisticated financial dealings such as money-market mutual funds, bank credit cards, commercial paper, computer transfers of funds, twenty-four hour banking, and derivatives. Today, over $1 trillion in funds daily sloshes through the world's financial system; those who wrote Glass–Steagall could not have imagined either the amount or means.

Laws forbidding banks and corporations from owning each other hobble American competitiveness in a world where other governments encourage such cross-holdings. By owning stocks of their own corporate customers, Japanese banks can finance their long-term expansion. Because they often make more from stocks than loans, Japanese banks can charge their corporations less for loans, thus granting them a vital capital cost advantage.

Sweeping reforms are unlikely anytime soon, if ever. Too many vested interests have a stake in the status quo. The financial industrial complex will remain a vast, lumbering giant whose productivity and wealth falls far short of its potential. And it was government policies which were responsible for making it what it is today.

3 Chips and Networks: The Microelectronics Industrial Complex

In an ever more interdependent world, national security is synonymous with economic dynamism and power.[1] The guts of that power are microelectronics – computers, chips, networks, fiber optics, software, virtual reality, flat panel displays, x-ray lithography, optical storage devices, high definition television and hundreds of other related products and components.

During his 1991 State of the Union address, President Bush lauded the sophisticated "Made-in-America" weapons that the United States and its allies were then launching to destroy systematically Iraq's economic and military infrastructure. The President's enthusiasm was somewhat misplaced. During the Persian Gulf War, America's high-tech weapons such as cruise missiles, stealth fighter-bombers, radar, satellites, and so on did indeed perform spectacularly. However, the microelectronic innards that made those bombs so "smart" were crammed mostly with foreign and largely Japanese parts. And the technologies upon which most of those weapons were based had been developed a decade or longer ago, and were currently obsolete. Thus the missiles flying down Iraqi ventilation shafts symbolized not America's technological triumphs, but how much and why it has lost out to others. The microelectronic revolution was pioneered by American entrepreneurs and corporations, but is increasingly capitalized on by foreign rivals.

Of course, microelectronics can just as easily run a toaster as a cruise missile. Here again, the United States has fallen short of its potential. In his rebuttal to Bush's speech, Majority Leader George Mitchell asked, "If we can make the best smart bomb, can't we make the best VCR?" The VCR is a classic example of a technology and product invented by Americans but mass-produced by others.

100

Policy is the answer to Mitchell's rhetorical question. The weapons and microelectronics industries are Siamese twins, each nurturing the other. Washington was responsible for nurturing both industries into global leaders. To help fight first World War II and then the Cold War, Washington founded, organized, financed, and developed America's microelectronics industry. Although a microelectronics industry would undoubtedly have eventually emerged, Washington created it decades earlier than market forces could have done alone. Federal policies have guided nearly every revolutionary step in computers, from vacuum tubes, cathode rays, transistors, magnetic storage, solid state (semiconductor) logic, integrated circuits, magnetic amplifiers, parallel processing, and photolithography – to name some of the more prominent.

Behind nearly every development was some combination of federal tax dollars, procurements, technology transfers, and laboratories. For example, although Bell Laboratory is credited with inventing the transistor, defense contracts provided one-quarter of the institute's funding from 1949 through 1958. In 1959, Washington still provided 85 percent of all microelectronics research and development; even well into the 1970s, it continued to provide half of all funding. During the 1960s, the Pentagon accounted for 20 percent of all integrated circuit sales. And today, astride the 1990s, defense procurements fatten the bottom lines of 10 percent of all microelectronics sales.[2]

America's microelectronics policies have married the best of public and private initiatives and strengths. Despite its early heavy subsidization of the industry, all along Washington has tried to maintain a competitive microelectronics market. For example, the Justice Department launched antitrust suits against AT&T and IBM when it appeared that those firms were establishing monopolies within the industry. The Justice Department sued AT&T in 1949 when it patented the transistor. The suit was finally settled in 1956 when AT&T agreed to license all of its patents, royalty-free, to any domestic firms. Throughout the 1970s into the early 1980s, the threat of an antitrust suit restrained IBM until it was clear to the Justice Department that its monopoly fears were no longer realistic.

So, if Washington's microelectronics policies have been successful, what explains cruise missiles packed with Japanese chips? What doomed America's consumer electronics market and almost its microelectronics industry as well? The answer again is policy – a policy, however, of neglect rather than guidance. If Washington can take credit for developing the microelectronics industry, it must also take the blame for allowing other nations to dominate one sector after another.

After inaugurating the revolution, policy makers succumbed to "free market" ideology and neglected their creation. "Free markets" first devastated America's consumer electronics market and threatened to do the same for its semiconductor industry before Washington belatedly intervened. In reality, of course, a free market exists no more in microelectronics than in any other industry: "Oligopolistic competition and strategic interaction among firms and governments rather than the invisible hand of market forces condition today's competitive advantage and international division of labor in high-technology industries."[3] Although Japanese neomercantilist strategies such as dumping, import barriers, and cartels bankrupted one American firm after another, Washington was ultimately responsible for allowing it to happen. The policies of most Republican and Democratic administrations and congresses remained mired in economic theories that had no basis in the real world. In an interdependent world, launching an industrial revolution is not enough – governments must continue to nurture their creation or watch it become devastated by foreign rivals. Free market rhetoric aside, in the real world the government's role in aiding economic development will forever remain decisive. For example, when the cost of a computer-chip plant is $1 billion and rising, government assistance becomes imperative for all but the most powerful firms. For several decades, American policy makers lost sight of that simple truth.

An information revolution is currently transforming not just America, but the global economy. Computers enhance our lives in ever widening ways, from assisting brain surgeons through calculating taxes to running the Fourth of July fireworks display in New York's harbor. The real price of computers has fallen by 20 percent a year for the last forty years, making them accessible to virtually every business and household. Indeed, personal computers are becoming as ubiquitous in American homes as television sets. And all those computers, fiber optics, and virtual realities are being knitted into one vast global microelectronics network which at once liberates and entangles us all.

How did Washington launch the microelectronics revolution? How did it almost lose it? What recent policies has Washington undertaken to reestablish America's lead? This chapter will address those and related questions.

HISTORY OF TECHNOLOGY POLICY

Before World War II, goverment aid for private firms to develop technology was rare, but at times decisive. An industrial policy, for example, jumpstarted America's telecommunications industry. In 1836, Congress granted Samuel Morse $30,000 to link Washington and Baltimore by telegraph. The investment was successful and encouraged entrepreneurs to invest in an ever thickening web of telegraph, and later telephone, and eventually satellite communications.

Although Washington mostly just patented the electronics revolution that Thomas Edison and others spawned in the late nineteenth and early twentieth centuries, it did make some contributions. The US Census Bureau procured Herman Hollerith's electromechanical calculating machine for the 1890 census. During World War I, the Navy Department employed Edison and other electronics experts to screen proposals for its anti-submarine laboratory. This research continued with the Naval Research Laboratory founded in 1923 to develop radar, improve radio technology, and encrypt foreign messages. Of these ventures, cryptology became the most important. In 1935, the Navy Department created the Navy's Communications Security Group (OP-20-G) to secure American codes and break foreign codes. To lead the effort, the Navy hired Vannevar Bush of MIT. Bush organized a secret group of MIT researchers who would eventually produce America's first computer.

Meanwhile, during the 1930s, Bell Laboratories developed a series of electromechanical calculators that stored and arranged numbers in binary form. Other companies like International Business Machines (IBM), Remington Rand, and National Cash Register (NCR) developed similar devices called "differential analyzers." The components of what would become the computer revolution were there. It remained for Washington to combine them.

During World War II, Washington knitted together disparate strands of leading technologies and theories to create the microelectronics industry. Washington and London worked closely together on developing the industry by exchanging research and researchers in joint projects. The Americans benefited greatly from British advances in cryptology. Although many old and newer institutions within America's military industrial complex contributed, the most innovative was OP-20-G, whose most important units were the Communications Supplementary Activities Washington (CSAW), and its engineering facility, the Naval Computing Machinery Laboratory (NCML), which was located within the NCR plant in Dayton, Ohio. NCML eventually employed 1,100 scientists and technicians who built over 140 different machines for various needs. The navy built other machines through IBM and Eastman Kodak. The most important of the navy projects were the computers it sponsored through Harvard University's Mark I, and MIT's Whirlwind efforts, which continued for years after the war. MIT's Whirlwind project received the lion's share of wartime research money – $56 million or 20 percent of the $250 million funneled into universities and $1 billion into private corporations.[4]

Meanwhile, the army developed its own encryption devices through its own facilities, Bell Laboratories, and the Moore School at the University of Pennsylvania. The army assigned the Moore School to build what became ENIAC, the world's second electronic digital computer. (Unknown to the ENIAC researchers, Britain had completed the first, Colossus, in 1943.) ENIAC was not tested until November 1945 and was as big as a small house – 1,800 square feet with almost 18,000 vacuum tubes, which consumed 174 kilowatts. It cost $800,000 to build. Despite all the cost and energy, it had a limited memory and speed. The great mathematician John von Neumann helped develop an improved version of ENIAC code-named EDVAC. Von Neumann's architecture for EDVAC became the computer industry's standard for another quarter century.

While working on EDVAC, von Neumann also headed Princeton University's Institute for Advanced Study (IAS) computer project, which was partly funded by the navy. Once completed, the IAS computer plans were distributed to related computer projects, including Oak Ridge Laboratory's ORACLE, Los Alamos Laboratory's MANIAC I, the University of Illinois's ILLIAC I, Argonne National Laboratory's AVIDAC, the Rand Corporation's JOHNNIAC, and Aberdeen Proving Ground's ORDVAC.

The thousands of researchers and scores of firms employed by Washington during World War II became the seedbeds for the subsequent microelectronics revolution. Even after the war, the government continued to help underwrite many of these private projects. Yet, for a while following World War II, politicians were torn over whether to curtail or carry on the symbiotic relationship that had developed between the government and the microelectronics industry. It took the Cold War with the Soviet Union before Congress wholeheartedly agreed to continue that relationship.

In 1946, President Truman approved a congressional plan to establish an Office of Naval Research (ONR), which would contract work in private universities, laboratories, and corporations. By 1948, the ONR employed over 1,000 of its own researchers while its contracted work projects included $29 million in public funds and $14 million in university funds. Among these computer projects were MIT's Whirlwind, Raytheon's Hurricane, Harvard's Mark III, and the University of California at Berkeley's CALDIC.

In March 1947, President Truman delivered his famous speech in which he called on the nation to contain communism. Later that year, Truman pushed through Congress the National Security Act, which created the National Security Advisor, Defense Department, and Central Intelligence Agency (CIA). Truman, however, wanted to confine government research to military projects. That same year he vetoed the National Science Foundation Act, citing his fears that it would lack accountability. Despite Truman's fears, although the Defense Department would remain by far the biggest sponsor, eventually nearly every government department and agency chipped in to the microelectronics revolution spreading across universities and private companies alike. In 1950 alone Washington directly injected as much as $20 million into the nascent computer industry.[5]

Firms capitalized on these taxpayer-donated start-up costs. The technological advances and cost reductions achieved by various computer companies allowed them to develop commercial models in the 1950s. For example, in 1949, the US Census Bureau got back into the industrial policy business when it contracted with two leading wartime scientists, Presper Eckert and John Mauchly, to build a stored-program computer based on the Binary Automatic Computer (BINAC) prototype they were developing in conjunction with Northrop Aircraft Company. When BINAC's development costs rose to $278,000, nearly three times the original estimate, Northrop dropped out. Strapped for cash, in 1950, the two entrepreneurs joined Remington Rand. By 1951, they built and delivered to the Census Bureau the Universal Automatic Calculator (UNIVAC). Remington eventually built 46 UNIVAC-Is.

The Commerce Department's National Bureau of Standards (NBS) was less successful in developing its own computer project. NBS first got involved in the microelectronics industry during World War II. In 1947, NBS established the National Applied Mathematics Laboratory (NAML) to build an electronic computer. Jealous rival agencies got NAML to spend most of its efforts in evaluating their own computer proposals. But it was McCarthyism rather than bureaucratic politics that eventually killed NAML's own efforts. The Committee on Un-American Activities accused two leading scientists of being Soviet agents. In 1954, NBS's budget was halved and its staff cut from 4,600 to 2,800.[6]

The Engineering Research Associates (ERA) was formed in 1945 by a group of researchers who had worked on wartime projects. In 1947, the Navy Department contracted ERA to build the first general purpose digital computer, code-named Atlas. In 1950, ERA completed and delivered Atlas, and received permission to build a commercial version. The ERA 1101 and 1103 computers captured 80 percent of the commercial market in the early 1950s. But ERA eventually foundered because it lacked marketing expertise, to be surpassed by IBM, which enjoyed both engineering and marketing prowess.

Two projects conceived during World War II – MIT's Whirlwind and Harvard's Mark – in turn spawned a range of technologies. The air force eventually supplanted the navy as the largest government sponsor of MIT's Whirlwind Project. In 1951, the air force set up MIT's Project Lincoln, which oriented Whirlwind toward an air defense system or Semi-Automated Ground Environment (SAGE). While the $8 billion SAGE project never achieved the air force's dream of an air-tight defense system, it introduced such industry standards as graphic displays, cathode-ray tubes, digital switches, ferrite core memory, a wide-area computer network, real-time transactions, mass-produced circuit boards, and digital data communications.[7]

IBM seized a dominant market share in the mid-1950s and has held it ever since. Three government projects provided IBM's initial advantage. By the early 1950s, IBM had acquired enormous expertise through its collaboration on Harvard's Mark series. By 1952, IBM had spun off from the Mark series its Model 701, an electronic digital computer, which in turn evolved into the 650, 702, 704, 705, and finally the 1401 model or computer industry's "Model T", of which 12,000 were sold. Then, in 1952, MIT's Lincoln Laboratory contracted IBM to build 56 computers for SAGE worth $30 million each. Altogether, IBM earned about $500 million from SAGE contracts alone; SAGE employed as many as 8,000 of IBM's 39,000 workers. Finally, in the late 1950s and into 1962, the Atomic Energy Commission (AEC) and National Security Agency (NSA) used IBM as the central contractor for its Stretch Project, in which a Harvest Computer's capacities would be "stretched" a hundred times to perform various functions. During the 1950s, IBM's various government contracts supplied about half of its R&D expenses.

IBM president Thomas Watson capitalized on these advantages with a winning strategy that involved targeting market niches, huge R&D investments, and an integrated global market and production outlook. IBM's decisive action occurred in 1964 when it introduced the 360 series. Until that time, IBM had six incompatible commercial computers. The 360 series was a family of computers a thousand times more powerful than existing ones and that used the same software. The result was the world's most powerful, versatile, and inexpensive commercial computer. Subsequent versions have built upon the 360's basic software and architecture.[8]

Given IBM's emergence as the dominant computer maker, the 1950s was a tumultuous decade for the industry. Altogether more than eighty firms formed, merged, or went bankrupt. Frequently, veterans of government-funded projects dropped out to form their own companies. For example, dissatisfied with their firm's commitments, a group of scientists left Bendix to form Packard-Bell, and eventually Scientific Data Systems. Another group left Northrop to start the Logistics Research Corporation while others formed the Computer Research Corporation. Other weapons and aerospace firms such as Hughes Aircraft and the Rand Corporation created their own computer divisions.

Although many of the products which flowed from these ventures were innovative, none managed to challenge IBM's dominant market position. IBM's competitors mostly competed with each other, with each jockeying fiercely for the number two spot. During the 1960s, the second rank included Sperry Rand, Philco, and Control Data, and the third rank Burroughs, GE, Honeywell, and NCR. By the late 1970s, the pecking order had changed considerably with DEC, Burroughs, Control Data, and NCR fighting for number two while Hewlett-Packard, Data General, and Wang Laboratories struggled in the third rank. Then newcomer Steven Jobs posed the most serious domestic challenge to IBM when he marketed his Apple I and II microcomputers as an alternative to the IBM standard. Although Apple initially captured huge market shares, IBM unveiled its own microcomputers in the early 1980s, which recaptured lost ground. By the mid-1990s, IBM held a 70 percent share of the mainframe computer market, and 35 percent of all computer-related sales.

Over time, those IBM competitors which survived did so by capturing niche markets that complemented rather than competed head on with IBM. All along, corporations traded divisions, technology licenses, and sometimes themselves to each other, formed joint ventures, and often just gave up on the computer business when the competition proved too tough.

From the 1960s through today, as a commercial computer market expanded exponentially, the importance of govern-

ment contracts to the industry has correspondingly diminished. Between the mid-1950s and mid-1980s, the federal
contribution to R&D efforts fell from 75 percent to 20 percent. Nonetheless, defense contracts for various weapons
systems have fattened the profits of all those computer firms
lucky enough to be involved, and often made the difference between profitability and insolvency.

Washington's guidance of the industry declined just when
the Europeans and Japanese targeted their own computer
sectors for development. Britain, France, Italy, the Netherlands, and Germany launched the most extensive efforts to
develop national computer industries. Their strategy largely
focused on creating "national champion" firms in computers,
semiconductors, and peripherals which could compete with
IBM and other American firms. The strategy failed. None
of the countries had the dynamic triad among entrepreneurs,
university laboratories, and vast government defense projects
that had given birth to America's microelectronics revolution. Today, European microelectronics firms enjoy about
50 percent shares of European markets, which comprise about
80 percent of their global sales.

In stark contrast to the Europeans, Japan succeeded in
developing a computer industry which competes directly and
successfully with America's.[9] Rather than target one firm,
like the Europeans, Tokyo nurtured groups of national champions. Japan's Ministry of International Trade and Industry
(MITI) and Nippon Telephone and Telegraph (NTT) managed the corporations' participation in various research, production, and market cartels, protected them from American
imports or investments, and promoted their exports. A three-
stage strategy involved first achieving global preeminence
in consumer electronics, then in semiconductors and other
peripherals, and finally in computers themselves.

As in so many other industries eventually dominated by
Japan, American inventors and manufacturers gave birth to
and developed the consumer electronics industry:

> The American era of consumer electronics manufactur-
> ing began in 1887 with Thomas Edison's invention of the
> phonograph. That breakthrough was followed by a string
> of other US inventions, including the cathode ray tube

(1897), wireless transmission of speech (1900), radio broadcasting (1920), television receivers (1923), magnetic wire recorders (1946), transistors (1947), color televisions (1954), portable radios (1954), and home videocassette recorders (1963).[10]

America's consumer electronics industry's strength peaked in sales during the 1960s and has been systematically destroyed ever since, the victim of sustained Japanese neomercantilism. Where once there were twenty-four American television manufacturers, none exists today. The last, Zenith, sold out to Goldstar, an affiliate of the South Korean conglomerate L. G. Electronics, in 1995. Although televisions, stereos, radios, walkmans, telephones, CD players, VCRs, facsimile machines, electronic cameras, laser printers, videocassette recorders, computer disks systems, digital audio tapes, personal copiers, and the like were nearly all developed in the United States, they are nearly all foreign and mostly Japanese made.[11]

Japanese firms succeeded in simultaneously devastating America's consumer electronics industry and becoming world leaders because of Washington's indifference. All along, Washington responded with a laissez-faire shrug to the pleas by American firms for relief from the Japanese dumping that was bankrupting them. It was not until 1980 that the Commerce Department overcame opposition from other bureaucracies and finally levied $76 million of fines for dumping and $10 million for fraud from Japan's television firms. By that time it was too late, America's television industry had nearly disappeared.

Zenith was called America's last television manufacturer, despite producing most of its TVs in Mexico. Although its share of America's television market had dwindled to 10 percent by the 1990s, Zenith had been an industry leader – it pioneered FM stereo in 1961 and stereo sound for televisions in 1984. But its consumer electronics division had not turned a profit since 1984. In 1989, in order to pay off a worsening debt, it sold off its computer business to the French corporation Groupe Bull. In 1990, Zenith enjoyed a 12.0 percent share of America's television market, second only to the French Thomson's RCA brand with 16.3 percent. Then, in 1991, Zenith sold off 5 percent of its stock to the Korean microelectronics firms, Goldstar. Finally, in July 1995, Goldstar bought 57.7 percent of Zenith.[12]

The consumer electronic and microelectronic industries are ever more intricately linked, a reality that Japanese corporations have long recognized and exploited – each Japanese corporation has both consumer and microelectronics divisions. When, one by one, American corporations abandoned their consumer electronics divisions in the 1970s, they unwittingly handicapped themselves in their rivalry with the Japanese and others. Unfortunately, they had little choice but to amputate those firms whose gangrenous wounds were inflicted by Japanese neomercantilism abetted by Washington's apathy. Today America's microelectronics industry is mostly fragmented among speciality producers. Only a few, like IBM, produce both components and consumer products.

America's semiconductor industry almost suffered the same fate as its consumer electronics industry. Initial Washington promotion of semiconductors followed by decades of neglect allowed the Japanese nearly to destroy America's industry. The semiconductor industry emerged in 1959 when Robert Noyce of Fairchild and Jack Kilby of Texas Instruments independently invented integrated circuits. Until the mid-1960s, only the military used semiconductors. Prices dropped steadily and chip capacities soared as the industry achieved economies of production, investment, and technological breakthroughs. Chips increasingly found their way into consumer electronics. Yet, government subsidies and procurement remained essential. By 1968, Defense Department procurements continued to take 40 percent of the output. Government subsidies had contributed 85 percent of the industry's start-up costs in 1958 and continued to supply half of the industry's research and development funds into the mid-1970s.[13]

By the early 1970s, over thirty firms were making semiconductors, most of which were small specialists. Government largess, expanding demand, easy credit, the diffusion of knowledge, and antitrust provisions encouraged entrepreneurs to start up firms and scientists to skip from one firm to the next. Government policy was responsible for this relatively free market for technology. A 1956 antitrust decision not only required AT&T to forgo making its own chips, but forced it to license its technology to anyone who demanded it. IBM made chips for its own products but, fearing a similar antitrust constraint, did not sell on the open market. These various policies succeeded in creating a semiconductor industry. By 1975, American firms enjoyed a 98 percent market share in the United States and 78 percent in Europe, although Tokyo granted them only a 10 percent share in Japan.[14]

Unfortunately, America's global preeminence in semiconductors was short-lived. As in other strategic industries, the Europeans and Japanese targeted semiconductors for development, although they did so in very different ways. Tyson explains that "the explicit objective of Japanese strategy was the creation of a Japanese industry, whereas the de facto objective of the European strategy gradually became the establishment of a European production base, regardless of ownership."[15] The Europeans were content simply to make semiconductors for American and eventually other foreign firms. They encouraged direct investments by foreign firms by erecting tariff barriers against semiconductor imports. In contrast, Tokyo wanted a Japanese controlled industry that would eventually dominate global markets.

To accomplish its goals, Japan's MITI blocked foreign semiconductor investments and imports, thus forcing American firms to license their technology if they wanted to make any money there at all. Only Texas Instruments and IBM were able to use their technological power to negotiate from MITI the very restricted right to build plants in Japan. Meanwhile, MITI organized its electronics firms into research, development, and marketing cartels. Like the Defense Department in the United States, Nippon Telegraph and Telephone (NTT) helped nurture Japan's industry with massive procurements. As in their other industries, Japanese bought homemade semiconductors even though they were of inferior quality and more expensive than American chips.

It was during the 1970s that MITI nurtured Japan's semiconductor industry from infancy into global maturity. Between 1971 and 1977 alone, Tokyo helped underwrite over 60 microelectronics research and development projects related to semiconductors. The most important of these cartels operated from 1976 to 1979 under the guidance of MITI's very large-scale integration (VLSI) project. Although, under Washington's pressure, Tokyo dismantled its formal semiconductor import and investment barriers by 1978, it continued to use the informal barrier of cartels to restrict foreign sales to less than 10 percent.

The Japanese enjoyed not only nearly exclusive control over their home market but free access to America's vast market. By 1979, Japanese firms had captured 43 percent of America's market for 16K DRAMs, and from there marched upscale through increasingly sophisticated chips. By 1981, they had taken 70 percent of America's market for 64K DRAMs (dynamic random-action memory), and in 1985 90 percent for 256K DRAMs. They conquered this market share and drove dozens of American firms into bankruptcy through dumping chips at well below production costs.

While Tokyo laid the groundwork for eventually developing a computer industry by nurturing its consumer electronics and semiconductor industries, it directly targeted computers in 1960 when MITI announced a "Five-Year Program for National Production of Electronic Computers." The following year, Tokyo raised tariffs on computers from 15 to 25 percent and established the Japan Electronic Computer Corporation (JECC), which would buy Japanese computers and then lease them to users. MITI coordinated JECC's purchases while the Japan Development Bank helped finance it. As with consumer electronics and semiconductors, MITI organized Japan's computer makers into research, development, and market cartels. By 1966, Japan's computer makers had seized half the domestic market, despite the fact that their products were more expensive and of poorer quality than American computers.

In 1966, MITI launched its Very High Speed Computer System (VHSCS) program, in which it organized Fujitsu, Hitachi, and Nippon Electric Corporation (NEC) into a research cartel to build the hardware, and Oki and Toshiba (later joined by Mitsubishi Electric) the peripherals, for a clone of IBM's 360 and 370 computers. A half-dozen other Japanese electronics firms contributed components. That same year, MITI organized a related project among Japan's electronics giants called the Pattern Information Processing System

(PIPS) to develop artificial intelligence. In the late 1960s and into the 1970s, MITI formed yet other R&D cartels to develop a range of other computer products and peripherals, including the aforementioned VLSI chip project. In the late 1970s, NTT formed its own VLSI project geared toward telecommunications.

One of Tokyo's most important strategies was to force American producers such as IBM and Texas Instruments (TI) into joint ventures with their Japanese rivals in return for shares of Japan's market. Sometimes, however, an American firm or entrepreneur sold out to Japan because of misguided American policies. For example, in 1970, not just IBM but America's whole computer industry suffered a terrible blow when one of its leading architects, Gene Amdahl, left to form his own company to build an IBM clone. Unable to attract enough venture capital, Amdahl sold out a 24 percent share to Fujitsu in 1972. Although Amdahl did the research in Silicon Valley, Fujitsu actually manufactured the machines. The computer that Amdahl and Fujitsu marketed in 1975 cost less than IBM's equivalent, used superior components, and was sold world-wide. Fujitsu bought 50 percent of Amdahl in 1984. During the 1970s and 1980s, lacking capital and government support, other American firms sold out to their Japanese rivals. Intel, for example, licensed its microprocessor production to Hitachi.

Tokyo's strategy was eminently successful. By the late 1970s, Japanese computers were as good as American ones. Throughout the 1980s, Japanese dumping either destroyed or damaged key links in America's microelectronic food chain. A 1990 Commerce Department study warned that such industries as silicon wafers, memory chips, computer displays, telecommunications network switchers, x-ray lithography, optical storage devices, and flat panel displays were rapidly losing global market shares. Japan would leapfrog the United States in microelectronics during the 1990s. The report concluded that only a concerted government effort including antitrust exemptions for research consortia, tax credits for research, export-control regulations, and capital gains tax cuts – in other words, a comprehensive industrial policy – could save America's microelectronics industry.[15] The Bush White House ignored the report.

What went wrong? As with the consumer electronics war, Washington sat indifferently on the sidelines throughout the computer conflict. It did, however, eventually get involved in the semiconductor war and thus saved America's industry from destruction. And ironically, it was the rhetorically free market Reagan Administration which did so.

America's share of the global semiconductor market fell from 53 percent in 1981 to 43 percent in 1988 while Japan's rose from 34 percent to 46 percent. During those years, American chipmakers racked up $2 billion in debt and shed 27,000 jobs. As threatening was the devastation of America's semiconductor equipment makers. In 1983, of the top ten semiconductor equipment makers, the top seven were American firms followed by three Japanese firms; by 1990 only one American firm remained in the top ten. Meanwhile America's share had plummeted from 74 percent in 1981 to 45 percent in 1990 while Japan's share rose from 20 percent to 48 percent. Even more alarming was the devastation of America's makers of wafer steppers, one of the key components of semiconductor manufacturing equipment. America's share plunged from 65 percent in 1983 to 20 percent in 1989, while Japan's soared from 30 percent to 73 percent. The relative market shares have remained steady ever since. Overall the cost of building a chip making factory rose to $150 million by 1985, making entry by entrepreneurs all but impossible. By 1986, American chip producers had stopped making DRAMs and had retreated up-market to more sophisticated EPROMs. It seemed as if the Japanese had successfully devastated yet another American industry.[17]

In addition to dumping and import barriers, Japan's chipmakers had an additional advantage over their American rivals. While most American firms were small, independent speciality producers, Japan's chipmakers were parts of huge industrial groups (keiretsu) that were thoroughly entwined vertically and horizontally. The keiretsu had virtually endless financial pockets with which to afford dumping, research and development, marketing, and, eventually, the buying out of bankrupt American firms. The Big Six Japanese semiconductor makers – NEC, Matsushita, Hitachi, Toshiba, Fujitsu, and Mitsubishi – were giants in all aspects of the microelectronics industry. The chip war between Japanese

firms and all but a few large American firms was like battle-
ships fighting gunboats. Japan's industry was formally organized into the Electronics Industries Association of Japan
(EIAJ), which breeds the array of cartels and buys the loyalty of politicians and bureaucrats at home and abroad.

America's chipmakers had formed the Semiconductor
Industry Association (SIA) in 1977 to lobby the government
to protect its increasingly endangered interests. Throughout the early 1980s, SIA debated bringing an anti-dumping
suit against the Japanese. American firms dependent on chips
benefited from the cheap prices and feared the higher prices
that a successful suit would bring. But by 1985, America's
chipmakers faced bankruptcy and the SIA finally filed a suit
under Section 301 of the 1974 Trade Law against Japan's
firms for dumping computer chips in the United States to
destroy America's industry. The SIA demanded not only that
Japan's corporations stop dumping but that they allow
American firms a 20 percent market share in Japan. Individual American firms also sued their Japanese rivals for
EPROMs as well. Finally, the Commerce Department filed a
suit against the Japanese for dumping 256K and 1M DRAMs.

The immediate Reagan White House reaction was to let
the "market" prevail. Not everyone in the administration was
so complacent. Defense Secretary Caspar Weinberger had
become increasingly concerned about the deterioration of
America's technological prowess and growing dependence
on high technology from Japan and other sources. In 1986,
he was shocked to learn that the microchips for the F-16's
fire-control radar were Japanese. American firms no longer
made that vital chip. Weinberger asserted that the "ability
of our industrial base to support flexible responses to national emergencies is critical to the overall national security
objectives of the United States." Although other pragma-
tists within the Reagan White House called for retaliation
against Japan's neomercantilism, the Defense Secretary's
pressure was decisive.

Two policies saved America's semiconductor industry from
destruction. In July 1986, after months of heated and prolonged negotiations, Washington got Tokyo to agree to set
separate global floor prices for each Japanese chipmaker,
based on its production costs, and allow American producers

a 20 percent market share in Japan by 1991. MITI would monitor its firms' prices and behavior to ensure compliance. In return, Washington and American firms suspended their dumping suits against the Japanese. Wisely, the American negotiators had rejected a Japanese offer to simply restrain chip exports to the United States. To have accepted that would have allowed the Japanese to make the United States a "high-price island," which would have further undermined the competitiveness of America's entire microelectronics industry. By making the deal global in scope, Washington avoided a price island for the United States but at the cost of allowing Japanese as well as American producers windfall profits.

As always, getting Tokyo to make a promise was tough enough, enforcing compliance was almost impossible. Japanese corporations continued to dump chips around the world and block additional foreign sales in Japan. On April 17, 1987, to the surprise of many, Reagan announced 100 percent tariffs on $300 million of Japanese electronics imports to force them to comply with the agreement. The Japanese shrilly protested the sanctions even though they were guilty of violating an agreement and the affected goods were a minuscule part of Japan's then $60 billion trade surplus with the United States.[18]

Once Tokyo began partially to fulfill the agreement, America's semiconductor makers benefited from an additional $1 billion in sales when their market share expanded from 8 percent to 15 percent by 1990. If Tokyo had allowed the American chipmakers to reach the promised 20 percent market share, the United States would have been richer by an additional $1.16 billion, which would have translated into $130 million in capital investment, $137 million in R&D, and 5,470 jobs.[19]

In all, the deal and its enforcement not only saved America's semiconductor industry from destruction but included a series of diplomatic firsts. According to Tyson, the 1986 deal was:

the first major US trade agreement in a high-technology, strategic industry, and the first one motivated by concerns about the loss of high-technology competitiveness rather than concerns about employment. It was the first US trade agreement dedicated to improving market access abroad rather than restricting it at home. Unlike previous bilateral trade deals, it attempted to regulate trade not only in the United States and Japan but in other global markets as well. It was the first time the US government threatened trade sanctions on Japan for failure to comply with the terms of a trade agreement.[20]

While Tyson lauds the agreement, she argues that a better solution would have been for Washington to offer matching subsidies to America's chipmakers so that they could resist Japan's dumping. However, she admits that in the budget and ideological climate of the mid-1980s, such subsidies would have been politically infeasible.

Washington also finally got around to taking advantage of a 1984 bill designed to revamp America's microelectronics industry. The National Cooperative Research Act relaxed antitrust laws affecting research consortia. Congress passed the law in response to powerful lobbying from America's industry that Tokyo was spending $1.3 billion on a Fifth Generation Computer program that could push Japan's computer industry far ahead of America's. The first consortium allowed to form under the new law was the Microelectronics Computer Technology Corporation (MCC). Unfortunately, without government funds or direction, it failed within years of its inception.

However, in 1987, Congress agreed to appropriate $100 million in matching funds through the Defense Advanced Research Project's Administration (DARPA) for a different consortium of America's leading semiconductor firms to help the industry avert destruction at the hands of Japan's microelectronics behemoths. Fourteen firms joined what became known as the Semiconductor Manufacturing Technology (Sematech), each chipping in a share of the $100 million in matching federal funds. In 1988, Robert Noyce, who had invented the integrated circuit, agreed to become Sematech's head. Of Sematech's 700 employees, 450 are permanent and the other 250 are on loan from their various member firms. Among Sematech's current eleven members are IBM, Intel, Motorola, National Semiconductor, and Texas Instruments. Congress initially allowed Sematech a five-year existence.

Sematech has been a decisive force in rescuing America's semiconductor industry from destruction. Between 1987 and 1994, Sematech invested $1.5 billion in generating new and better semiconductor and computer technologies, of which half was contributed by the member firms and the other half by the Defense Department. Its primary goal was to reduce the distance between a chip's circuits to make it more efficient and thus competitive. To do so, Sematech had to improve the quality of chip making equipment, which in turn meant saving the semiconductor equipment producers from an oblivion that would have made American chipmakers dependent on equipment from their Japanese rivals. Sematech thus saved America's entire microelectronics industry from destruction.

Today, America's DRAM (dynamic random-action memory) chips can hold 16 megabytes or 16 million bits of data; within years, a thumbnail-sized computer chip will hold 256 megabytes. Sematech was largely responsible for this revolutionary turnabout in the industry. In 1993, Sematech declared its mission of reviving America's semiconductor industry accomplished, and would wean itself of all federal funds by 1997. Like many, President Clinton called Sematech "a model for Federal consortiums funded to advance other critical technologies."

Along the way, Sematech has overcome numerous setbacks and obstacles. Neoclassical economists decried Sematech as a violation of market principles – for the same reason political economists hailed it. First the Reagan and then the Bush Administrations continually tried to cut off Sematech's federal funds. Overwhelmed by the harassment, three of the fourteen firms quit. Noyce died in 1990. His place was taken by Xerox's chief technical officer, William Spencer.

Not all of Sematech's actions were effective. It tried to rescue Semi-Gas Systems, which made the gas-purification equipment that purified the labs in which chips are manufactured. By working together, Semi-Gas and Sematech achieved a ten-fold increase in purity levels, giving the equipment a two-year leap over the best Japanese equivalent created by Nippon Sanso. But quality was not enough to save Semi-Gas. The company went further into debt and Nippon Sanso eventually bought it for $23 million. America's dependence on Japan deepened. Sematech also failed to save GCA, which in 1990 was one of the two remaining makers of photolithography equipment, which etches the fine lines on computer chips. Once again, although Sematech's guidance and $60 million of investments enabled GCA to make the world's best equipment, the company went bankrupt. Sematech invested $30 million in the Silicon Valley Group Lithography (SVGL) to help it design and produce equipment as fine as GCA's. But once again, quality was not enough. Canon bought a controlling share of the financially troubled SVGL. In all three cases, antitrust laws prevented Sematech from buying out those firms; it did not prevent the Japanese or another foreign power from doing so.

There seems to be no consistency to Washington's policies. What it divvies out to one group it may well refuse a similar group. Another research consortium, US Memories, was formed to develop and produce memory chips which could overtake Japan's lead. It asked for $1 billion in federal matching funds. Congress refused to grant it.

In the global microelectronics war, defeat can be averted by decisive joint government and corporate action, but ultimate victory in terms of restoring America's industry to global predominance is probably an impossible dream. To simply maintain its industry, Washington must remain ever vigilant and counter any foreign dumping, cartels, or trade barriers. In 1991, Washington negotiated a second five-year semiconductor agreement with Tokyo similar to the first agreement. By 1993, Tokyo had finally complied with its promise to ensure a 20 percent market share for American producers in Japan, but only after the Clinton Administration threatened sanctions.

As a result of Washington's policies, by 1994, in a dazzling reversal, American semiconductors captured 43 percent of the $102 billion global market, surpassing Japan's 40 percent share. While the Japanese dominate the commodity memory chips at the lower market end, they have yet to penetrate deeply the much more sophisticated microprocessors dominated by American firms. Meanwhile South Koreans are snatching away ever larger market share from the Japanese in memory chips. There was a similar turnaround in semiconductor manufacturing equipment makers.

America's global market share reached a nadir of 45 percent in 1990 but has since risen to 54 percent in 1993 while Japan's fell to 38 percent. By 1993, the top firm was America's Applied Materials, followed by four Japanese firms, and then five American firms.[21]

Despite this dramatic comeback, America's microelectronics industry remains vulnerable to the Japanese and may never regain its former power. Many American firms survived in the short-run by forming joint ventures with their Japanese rivals, such as Motorola with Toshiba, Texas Instruments with Hitachi, AT&T with Mitsubishi and NEC, and IBM with Toshiba, to name the more prominent. They did so primarily because they needed money, and Japan's industrial groups had plenty of that.

Even more troubling was the acquisition of American microelectronic firms by Japanese and other foreign rivals. Between October 1988 and April 1992, foreign firms acquired 60 firms in America's semiconductor industry – Japan's microelectronics behemoths accounted for 51 of those buy-outs. During the same period, no American firms bought a firm in Japan's semiconductor industry; the reason was simple – none were for sale to foreigners. A Commerce Department study concluded that America's loss of technological and industrial leadership in the semiconductor industry was directly related to "the high level of foreign acquisitions throughout the semiconductor food chain."[22] Tyson reveals the devastating effects that Japanese acquisitions of key links in the semiconductor industrial chain can have not only on the entire industry but on American national security:

> Sony's acquisition of Materials Research Corporation, a major US manufacturer of semiconductor equipment, caused the share of the world market for so-called sputtering equipment supplied by US-owned companies to drop from 60 percent to 2 percent. By acquiring Semi-Gas Systems, which accounted for 38 percent of the American market for gas cabinets, Nippon Sanso raised its share of the market from 2 percent to 40 percent.[23]

And the Japanese have not hesitated to use their takeover of America's vital microelectronic industry links to weaken adjacent ones. Several government studies have revealed that the Japanese are using their monopoly over key electronics components to further weaken dependent American firms. A General Accounting Office (GAO) survey of 59 American firms revealed that 43 percent had experienced problems sourcing state-of-the-art components from Japanese firms, with common delays of half a year. For example, Nikon has delayed shipments of its most advanced semiconductor-making equipment to American firms for up to two years after it supplies the same machines to Japanese corporations.[24]

Ironically, Washington has the power to block these sales of strategic American firms that undermine national security, yet refuses to use it. The interagency Committee for Foreign Investment in the United States (CFIUS) is empowered to review any proposed foreign acquisition of a high-technology American company and block the sale if it is deemed detrimental to American national security. Between 1988 and 1992, CFIUS reviewed over 700 applications and rejected only one – a Chinese purchase of an aerospace components maker.[25]

Throughout the 1980s, Japanese attacks on America's supercomputer industry grew increasingly destructive. At the last minute, the Reagan Administration stepped into the "marketplace" to save America's supercomputer industry. Cray, America's leading supercomputer producer, was yet another victim of Washington's failure decisively to counter Japanese neomercantilism. Cray unveiled the world's first supercomputer in 1976; the first Japanese prototype did not emerge until 1983. Despite its overwhelming comparative advantage, Cray was unable significantly to penetrate Japan's lucrative market and was completely denied a chance to sell to government agencies.

Washington got Tokyo to sign a supercomputer agreement in 1987 whereby it would open its market. In 1989, Tokyo did get its agencies to buy five Cray supercomputers of the fifty-one supercomputers it purchased that year. Those five sales occurred only after years of pressure by Washington. Meanwhile, Japanese supercomputer producers dumped their products abroad to capture market share. While Cray commanded a 63 percent share of the global supercomputer market in 1989, it held only 15 percent of Japan's market compared with 84 percent of the European and 81 percent of the American markets. Japanese firms enjoyed an 84 percent share of their home market but only 10 percent of the European market and 2 percent of the American market.

In April 1990, Washington warned that it would retaliate under Section 301 of the 1988 Trade Act if Tokyo did not genuinely accept free trade. In June 1990, Tokyo signed yet another agreement promising to open its supercomputer market. The promise, of course, remained unfulfilled. Having failed to get Tokyo to play by American rules, Washington began playing by Japanese rules. In 1991, the Commerce Department pressured MIT not to accept an NEC supercomputer. NEC had won the contract by dumping a bid against Cray, Amdahl, and CDC. That same year, Congress pressured a private environmental think tank in Boulder not to accept a "gift" from Fujitsu of a supercomputer.[26]

Meanwhile, Washington tried to beef up its own industry. Conventional supercomputers relied on powerful central processing systems to compute data. The most powerful of these machines could process 100 billion bytes of information per second. In 1989, DARPA gave Thinking Machines Company $12 million to create a next generation supercomputer that could compute a trillion operations a second, or 500 times quicker than existing machines. Thinking Machines succeeded by pioneering the use of massively parallel design, or thousands of microprocessors packed together. Parallel processing works by breaking down complex problems among all those microprocessors, which then separately solve and then reintegrate the pieces. The technology has brought the price of the average supercomputers down from about $15 million to $500,000, thus making them far more accessible to corporations, laboratories, and universities. The price will drop further as ever more powerful microprocessors allow ever more information to be processed in less space.

While lauding DARPA for creating the supercomputer market in the first place, some criticize it for concentrating on developing top-of-the-line machines for the Pentagon rather than for the commercial market – the target of Japan's industrial policies. Despite America's innovation of parallel processing, Japan's corporations continue rapidly to catch up. In 1993, Japanese supercomputer makers Hitachi, Fujitsu, and NEC made only two of the world's twenty fastest supercomputers; in 1994, they made ten of the fastest twenty. Supercomputers were a $1.7 billion global business in 1994.

High definition television (HDTV) is yet another strategic industry that Washington allowed to languish until finally stepping in to save it. HDTV has the ability to make television screens as clear as that of a movie theater. American and Japanese televisions have 525 scanning lines; European televisions, 625. HDTV could have as many as 1,250 scanning lines, making the picture twice as sharp as present televisions. Yet, infinitely more important than clarity is HDTV's potential to be to consumer and microelectronics what steel is to heavy industry: a basic, strategic industry that feeds countless others. The nation that can develop HDTV will reap hundreds of billions of dollars in more wealth for itself, at the expense of its rivals.

The Japanese were the first to recognize this. Since 1970, Japan's Ministry of Posts and Telecommunications (MPT), National Broadcasting Company (NHK), Sony, Matsushita, Toshiba, and Hitachi have spent over $1 billion jointly trying to develop HDTV. A consortium of European firms, including Philips, Thomson, Bosch, and Thorn-EMI, joined the race in 1986, and have since invested $300 million in HDTV research. The Japanese and Europeans based their efforts on analog technology, which breaks down signals into electromagnetic waves. The trouble with analog transmissions is that they are easily disrupted by static electricity, must be broadcast by satellite, and are incompatible with computer networks. Nonetheless, in 1990, the Japanese marketed an HDTV which sold for $30,000. There have been few buyers.

A powerful but underappreciated industrial policy tool is the government's ability to set standards. The Japanese understand this and for decades have used standards to promote their own industries and block foreign rivals. Tokyo has pushed its MUSE standard and Brussels its MAC standards to become the global HDTV standard.

The standoff allowed an opening for American entrepreneurs. But only if Washington developed its own standard that favored American firms. Even then, any revival of America's consumer electronics industry would be a long-shot. The Japanese had virtually wiped it out in the 1960s and 1970s through dumping, import barriers, and other neomercantilist strategies. And in the 1990s, American firms had to contend not only with the Japanese but with a host of Asian and European firms. However, one advantage the Americans had as late-comers was that they could capitalize on the mistakes of their rivals who had spent billions of dollars developing analog technology. The Americans concentrated on digital technology, which breaks down the transmission into pulses that replicate the ones and zeros of computer codes, and shoots it through the system. Digital can be broadcast over existing channels; satellites are unnecessary. It can also be meshed with computer networks thus vastly expanding the types of available HDTV programs.

In 1988, the Federal Communications Commission announced that it would choose an HDTV standard within five years, and encouraged all those developing the technology to submit proposals. In February 1989, the House Telecommunications and Finance Subcommittee began hearings on HDTV, followed in May by the Senate Commerce Committee. At these hearings, the American Electronics Association submitted a plan by which the government would create a Sematech-like consortium to develop HDTV, funded by $1.3 billion in federal loans, loan guarantees, and research grants. The Bush White House split over the issue, with the political economists supporting and economists opposing the policy. President Bush finally gave thumbs down and the proposal died.

Meanwhile, six consortia – four American, one Japanese, and one European – submitted their respective HDTV standard proposals to the FCC. The FCC began testing the proposals in 1991. Along the way, the FCC announced more details of the future HDTV industry. In 1991, it ruled that any HDTV must not make existing televisions obsolete; broadcasters would have to run both HDTV and regular television. In 1992, it announced that it would choose an HDTV standard and that the then current transmission technology would be entirely phased out by 2008. To ease the transformation, television networks would be given a second channel in which to transfer their broadcasts and technology.

By 2008, consumers will have to buy either an HDTV or a decoding device for their televisions. It also asserted that any firm that developed the HDTV standard had to license it at reasonable terms to anyone who requested it. Yet, the FCC remained silent on its most important decision – the specific HDTV transmission standards. When asked, the FCC admitted it was still studying the issue. These studies were strongly influenced by House telecommunications subcommittee hearings in 1993.

By spring 1993, only three applicants remained viable contenders, two American and one European. Of the Americans, one was an alliance between Zenith and International Telephone and Telegraph (ITT), and the other was between General Instrument Corporation and the Massachusetts Institute of Technology (MIT), the first to develop an entirely digital transmission system. The MIT and General Instrument Corporation consortium did not even plan to produce HDTV even if it could develop it, but instead would license the production. The Advanced Television Research Consortium is controlled by the Dutch Philips Electronic and French Thomson Consumer Electronics, but includes such American investors as the NBC television network and David Sarnoff Research Center. To garner support for their standard, the European Consortium promised to build HDTV in their factories currently employing 20,000 workers in Indiana, Pennsylvania, Ohio, North Carolina, and Tennessee, leading the governors of those states and the International Brotherhood of Electrical Workers to lobby vigorously on its behalf.

The two American consortia argued that standards and jobs are separate issues, and that the standard has no bearing on where the sets will actually be made. Under the FCC rules, any firm can produce HDTVs under the standard. Thus the European consortium will be likely to build HDTVs at their American plants regardless of whether the standard is based on the technology they are developing. In fact, every corporation which can develop or license HDTV technology will produce the sets in the United States because the sets are too fragile and expensive to gamble on long shipping routes. To further complicate the FCC's decision, America's computer industry, led by Apple and Digital Instrument, pressured Washington not to adopt an HDTV standard that would favor broadcasters over computer firms. Televisions and computers will soon merge, the industry argues, and if the government does not include computers in its HDTV standards, it will block that merger.

The FCC continually pressured the three survivors jointly to develop HDTV. On May 24, 1993, the two American and the European consortia announced their decision to work together on HDTV, thus creating one super-joint venture. The decision advanced HDTV development not just by allowing more financial and scientific resources to be devoted to the effort, but also by removing the inevitable future lawsuits and other delaying tactics the losers would have employed.

Who will eventually win the HDTV race? The United States, Europe, and Japan are each already committed to their own standards and are unlikely to adopt another. While America's digital technology is revolutionary, without a domestic consumer electronics industry, its developers may have to license it to Japanese and European firms.

Ironically, the United States has a budding HDTV industry only because the Europeans decided in 1986 to enter the fray. Had not the Europeans targeted HDTV, they and the United States would have adopted the Japanese standard, thus surrendering to Japan without a fight that strategic industry which may eventually be worth hundreds of billions of dollars annually and allow those who master it enormous geoeconomic power. The next decisive step came in 1988 when the Federal Communications Commission (FCC) rejected the Japanese standard as incompatible with American broadcasting standards. This gave American entrepreneurs the incentive to develop their own standard. DARPA then provided seed money to several groups of investors.[27]

Liquid crystal displays (LCDs), like the one upon which this book is being written, are an increasingly vital link in the microelectronics food chain. As in so many other technologies, although LCDs were developed by Americans, they were mastered by Japanese. Some of the most powerful American microelectronics firms – Hewlett-Packard, AT&T, Texas Instruments, and Control Data – tried to make them. But the Japanese microelectronics giants acquired the technology, mass manufactured and dumped LCDs, and virtually destroyed the American industry. By the mid-1990s, the

Japanese controlled 90 percent of the global LCD market. Of America's microelectronic firms, only IBM makes LCDs – in Japan!

Washington thus faces a dilemma with the remnants of America's LCD makers. Any attempt to revive the industry would be costly for both taxpayers and American microelectronic makers with no guarantee of success. But if Washington does nothing, the domestic industry will die and the United States will be dependent for all of its LCDs on the Japanese. Tokyo can use that power to turn on and off the LCD spigot to assert its interests in countless other issues.

A 1990 anti-dumping suit by the Advanced Display Manufacturers of America (ADMA) forced the issue. In fighting back, the ADMA faced not just Japan's government and industrial lobbying machine and America's market ideology, but the resistance of American computer firms, which fear the higher prices that anti-dumping suits and restricted sales can bring. America's microelectronics producers joined with Japanese LCD makers in protesting the decision, warning that to compete they would have to move offshore if ADMA won the suit and prices rose.

In 1991, the ADMA did indeed win its suit. Washington imposed 63 percent duties on Japanese active-matrix LCDs. Unfortunately, unlike the semiconductor agreements, there was no attempt to assert global floor prices or increase the share of American LCD makers in Japan. As a result, the United States became a "high-price island" to the economy's detriment. The decision was a

> kind of reverse (or perverse) industrial policy, pitting the interests of the successful American computer industry against the interests of the fledgling but doomed American display industry. Most US LCD companies – including all the companies involved in the antidumping suit – are speciality producers and cannot compete with their much larger, vertically integrated Japanese rivals on costs or access to capital.[28]

True to their promise, many American laptop computer firms did move production overseas. Those which remained demanded duty-free trade zones within which to produce.

In August 1992, DARPA unveiled a plan to create a consortium of LCD makers which would form a research consortium like Sematech. So far, the consortium has not proved as effective as Sematech. Meanwhile, the Japanese continue to dump their flat-panel displays in the United States to destroy completely the remnants of America's industry.[29]

INFORMATION SUPERHIGHWAY

While most policies have targeted industrial sectors, a few have promoted the entire industry. An information superhighway would revolutionize productivity and production in a range of industries, and spawn dozens of related industries. A primitive version of the information highway has existed since 1969 when the Defense Department began building what became a web of 9,000 networks among universities, research laboratories, and military bases in 102 countries. In the late 1980s, Washington also underwrote the construction of Internet, a global civilian version of the Defense network. But those networks are slow and their capacity limited, the technological equivalent of dirt roads compared with the envisioned information superhighway. Then, in 1991, Senator Al Gore succeeded in pushing through Congress the High Performance Computing Act, which allocated $2.9 billion for the development of the National Resource and Education Network (NREN). When completed, NREN will raise Internet's capacity from 45 million to 3 billion bytes of information. But even this would be just a step toward a genuine information superhighway.

In April 1993, shortly after taking office, President Clinton and Vice President Gore jointly announced that they would allocate $2 billion in federal funds to create an "information superhighway." One hundred million dollars of those funds would go to a new institution at the Los Alamos National Laboratory, which would use computer models to design new chip making equipment. In promoting the information superhighway, Clinton explained that it "could do for the productivity of individuals at their places of work and learning what the interstate highway system of the 1950s did for the productivity of the nation's travel and distribution system."[30]

Yet that $2 billion in government funds will provide only the system's start-up costs. The information superhighway will cost hundreds of billions of dollars to build over a score of years. Fiber optic cables must replace the current copper wires used in telecommunications. Software must be devised to run the systems. Thousands of supercomputers must be connected. Nonetheless, Clinton and Gore took the essential first step in creating the information highway – a step too expensive for any one firm or even a combination to take on its own.[31]

LEGACY

The popular view of inventors involves lone, driven, heroic geniuses from Benjamin Franklin to Steven Jobs tinkering at home, and then getting rich when they market their creations. More than ever, that image is the exception rather than the rule among innovators in the United States and elsewhere. Although the United States still spawns countless technological innovations, most of them come from multimillion-dollar facilities staffed with hundreds of scientists and technicians. There is nothing new in that. Even a century ago, Edison's thousand or so patents came from a vast laboratory complex filled with hundreds of scientists.[32]

Yet, even the most powerful American corporations have found that devising a better mousetrap is difficult enough, while producing and bringing it to market is increasingly a Herculean task. American innovators are severely hobbled in the global technological race. With so many safer investments available, conservative financial institutions simply do not want to risk the hundreds of millions and even billions of dollars it may take to convert a patent into a profitable product. When a firm can get the necessary venture capital, it often comes at a debilitating price. The result is usually bankrupt dreams. America's free-wheeling entrepreneurs may nourish great ideas, but often have to sell them to others for want of the necessary financial, manufacturing, and marketing clout.

And it is to the Japanese that American entrepreneurs usually sell out. Japan's corporate giants enjoy all the power that most American entrepreneurs lack, and more often than not it is to them that the Americans turn. Who can blame those that do defect. American innovators and entrepreneurs are trapped in a "catch-22." Once the Japanese have conquered an industry, it is nearly impossible for an American entrepreneur to obtain the capital to challenge let alone dislodge them. And the Japanese dominate those fields because the American firms lack the long-term, patient capital – along with the access to Japanese markets and government protection against Japanese dumping – to compete.

In stark contrast, as with its policies toward other industries, Washington's policies toward the microelectronics industry completely lack the strategic vision, determination, and resources mustered by Japan and other rivals.[33] Political rather than national interests tend to shape Washington's microelectronics policies. When Washington rides to the rescue of a beleaguered industry, it is usually only after that industry has been bashed to the brink of death, as with semiconductors, supercomputers, and liquid crystal display monitors. Sometimes, as with VCRs and televisions, Washington simply stands aloof, indifferent to the industry's pleas as it succumbs to foreign onslaughts.

An industry's relative strategic importance matters little to policy makers. Semiconductors are to microelectronics as steel is to automobiles. Yet, like its steel industry, America's semiconductor industry enjoyed an initial period of global preeminence followed by near collapse during the Reagan years, and then a hard struggle back into viability since. Washington's policies contributed decisively to all of those shifts in the industry's relative dynamism.

The microelectronics industry's strategic value is unquestionable. The industry is very research intensive. The average high-tech firm employs 82 research and development scientists for every thousand workers, compared with 45 for every thousand workers in other manufacturing firms. Microelectronics firms demand highly skilled workers and compensate them accordingly. The industry produces more wealth and employs more people than automobiles, aerospace, and steel. In 1989, the respective production values of those four industries were $295 billion, $250 billion, $106 billion, and $61 billion, while the respective employment figures were

2.6 million, 900,000, 800,000, and 300,000. That year, the electronics industry's $740 billion food chain led from a $19 billion equipment manufacturing segment, to a $57 billion semiconductor segment, to a $218 billion computer segment.[34]

Unfortunately, America's lead in microelectronics disappeared in Reagan's 1980s. Until 1983, the United States enjoyed a trade surplus in electronics; since then it has suffered annual deficits. In 1990, Japan spent $586 billion on new equipment and factories, surpassing America's expenditures of $524 billion, in per capita terms, two times more. In 1991, the three top patent winners in the United States were Japanese: Toshiba with 1,014, Mitsubishi with 927, and Hitachi with 863, followed by Eastman Kodak with 863, Japan's Canon with 823, and General Electric with 809.[35]

Washington's policies created the microelectronics industry. More recent policies are responsible for converting the United States from microelectronics leader to follower. The success of Japanese and other foreign neomercantilist strategies has caused many Americans to reevaluate their traditional reliance on markets and minimal government interference. However, as of yet, no alternative policy paradigm has emerged.

Until recently, the United States has lacked not only coherent high-technology policies, but an institution which could devise and implement such policies. From the early 1960s, the Defense Advanced Research Projects Agency (DARPA) has aided the computer industry's development. Yet, until recently, DARPA concentrated on military rather than civilian applications. And it never attempted to provide an overall strategy.

In America's free-for-all political system, policy becomes the outcome of a tug-of-war among countless domestic and foreign interest groups. America's microelectronic industry is most prominently represented by the American Electronics Association, whose members include 3,500 electronics and information processing firms. Other prominent interest groups include the Electronics Industry Association (IEA) and the Institute of Electrical and Electronic Engineers (IEEE). Yet, Japanese and other foreign industrial associations have become increasingly adept at manipulating America's political system in their own favor.[36]

America's microelectronics firms have finally realized that in order to survive in a neomercantilist global economy they must cooperate. Their efforts have had mixed results. Although Sematech succeeded in its goals, MCC and US Memories eventually folded. Meanwhile, IBM has increasingly attempted to assert leadership over America's computer industry. In 1990, it got the Silicon Valley Group to act as the White Knight for the lithography firm Perkin-Elmer when it almost sold out to Japan's Nikon. In 1993, it licensed its most powerful DRAM to Micron and Sematech to help rebuild America's memory chip industry.[37]

Whether these fragmented government and corporate initiatives will restore America's microelectronics industry to leadership remains to be seen. One thing is certain, the strategic importance of microelectronics will expand into the twenty-first century, and with it the power of the country that can master it.

4 Weapons and Spaceships: The Military–Industrial Complex

Every gun that is made, every warship launched, every rocket fired, signifies in the final sense a theft from those who hunger and are not fed, who are cold and are not clothed. The world in arms is not spending money alone. It is spending the sweat of its laborers, the genius of its scientists, and the hopes of its children.

Dwight Eisenhower[1]

The whole army and navy are unproductive labourers. They are the servants of the public, and are maintained by a part of the annual produce of the industry of other people. Their service, how honourable . . . produces nothing for which an equal number of services can afterward be produced.

Adam Smith[2]

In his farewell address in 1961, President Dwight Eisenhower warned Americans to prevent the growth of a military–industrial complex that threatened to undermine their economic dynamism and political freedom. Two years later, the former four-star general and president elaborated his views:

No matter how much we spend for arms, there is no safety in arms alone. Our security is the total product of our economic, intellectual, moral, and military strengths . . . there is no way in which a country can satisfy the craving for absolute security – but it can easily bankrupt itself, morally and economically, in attempting to reach that illusory goal through arms alone. The military establishment, not productive itself, necessarily must feed on the energy, productivity, and brainpower of the country, and if it takes too much our total strength declines.[3]

134

Just what is the military–industrial complex that Eisenhower argued was so threatening to America's freedom and prosperity?[4] Like any other political economic complex, it includes all those who share a common interest and are organized to defend that interest. The military–industrial complex combines all of those politicians, manufacturers, bureaucrats, financiers, stockholders, soldiers, shopkeepers, scientists, home-owners, factory workers, medical patients, retirees, and countless others who share a common interest in keeping military spending as high as possible.

Congress, thankfully, does not have enough money to fulfill the wish lists of every one of the myriad of interest groups that make up the military–industrial complex. Nonetheless, despite the often fierce competition among the interest groups for finite dollars, more often than not, the components will stand together rather than apart in lobbying Congress for ever more resources. As in any other political economic complex, success for each interest group depends on logrolling or backscratching with others. And no political economic complex in the United States is as powerful as the military–industrial one. For example, taxpayers subsidize not only the personnel and weapons that won the Persian Gulf War, but also a range of weapons that fail strategically and technically, the goods military members buy at their base post exchange (PX), and even $600 toilet seats and $1000 coffee pots.

The embryo for a military–industrial complex has existed from America's Revolution. Yet until World War I, the complex never developed to the point where its political power allowed it to continue long after the threat which brought it into existence disappeared. It did emerge during four years of Civil War only to recede for another half-century. The need to mobilize and send to Europe over 1.5 million personnel during World War I stimulated the development of a military–industrial complex which, unlike after previous wars, was never dismantled. Instead, during the interwar era, the military–industrial complex was simply pruned back – the institutions remained largely intact. World War II demanded an even vaster effort at mobilizing the nation for total war. Unlike after World War I, the complex was not cut but instead developed to unimagined peacetime heights to wage the Cold War.

Even with the Cold War finally won a half-dozen years back, the "peace dividend" has proven rather skimpy. Although the Pentagon's 1995 budget of $264 billion was only 3.8 percent of GNP, well below the average 6.5 percent of the 1980s, the military–industrial complex was hard-pressed to justify even that spending level in a world in which the only realistic direct military threats to American national security were Iraq, Iran, and North Korea.

How do we explain this? The Pentagon may be the complex's symbolic and spending center, but decisions are often determined by politicians and bureaucrats elsewhere. Congress and the White House frequently heap weapons systems, bases, and other expenses on the Pentagon that it had previously rejected as wasteful and unnecessary diversions of scarce resources from more pressing needs – the more spent on political pork means less available for essentials like training, supplies, and weapons systems that actually work. For example, Congress donated $9 billion more to the Pentagon's 1996 budget than the Defense Department had demanded. Those who voted for the higher spending justified their action by all the foreign "threats" facing America, but taking home the pork to voters or satisfying right-wing ideological obsessions were the real reasons.

Ultimately the Pentagon must bear responsibility for the budget's politicization. Over the last half-century, the Pentagon's decisions to spread the fruits of bases, subsidies, laboratories, and procurements to as many congressional districts as possible have made it the nation's most powerful political economic complex. Like Dr Frankenstein, the Pentagon has helped make a political economic monster it cannot fully control. As a result, the Pentagon is heaped with weapons systems and bases which it formerly rejected on strategic, technical, and economic grounds.

This chapter will explore the development and consequences of first the military–industrial complex and then its younger brother, the aerospace industrial complex.

THE MILITARY–INDUSTRIAL COMPLEX I: AMERICA AS A GREAT POWER

America's political economy has not always been dominated by a military–industrial complex. Until World War II, most Americans distrusted the military as a threat to their political liberties and wealth. The Founders who fought the Revolution and devised the Constitution were determined not to replace subjection to the Crown with subjection to a military dictatorship. The institutions they devised and values they codified ensured that civilians should always strictly control the nation's soldiers.

The Founders' fears were justified. Ironically, at no time since the Revolution has the United States been closer to military rule than during the war for independence. The Conway Cabal of 1777 and Newburgh Cabal of 1781 were both attempts to overthrow a weak and inefficient Congress and establish military rule. Fortunately for liberal democracy, alert patriots thwarted both conspiracies.

Alas, the tradition of a minuscule army and navy ill prepared the United States to fight let alone win wars. Allowing the free market to supply the military subjected its personnel and American taxpayers to the grossest corruption, expenses, and abuses by contractors. Those thefts from the public purse by private interests were so blatant and debilitating to America's ability to fight the 1812 War that Congress granted the military a Quartermaster Corps and Ordnance Department so that it could succor directly from the nation's factories and fields rather than through layers of rapacious middlemen.

During the four years of Civil War, President Lincoln helped organize a vast production, transportation, storage, and communications complex which gave the Union armies enough bread and bullets eventually to grind the Confederacy into oblivion. With the war over, the military–industrial complex was dismantled, its troops demobilized and its factories quickly converted to serve civilian needs. In those industrially and technologically simpler days, conversion was not the painful economic and political process it is today.

It was World War I which gave birth to a permanent, ever evolving military–industrial complex. How did this happen?

Having asked for and received a congressional war declaration, the Wilson Administration faced serious choices and dilemmas over just how to mobilize the nation for war. The demands of waging that war depended on the unprecedented mobilization of America's economy, which in turn demanded entirely new institutions, relationships, and values. Should Washington nationalize those industries necessary for supplying the armies in the field? Or could it somehow guide the private sector into supplying those needs on its own?

The debate had raged ever since the Europeans first went to war in August 1914 and seemed likely to drag the United States into it. In 1915, the Navy Secretary set up a Naval Consulting Board which brought together leading corporate executives, engineers, and bureaucrats to discuss ways to modernize the navy. The Board's most important subdivision was the Industrial Preparedness Committee, which began to inventory those factories that would be necessary for war. In 1916, the White House created a Council of National Defense, composed of six cabinet officers along with corporate, bureaucratic, and military leaders, which absorbed and expanded the Naval Consulting Board's duties. Beneath the Council was the National Defense Advisory Commission, which supervised what became over 100 committees that took responsibility for the war's every facet. In July 1917, the system was expanded with the creation of the War Industries Board (WIB), which was endowed with even broader powers and duties. By the war's end, the WIB presided over 57 commodity committees and more than 300 other committees, each of which was composed of bureaucratic, corporate, and military representatives.

The system looked good on paper but at first was executed poorly. "Dollar a year" corporate executives may have directly received a pittance for their service but reaped untold wealth for their businesses by funneling them as many taxpayer dollars as possible, whether or not the diversion could be justified militarily. Meanwhile, the War Department, fearing it would lose the procurement independence it had won a century earlier, at first refused to cooperate with the WIB. Unfortunately, the military was completely ignorant of just how to mobilize the economy to enable it to ship over a million troops to France and there wage modern war.

To break this deadlock, Wilson pushed through Congress the Overman Act of March 1918, which empowered the President to revamp his administration as he wished. Thus empowered, Wilson forced the War Department to reorganize itself in alignment with and subordination to the WIB. Almost as importantly, Wilson appointed the financial and managerial wizard Bernard Baruch to head WIB. It was only after the reorganization was complete that the war machine began to hum. And then, on November 11, 1918, the guns abruptly fell silent.

The military–industrial complex was not dismantled after World War I, it was merely reduced. The National Defense Act of 1920 authorized the War Department to plan not only its own logistics but the entire economy's mobilization in a future war. In 1930, the War Department unveiled an Industrial Mobilization Plan, which it then modified in 1933, 1936, and 1939.

Not everyone blindly accepted the transfer of unprecedented and constitutionally questionable power to the War Department. Between 1934 and 1936, the Nye Committee extensively reviewed the War Department's plans and power, along with the WIB's performance during World War I. It found that the WIB had engaged in shameless profiteering during the war that sapped rather than enhanced the war effort. Furthermore, since the War Department's Industrial Mobilization Plan was based on the World War I experience, its implementation would involve similar gross corruption and undermining of American military power. In all, the Nye Committee did not mince its words as it identified "an unhealthy alliance ... that ... brings into being a self-interested political power which operates in the name of patriotism and satisfies interests which are, in large part, purely selfish, and that such associations are an inevitable part of militarism, and are to be avoided in peacetime at all costs."[5] In all, the WIB's legacy was unnecessary waste, profiteering, debt, inflation, and the further concentration of industry. The Committee recommended that any future war be paid for with taxes rather than loans, and that laws be enacted which prohibited any conflict of interests among industrialists mobilized for the war, and that empowered Washington to draft any private enterprises into the war effort.

Congress and President Roosevelt ignored the findings and recommendations.

Contrary to popular belief, thanks to a combination of its World War I and New Deal experiences, and its Industrial Mobilization Plans, the United States was largely prepared to fight World War II. As in the years leading to World War I, Washington created most of the institutions it would need to fight World War II before war was formally declared. In May 1940, Roosevelt reestablished the National Defense Advisory Commission Board (NDAC) to work with the War and Navy Departments in implementing the Industrial Mobilization Plan. In December 1940, he replaced the NDAC with an Office of Production Management (OPM) with even greater duties and powers, and, in January 1941, renamed it the War Production Board (WPB). However named, the organization was subdivided into Industry Divisions which formulated and implemented mobilization policies for each industry, which in turn was represented by an Industry Advisory Council composed of the trade association. By 1943, two other institutions, the Production Executive Committee (PEC) and Office of War Mobilization (OWM), joined with WPB to coordinate the hundreds of industrial committees. As in World War I, it took the wartime bureaucracy two years to purge the system's kinks and begin smooth operations.

Washington spent almost ten times more for World War II as for the previous world war. Of the total $315.8 billion bill, the War Department expended $179.9 billion, the Navy Department $83.9 billion, and the rest was channeled directly into subcontracts with some 18,539 firms. Impressive as that range of subcontractors seems, in fact, a mere 30 firms took over half of all procurements while 100 enjoyed two-thirds of the contracts.[6]

THE MILITARY–INDUSTRIAL COMPLEX II: AMERICA AS A SUPERPOWER

Following the surrenders of Germany in May and Japan in September 1945, Washington began dismantling its military machine just as it had following previous wars. In 1945, the Defense Department directly employed 12.056 million troops

and 2.628 million civilians, while another 11 million people
worked in defense industries. By 1947, the number of troops
had plunged to 1.582 million, civilian employees to 859,000,
and defense industrial workers to 786,000. In 1987 dollars,
defense spending plummeted from the equivalent of $714.6
billion in 1945 to $64.9 billion in 1946.[7] The Cold War ended
and then reversed demobilization. Had it not, the military–
industrial complex would have been reduced to a skeleton
of the bloated giant it had become during World War II.
Instead, it quickly developed into an even more powerful,
sophisticated version.

Historians will forever debate the Cold War's central questions: Could it have been avoided or ended sooner? Why
did it end, and how and when it did? Which policies were
successful and which failures? Regardless, for our purposes
the key question is whether the military–industrial complex
had to develop as it did. The military–industrial complex's
power was shaped by the shifting political struggle between
adherents of two very different containment strategies.

George Kennan authored America's "containment policy"
toward the Soviet Union. Kennan was a brilliant diplomat
and historian who had served in Moscow during and shortly
after World War II. In his famous 1946 "long telegraph"
back to Washington and his 1947 "Mr X" *Foreign Affairs* article,
Kennan explained that the Soviet Union would assert control over Eastern Europe and try to subvert the democratic
governments of Western Europe. According to Kennan,
Moscow under the Communists was not very different in
mentality and foreign policy goals than it was under the
Tsars. Russia had traditionally sought to expand to Central
Europe, the Middle East, Central Asia, and the Pacific, all
in order to destroy any possible foreign threats and create
buffer zones to protect the Russian heartland from invasion.
This goal was reinforced by the imperialist ideology of communism. Victory in World War II gave Moscow the chance
to realize that ancient goal.

Yet, the Soviet threat to the West was limited in several
ways. Moscow really threatened only the industrial countries
of Western Europe and Japan, or oil-rich countries of the
Persian Gulf; a communist takeover in poor countries like
China or Vietnam did not pose a threat to American interests.

Revolutions in the Third World were based as much on nationalism as communism, and the new regimes would eventually break with Moscow. The Soviet threat was primarily rooted in economics and psychology rather than in the military. Taking advantage of postwar economic chaos and depression, Communist parties would subvert the West's economic and political systems, and then take over.

Just as the Soviet threat was limited in means and geography, so too should be the policy that contained it. Under Kennan's "selective" containment vision the Soviet threat could be thwarted through American economic and political aid which reconstructed the Western European and Japanese political economies. Communism flourishes in chaos, depression, corruption, and widening gaps between rich and poor. If the United States worked with Western leaders to reduce those problems, the communist threat would correspondingly whither. Likewise, Washington could exploit the nationalism of communist regimes which came to power around the world, aiding them against Soviet domination. Since the Soviet threat was non-military, it could not be contained by military means. Thus reconstructing the military–industrial complex was not only unnecessary and wasteful, but would scuttle any possibility of negotiating a rapprochement with the Soviets and instead provoke an arms race with them.

President Truman acted on Kennan's analysis. In March 1947, he announced what became know as the "Truman Doctrine" in which the United States would support any government threatened by communist subversion. Although Truman's containment seemed "global," in execution he confined it to the regions Kennan designated. In June 1947, Secretary of State John Marshall unveiled a plan to extend massive economic aid to Western Europe to restore its economic prosperity and political stability. The United States eventually gave Western Europe $14 billion and Japan $2.2 billion.

Despite Kennan's warning that containment should be a socioeconomic rather than a military strategy, the United States increasingly became entangled in defense issues. In 1947, Congress passed the National Defense Act, which created the Defense Department, National Security Council (NSC), and Central Intelligence Agency (CIA). In 1948,

Britain, France, Italy, and the Benelux countries signed the Brussels Pact and invited the United States to join. Moscow in turn responded by attempting to starve the western sectors of Berlin into submission from June 1948 to April 1949. The Berlin crisis convinced the Truman administration that it had to join the West European alliance. In 1949, the United States, Canada, and most West European states formed the North Atlantic Treaty Organization (NATO).

The growing military tensions between the American and Soviet blocs led an increasing number of policy makers to question Kennan's assumptions that the Cold War should be fought mostly with socioeconomic means. NSC analyst Paul Nitze led those in the United States who wanted to globalize and militarize containment. In April 1950, Nitze submitted to Truman NSC-68, which called for the United States to engage in a massive military buildup and network of alliances that bound all regions in order to contain what was primarily a Soviet military threat. Between 1950 and 1954 alone, NSC-68 recommended that the Pentagon's budget rise from $13 billion to $35 billion. Once the plan became widely known, some prominent White House voices joined Kennan's in protest. Joint Chief of Staff Chair Omar Bradley, for example, warned that such an explosion of the Pentagon's budget was not only completely unnecessary, it would pose dangers to American wealth and liberties worse than any threat from Moscow.[8]

The outbreak of the Korean War in June 1950 tipped the political balance between those who advocated "selective" and those "global" containment to the latter. The administration viewed communist North Korea's invasion of South Korea as orchestrated by Moscow in yet another attempt to probe the West's determination to defend themselves and perhaps as the prelude to another crisis in Berlin or elsewhere. Truman ordered American troops to reinforce the remnant of South Korea's army; the Seventh Fleet to intervene in China's civil war on the side of Chiang Kai-shek and the remnant of his army, which had retreated to Taiwan and was besieged by the triumphant Communist armies which had overrun the mainland; and military aid to the French colonial armies battling the Communist forces under Ho Chi Minh in Vietnam. Between 1951 and 1953, the

Defense Department's budget more than quadrupled from $11.9 billion to $47.7 billion, while the number of troops rose from 1.459 million to 3.636 million, civilian employees from 710,000 to 1.304 million, and defense industrial workers from 713,000 to 4.118 million.[9] Washington expanded its range of military commitments through defense treaties with Japan (1952), Australia and New Zealand (ANZUS, 1954), and the Southeast Asia Treaty Organization (SEATO, 1954), creating in the Pacific a loose version of NATO.

Perhaps more than any president, Dwight Eisenhower understood the dangers of a military–industrial complex and attempted to cut it back before it became too powerful. As president, Eisenhower tried to get "more bang for the buck" in both conventional and nuclear military power. He cut defense spending by three million dollars from $47.7 billion in 1954 to $44.6 billion in 1961 (nearly $100 billion in constant 1987 dollars from $315.2 billion to $217.9 billion), and the number of troops to 2.483 million troops, civilian employees to 1.012 million, and defense industrial workers to 2.600 million.[10] Eisenhower made up for fewer troops with more nuclear weapons and the policy of "massive retaliation" with nuclear weapons against any Soviet attack on Western Europe. But massive retaliation seemed increasingly unrealistic as Moscow built up its nuclear arsenal and in 1957 launched an inter-continental ballistic missile (ICBM) theoretically capable of hitting the United States. And even before that, America's four-year nuclear monopoly before the Soviets exploded their first atomic bomb in 1949 did not prevent Moscow from conquering Eastern Europe or going to the brink of war with the West over Berlin (1948–9). Nonetheless, in managing to trim back the military–industrial complex during his eight years in the Oval Office, Eisenhower not only managed to avoid harming national security but actually boosted it as billions of dollars were diverted from low-return military to high-return consumer research, development, and production.

His successors between 1961 and 1969, John Kennedy and Lyndon Johnson, abandoned Eisenhower's prudent policies and expanded America's conventional and nuclear forces. Defense spending rose to $78.7 billion in 1969 ($299.5 billion in 1987 dollars), while the number of civilian employees reached 1.275 million. The previous year in 1968 the number of troops had peaked at 3.548 million and defense industrial workers at 3.174 million.[11] Meanwhile, America's nuclear arsenal continued to grow in numbers and types. Recognizing that massive retaliation against a Soviet attack on the West would result in "mutually assured destruction" (MAD), the Kennedy Administration replaced it with the "flexible response" strategy whereby a Warsaw Pact attack on NATO would first be met with conventional arms alone. But if the Red Army seemed about to prevail, the United States would use tactical nuclear weapons to destroy Soviet armoured divisions and supply-depots within twenty or so miles of the front line. If the Soviets retaliated, the Pentagon would then use regional nuclear missiles to strike deep against the enemy's supply and industrial network in Eastern Europe and the western Soviet Union. If Moscow ordered retaliatory strikes against Western Europe, Washington would then order ICBM strikes across the Soviet Union. Flexible Response remained the Pentagon's deterrence strategy until the Cold War's end. The strategy was extremely expensive in its demand for large increases in nuclear and conventional forces alike.

Throughout the 1950s and 1960s, the global containment assumption that American interests existed everywhere in equal measure led the United States to intervene against revolutionary forces in every region and most countries around the world, mostly with military and economic aid, and CIA actions, but sometimes with American troops. Global containment's logic ultimately led to America's entanglement in an unwinnable war in Indochina. In that war alone, the United States squandered $150 billion and 58,000 American lives, and hundreds of thousands of other Americans physically or psychologically maimed for life. About 4 million Indochinese died during the war.

All along, Washington saw itself as engaged in a life-or-death game with Moscow in which the entire world was a giant chessboard in which no piece or square was safe, even within the United States itself. In the early 1950s, Senator Joseph McCarthy's congressional hearings and accusations that thousands of Americans were Communist agents bent on destroying the country were only the most blatant expressions of the paranoia that permeated American society and politics. Any American who was critical of American foreign or domestic policies, no matter how well documented or reasoned, was labeled a "red" by conservatives. The FBI and CIA frequently violated those Americans' civil rights through spying and dirty tricks.

President Richard Nixon had a more sophisticated understanding of global politics than his postwar predecessors. Nixon essentially embraced Kennan's vision that nationalism was more important than communism in the revolutions wracking the Third World, and that regardless, the United States had no significant interests in most of those countries and any intervention would simply fan nationalism's flames. In a 1969 speech at Guam, he outlined what would become known as the "Nixon Doctrine." Henceforth, the United States would aid only those governments with the will and ability to suppress a communist insurgency. Under his "Vietnamization policy," the White House simultaneously withdrew American forces from Indochina, bolstered the ability of its regional allies to defend themselves, and negotiated with the North Vietnamese. He pursued détente with both the Soviet Union and China, trying to manipulate the old nationalist antagonisms of those two communist giants against each other.

Nixon recognized that America's economic and political power had relatively diminished, not vis-à-vis Moscow, but also against Tokyo and Brussels. Japan and the European Community were rapidly catching up to the United States economically. The United States was suffering increasingly severe balance-of-payments deficits and, in 1971, its first trade deficit since the nineteenth century. In August 1971, Nixon responded by taking the dollar off the gold standard and imposing a tariff hike. In December of that year, he devalued the dollar by 15 percent against other major currencies. In 1973, the dollar floated freely. His administration confronted trade rivals on their dumping and import barriers. Finally, he tried to get America's allies to "share the defense burden" by increasing their own contributions.

All of those policies were attempts to revive American power and realign it in pursuit of genuine American interests at home and abroad. Recognizing that the military was a huge drain on America's economic dynamism, he sharply cut back defense spending. And he tried to negotiate nuclear treaties with the Soviet Union to rein in the arms race that threatened to bankrupt and devastate both countries. By 1974, he had decreased America's defense burden to 2.162 million troops, 1.013 million civilian defense employees, and 1.860 million defense industrial workers, while he cut the defense budget to $185.3 billion in constant 1987 dollars. Nixon's successors, Gerald Ford and Jimmy Carter, continued his "selective containment" policies. In 1979, American troops numbered 2.031 million, civilian defense employees 916,000, and defense industrial workers 1.860 million, while in 1980, the budget was $187.1 billion.[12]

A series of foreign-policy catastrophes around the world in 1979 caused the Carter administration to abandon "selective" and embrace "global" containment. A pro-American dictatorship in Nicaragua was toppled by communist Sandinista revolutionaries, and one in Iran by a fundamentalist Islamic revolution, global oil prices doubled, and, worst of all, in December the Soviets invaded Afghanistan. Carter responded by raising defense spending and declaring that the Persian Gulf was essential to American security and would be defended against aggression, a policy known as the "Carter Doctrine."

Claiming that Carter was soft on defense, Ronald Reagan took office in 1981 determined to double American military spending. He succeeded. In what was the biggest peacetime increase in American history, Reagan fattened the military budget from $140.7 billion to $291.4 billion ($187.1 billion to $283.3 billion in constant 1987 dollars) between 1980 and 1988, for a total defense spending of $2.3 trillion during his eight years in the White House. Ironically, those massive budget increases did not make the United States military any more prepared to go to war in the Persian Gulf, the most likely place a war might begin.

Most of the funds went to an array of conventional and nuclear weapons whose positive impact on national security was questionable at best. About 15 percent, or $300 billion of spending, went to the development, maintenance, or procurement of nuclear weapons. Reagan ordered the resumption of the B-1 bomber's development (which Carter had terminated as wasteful and unnecessary), the MX ICBM, the Trident II Submarine-launched ballistic missile (SLBM), the Midgetman mobile ICBM, the B-2 bomber, and the Strategic Defense Initiative (SDI). The 899 Trident II missiles alone were estimated to cost $35.5 billion and the 132 B-2s, $68.1 billion. By the time Congress finally pulled the plug on SDI in 1991, 44 billion taxpayer dollars had been spent on largely laboratory work. By the late 1980s, 70 percent of government research and development funds were going to military technology compared with only 50 percent when Reagan took office. In the emphasis on glitzy, exorbitantly priced weapons systems, Reagan's defense buildup slighted conventional forces in number, training, and readiness. By 1988, the number of troops had slightly increased to 2.209 million and civilian defense employees to 1.049 million, although the vast procurement orders did boost the number of defense industrial workers to 3.450 million.[13]

Unfortunately, America's economy was increasingly unable to afford Reagan's weapons buildup. Reaganomics had a devastating effect on American prosperity and dynamism – the United States ran ever worsening trade and payment deficits throughout 1987; in 1985, the United States was transformed from the world's largest creditor to worst debtor nation; Japan leapfrogged the United States by most trade, technological, manufacturing, and financial indicators. The Pentagon's war machines became increasingly dependent on foreign components. Even scientists, technicians, and laboratories were diverted from the mainstream economy where they were desperately needed to quell America's ever worsening trade deficits, productivity, and array of socioeconomic problems.

Between 1989 and 1992, the Soviet empire and communism collapsed. A series of revolutions toppled the communist dictators of Eastern Europe and eventually the Soviet Union itself. The Warsaw Pact and Soviet Union dissolved by 1992. The Cold War was over. What ended it? The collapse of communism and Soviet power was inevitable given the inability of Marxist Leninism to create wealth, freedom, or meaning for those under its rule. Soviet President Mikhail Gorbachev caused the inevitable collapse to occur sooner rather than later with his revolutionary policies of perestroika (restructuring), glasnost (openness), democracy, and allowing freedom to the Eastern European countries. And finally, nearly five decades of American containment policies had helped grind down the Soviet empire and communism.

THE COSTS OF COLD WAR

America's Cold War victory was very costly. Over a half-century, the United States is estimated to have diverted directly or indirectly $16 trillion of its wealth into its containment policies, of which one-quarter went into the various costs of nuclear weapons. A September 1995 Brookings Institute report entitled "US Nuclear Weapons Cost Study Project" broke down the $4 trillion spent on nuclear forces that included, among hundreds of billions in other expenses, $200 billion for strategic bombers, $375 billion for nuclear warheads, $371 billion for 50 types of nuclear missiles, $100 billion for nuclear missile-firing submarines, $182 billion for command, control, and communications systems that control nuclear forces, $270 billion into spy satellites, and $400 billion in handling the subsequent nuclear waste. Was that money well spent? How much more security did $4 trillion in nuclear weapons spending purchase for the United States than $2 trillion would have? Would the United States have been any less secure if it had spent only $1 trillion on nuclear weapons? In retrospect, could the United States have won the Cold War at a much lower cost in treasury and blood?[14]

Clearly, the United States squandered enormous amounts of financial, human, and scientific treasures in the nuclear arms race. Both the "massive retaliation" and "flexible response" nuclear strategies demanded an ever burgeoning horde of nuclear weapons. Under massive retaliation, deterrence theoretically rested on America's nuclear superiority in bombers and, later, missiles capable of destroying the Soviet Union. Under flexible response, deterrence supposedly rested on the ability to "prevail" at each rung of the nuclear escalation ladder. Both strategies were supposed to "deter" Soviet aggression by making its costs too great. Deterrence assumes the other side's rationality. If the enemy is irrational, it will not be deterred even in the face of destruction.

Rationality, in turn, depends on information and communication. One must communicate unambiguously one's own capability and resolve to resist the other side's unacceptable behavior. Deterrence will not work if the enemy does not understand what it had better not do, and the consequences if it does do it.

Throughout the Cold War, the Soviet Union proved as rational as the United States in stepping back from the brink of nuclear holocaust in the various Berlin, Middle East, and Cuban crises. Yet, there is no evidence that nuclear deterrence worked. Moscow might not have wanted to go to war with the West even if it had had no nuclear weapons. And America's nuclear arsenal certainly never deterred North Korea from invading South Korea, North Vietnam from South Vietnam, the Soviet Union from Afghanistan, or Iraq from Kuwait. It is difficult not to conclude that the nuclear arms race was a tragic misallocation of trillions of dollars, millions of people, and thousands of laboratories and factories, based on unwarranted fears and flawed strategies.

But what if irrational leaders determined to invade Western Europe had ruled the Kremlin? Would any president have retaliated with nuclear weapons against a successful Soviet assault on Western Europe? It is unlikely that the White House would have ordered an attack on the Soviet Union when such an attack would have resulted in a Soviet counter-strike that devastated America. Once the Soviet Union acquired the ability to strike the United States, massive retaliation and flexible response alike became myths. As nuclear war expert Lieutenant Colonel Dean Darling put it, "We have built our strategy in Europe on nuclear weapons systems that we will refuse to use when the time comes to use them. Not only that – by relying on this nuclear facade, we have undermined the war-fighting abilities of our conventional forces as well."[15]

It was clear to many at the time and most in hindsight that there was never any strategic need for Washington or Moscow to develop enough nuclear power to destroy all human life on the planet dozens of times over. Politics compounded by paranoia and ignorance about the other side's capabilities and intentions propelled the nuclear arms race to insanely high levels of destruction. The United States weak-

ened rather than strengthened itself by spending hundreds
of billions of dollars on such redundant and often unworkable weapons as the B-1 and B-2 bombers, Star Wars, MX
and Midgetman ICBMs, and Trident II SLBM programs. To
the direct costs of those unnecessary weapons must be added
the indirect cost of diverting America's best minds and laboratories from productive to destructive ends. The nuclear
arms race left the United States economically and socially
much weaker than it otherwise might have been.

America's conventional force strategy was just as flawed.
For example, throughout the Cold War, nearly two of every
three Pentagon dollars underwrote American participation
in NATO. Between 1980 and 1989, NATO's cost to American taxpayers rose from $100 billion to $200 billion. In 1986,
every American spent $1,155 on defense compared with an
average $318 for each citizen of its democratic industrial
allies. Altogether the other NATO members devoted an
average 3.5 percent of their collectives GNPs for defense.
Japan's contribution to the alliance was even more miserly
– defense spending averaged only 1 percent of Japan's GNP.
Although the Nixon Administration was the first strongly to
advocate allied burden-sharing, and subsequent presidents
mouthed similar sentiments, no one pressed the Europeans
or Japanese to pay more so that Americans could pay less.[16]

America's military allies were also its economic rivals. While
the United States was pouring hundreds of billions of dollars annually into defense, its rivals were concentrating on
creating and distributing wealth, and increasingly wielding
the power that accompanies greater wealth, mostly to the
end of creating yet more wealth. Economists estimate that
a nation loses 20,000 jobs for every $1 billion of its trade
deficit. When America's trade deficit peaked at $169 billion
in 1987 under the Reagan administration, that meant that
3.8 million more Americans were jobless than if the United
States had had a trade balance. Meanwhile, the Europeans
and Japanese enjoyed such higher living standards as universal health care, lower crime, better education, inexpensive college education, day care, lower divorce and unwed
mother rates, and less poverty.

None of America's economic rivals was more voracious
than Japan. Starting in 1965, Japan enjoyed ever larger annual

trade surpluses with the United States. Japanese corporate groups used dumping abroad, trade barriers at home, and a range of other neomercantilist strategies to devastate their American rivals in such industries as consumer electronics, steel, semiconductors, automobiles, and machine tools, to name some of the more prominent. If the economists are to be believed, Japan's trade surpluses of $60 billion in 1987 and 1994 translated into 1.2 million lost American jobs in those years.

All along, most American policy makers grossly exaggerated the Soviet threat. At worst, the Soviet threat involved the political and economic subversion of the Western democratic nations. As George Kennan argued from the Cold War's beginning, political and economic means were the best way to contain Soviet ambitions.

Even during the Cold War's height, the chances of a Soviet attack on Western Europe were virtually nil. Moscow's conventional military forces were largely a paper tiger. Training, morale, supply, and tactics were second-rate at best.[17] Soviet forces would have had enormous logistical difficulties launching a sustained campaign in central Europe, compounded by worries about the loyalty of their Warsaw Pact allies. And even if the Soviet Union had somehow magically replaced its military jalopy with a Ferrari, would World War III have broken out?

Strobe Talbott very nicely captured the tragically mistaken assumptions behind America's Cold War policy:

> For more than four decades, Western policy has been based on a gross miscalculation of what the U.S.S.R. could do if it wanted, therefore what it might do, therefore what the West must be prepared to do. Gorbachev has shown that, in some respects, where the West thought the Soviet Union was strong, it was in fact weak. . . . Gorbachev is admitting that much of what has been perceived by the outside world as his country's collective "discipline" is actually an ossifying, demoralizing, brutalizing system of institutionalized inefficiency.[18]

Why did the nuclear and conventional arms races persist despite the abundant evidence that neither side had any intention of attacking the other? Paranoia certainly played a major role – and people tend to act on their fears. Communist and Russian xenophobia is deeply ingrained. American fear of the Soviet Union was understandably exacerbated by Moscow's own Marxist Leninist creed of class struggle and world conquest. And the Soviet Union did possess a vast nuclear and conventional arsenal.

But perhaps even more important forces behind the arms race were the military–industrial complexes of both the United States and the Soviet Union. The defense-related bureaucrats, politicians, and contractors had a vested interest in taking as much of the financial, human, technological, and institutional assets from their nations as they could. And they succeeded in doing so.

THE POST-COLD WAR

What should be America's military strategy into the twenty-first century? What threats linger in the world, and how can they best be countered? Just where is that elusive line between just enough military spending to provide national security, and too much that drains vital personnel, money, technology, institutions, energies, and attention from creating a more prosperous nation?

Presidents George Bush and Bill Clinton have wrestled with those questions but neither offered comprehensive answers. The Bush Administration did agree to reduce the military, with cutbacks in troops from 2.202 million in 1989 to 1.705 million in 1993, civilian defense employees from 1.037 million to 915,000, and military industrial workers from 3.295 million to 2.725 million, while he pared the Pentagon's budget from \$292.9 billion in 1990 to \$288.4 billion (\$272.3 billion to \$240.6 billion in constant 1987 dollars).[19] Defense Secretary Richard Cheney tried to drop unnecessary weapons like the V-22 Osprey vertical-takeoff transport for the marines, the navy's F-14 fighter, and air force's F-15E. Acting on behalf of the military–industrial complex, Congress restored them.

The Clinton Administration went far beyond its predecessor in trying systematically to assess possible military threats to

American interests and the force structure to meet those possible threats. It narrowed the choices to three force structures that would shape Pentagon planning, procurement, and deployments for a generation. Option One was designed to fight two regional wars at once, and included 12 carrier fleets, 12 army divisions, and 24 air wings. Option Two would fight one regional war while holding the line elsewhere, then fight that second war, and included 10 carrier fleets, 10 army divisions, and 20 air wings. Option Three would fight only one regional war, and included 8 carrier fleets, 8 army divisions, and 16 air wings. The most likely scenario, of two regional wars simultaneously breaking out which threatened American interests, would be attacks by Iraq against Kuwait and North against South Korea.

In May 1993, after careful consideration, President Clinton chose Option Two, the win–hold–win strategy, but held off determining its exact force structure until he had studied the issue more. On May 23, the Pentagon issued a policy paper which emphasized collective security among America's allies to deter any regional aggressor. It also spoke of converting old rivals such as Russia into new allies. The means of securing American interests would largely involve diplomatic and economic rather than military means. The draft replaced an earlier one developed under the Bush Administration, issued on February 18, which called for a one-superpower world in which the United States contained the rise of any military competitors, including the extremely unlikely reemergence of Japan and Germany as military aggressors.

On September 1, 1993, President Clinton unveiled the military's future force structure. After listening to the various arguments and assessing the political strength behind them, Clinton essentially split the difference between the two options' force structures. In all, the Clinton military would be a leaner, tougher, and more mobile version of the old. The army would have 11 active divisions and 15 reserve brigades, 4 fewer active divisions than at the Cold War's end. Concerned with the military's ability to respond quickly to crises, Clinton actually decreased the marines' strength less than Bush would have done, from 182,000 to 174,000 compared with his predecessor's proposed cuts to 159,000. The navy would have 11 carrier battle groups and one reserve training group, compared with its then 13 carrier groups. The air force would be composed of 13 active fighter wings and 7 reserve wings rather than its then 16 active wings and 12 reserve wings.[20]

Critics assailed Clinton's choice as dangerously weakening American military power. Yet, the furor between advocates of Option One and of Option Two is ironic considering that as recently as 1990 the Pentagon claimed that it could simultaneously fight a major land war against the Soviet Union in central Europe and a smaller regional war elsewhere. Although spending has declined slightly in relative and absolute terms recently, surely the American military has not fallen apart like the Soviet military, as some would have the public believe.

Military spending remains enormous in the post-Cold War. In 1994, the Pentagon's budget was $264 billion, the equivalent of 4.5 percent of GNP. If the military has weaknesses today, it is not from a lack of money, but from a misallocation of resources which goes back decades. For example, most analysts would agree that the United States does not need a third Seawolf Submarine that costs $3.5 billion or another nuclear aircraft carrier that costs $5 billion, but does need many more cargo ships and planes. Clinton, however, retained plans to develop the Seawolf and carrier so that the last shipyards which can build those kind of ships, in Groton, Connecticut and Newport News, Virginia, would not shut down. That decision was as much about retaining the potential votes as it was about the skills of those workers. And, although American hawks are running out of enemies with whom to justify the current military–industrial complex, that does not stop them from boosting America's defense spending. In May 1994, Congress appropriated $1.2 billion more than even the Pentagon asked for, including $274 million to support an executive aircraft purchasing program that had been dropped.[21]

Recently the Pentagon has experimented with more effective industrial policy tools to supply more weapons at a cheaper cost. Traditionally, the Defense Department paid private firms to build a factory to manufacture some key component or final product. During the 1970s and 1980s, as Japanese and other foreign firms devastated one American industry after another, the Defense Department faced an increasingly severe dilemma. It could buy from and thus become dependent on the foreign source, or prop up the often inefficient and dwindling American survivors.

The Clinton White House has attempted to finesse that dilemma by pressuring the Pentagon into subsidizing an entire industry rather than simply an assembly line. Over the long-run, it was hoped that bolstering an industry would save more money than simply making small, highly specified purchases from a firm. Private firms would develop products for mass consumer markets, and the Pentagon would simply be one of many purchasers. If one company foundered, the Pentagon could switch its purchases to another firm. Thus, it would avoid getting trapped into buying outdated, grossly overpriced products from one source.

The policy's first venture was with the remnants of America's flat-panel computer display industry, which had been nearly wiped out by Japan's microelectronics giants. Flat-panel displays are one of the cutting edge, strategic, dual-use industries for the 1990s and into the twenty-first century. They not only provide displays for jet bomber cockpits but for computers, car dashboards, and even maps for soldiers and civilians alike.

In a concerted action directed by the National Economic Council, the Defense and Energy departments provide direct subsidies to the industry, while the Commerce Department helps it market its goods overseas, the US Trade Representative attacks foreign trade barriers, and the Justice Department monitors and retaliates against Japanese dumping, cartels, and other nefarious business practices within the United States. The subsidies – $1 billion over a decade – are in the form of matching funds for research and development by the industry's firms. American flat panel producers currently cling to a 3 percent global market share. It was hoped the policy would be a model for countless others. Predictably, political economists applauded the new policy as a means of boosting economic development and national security; theoretical economists blasted it as an infringement of "market magic."

Clinton's policy will be less expensive and more effective than the traditional means of subsidizing the military–industrial complex. By 1998, Clinton will have boosted that portion of the government's research and development budget devoted to civilian technologies to 50 percent, up from 41 percent in 1993. It will require federal laboratories to divert 20 percent of their spending to joint ventures with private industry, up from 5 percent in 1993. Consortia rather than single companies would be the preferred partners. The model was Sematech, formed in the mid-1980s by a dozen high-technology firms to promote basic research and development and backed by matching government funds.[22]

The chief implementer of these reforms would be the Defense Advanced Research Project Agency (DARPA), the Pentagon's leading industrial-policy agency. While the Reagan and Bush Administrations blocked DARPA's efforts to expand its research efforts, Clinton's White House encouraged it. In 1994, the Clinton Administration boosted DARPA's budget to $1.4 billion and encouraged it to support commercial research, with an additional $473 million to help military contractors convert to civilian production.

Yet another way in which the Clinton Administration is trying to ease the military–industrial complex's transition to the post-Cold War is by encouraging exports. Washington spends a half-billion dollars annually to promote weapons sales, a figure which in 1993 reached $31 billion or 75 percent of a shrinking global market. Given the sales figures, that money appears to have been well spent. These sales simultaneously ease the economic impact of converting unneeded guns to butter, maintain needed weapons production, help alleviate the trade deficit, generate more national wealth and jobs, and undermine the military–industrial complexes of other countries.[23]

Critics have blasted America's arms exports on several grounds. William Hartung's book on the subject argues that the United States actually spent $7 billion rather than $500 million in subsidizing that $31 billion in sales.[24] The subsidies included $3.2 billion in grants and $800 million in low-interest loans to finance buyers. To promote sales, the Pentagon deployed a small army of 5,000 armed with a $300 million budget. It spends an additional $25 million annually on trade shows. To secure a deal, the Pentagon and American manufacturers often must conclude an "offset" agreement in which some production is transferred to the foreign country. These deals result in a loss of wealth, jobs, and technologies to other nations. Nations which spend more on arms, have less to spend on consumer goods. The International Monetary Fund estimates that a 20 percent drop in world-wide military spending would stimulate a $190 million increase in global wealth.

Another downside to these sales is that they can aggravate regional tensions and encourage aggression. The Reagan and Bush policy of financing and arming Iraqi President Saddam Hussein was a grievous blunder that cost the United States and its allies enormous treasury and blood to correct. Between 1980 and 1988, the Reagan White House tilted toward Iraq in its war with the more radical Iran, supplying it with arms, intelligence, and finance. This aid continued even after Iraq and Iran signed an armistice in August 1988. The Republican presidents discarded reports that Hussein was simply milking the Americans while gathering strength for further aggression. The Bush Administration continued to support Hussein during the six months before his forces actually invaded Kuwait, even though all along he continually stated his intentions of doing so. Money from the Commodity Credit Corporation and Export–Import Bank, which was supposed to subsidize American grain shipments to Iraq, was used instead to finance arms exports.

In an era of declining defense budgets, military bases have been increasingly controversial. Like most of its weapons systems, the Pentagon's bases were selected as much for political as for strategic reasons. The greater the number of electoral districts in which the Pentagon located military bases, the wider the support it would receive for its yearly budget, which would enable it to pour more money into even more electoral districts, receive even more political support, and so on. That Pentagon strategy made political if not military sense as long as the Cold War raged, but has returned to haunt the generals and their minions throughout the 1990s.

Where are military bases located? Where does the base money come from? Some rural residents complain that many of their tax dollars go to welfare mothers in big cities. Of course, anti-poverty programs exist in both urban and rural areas. However, when it comes to military spending, not surprisingly, most military bases are located outside of major cities. A study revealed that in 1990 alone, New York experienced a net loss of $8.38 billion to the Pentagon, Los Angeles $3.27 billion, and Chicago $3.1 billion, for an average loss of $3,000 per family in all three cities. This outflow of tax dollars translated into 250,000 fewer jobs for New York and 100,000 less for Los Angeles and Chicago. Altogether, nineteen of America's twenty-five largest cities paid out more to the Pentagon than they received. Among those six cities which did enjoy a net gain, San Diego was the largest with $3.97 billion, followed by Washington with $1.49 billion, and smaller amounts for Seattle, New Orleans, and Baltimore. All those cities which gained money were ports.[25]

In an attempt to provide political cover for politicians with military bases in their districts, a presidential commission of seven experts, called the Base Realignment and Closure Commission (BRAC), was set up in 1988 to study the issue and make recommendations based on several criteria including: the base's military value, its return on investment, and the economic impact its closing would have on the community. Congress and the president would then accept or reject the entire package of suggested cuts. The first three rounds in 1988, 1991, and 1993 resulted in 250 bases closed and 109 others realigned, at total savings of about $4.5 billion annually. In 1995 BRAC recommended that 79 bases be closed and 26 others realigned, for savings of $19.3 billion over two decades. The employment cost of the 1995 cuts would be high – 43,742 soldiers and civilians.[26] Although most of the cuts would occur in politically vital California, Clinton reluctantly approved the BRAC recommendation and sent it to Congress, which also approved it.

THE AEROSPACE INDUSTRIAL COMPLEX

Man has longed to fly ever since he first looked skyward to watch birds race across the heavens. Mythical Icarus flew briefly until hubris plummeted him into the sea. Leonardo da Vinci composed elaborate blueprints for flying machines that never took off. It was not until the late eighteenth century that silk hot-air balloons first took men aloft. A century later, machine-age tinkerers in Europe tried to attach engines to wings and fly away, but the attempts all failed. Then, on December 17, 1903, after three years of experimentation, Orville and Wilber Wright became the first humans success-fully to fly an airplane. Others on both sides of the Atlantic soon emulated the Wrights. Within a decade, hundreds of airplanes had been built and flown.

Despite these advances, the United States had no airplane industry on the eve of World War I. The forty-nine planes built in 1914 rolled from machinist shops as dangerous novelties for the few wealthy and brave enough to fly them. Patent disputes limited American production. Meanwhile, European producers threatened to swamp America's airplane makers with cheaper, better made flying machines. Although airplanes were relatively easy to put together and fly, it took government policies to convert that rich man's toy into what is today the vast aerospace industrial complex.

World War I demanded airplanes, first for reconnaissance, then air combat, and finally bombing. Each European bel-ligerent built an aircraft industry to supplement its war effort. When the United States entered the war in April 1917, Washington also had to create its own airplane industry. A Bureau of Aircraft Production and National Advisory Com-mittee for Aeronautics were established to manage the con-struction of the 25,000 planes considered essential for America's war effort. Washington solved the patent disputes by bringing together all the existing and possible producers into the Manufacturers Aircraft Association and cutting a cross-licensing deal whereby the government would pay $200 extra per plane to be distributed as royalties. Plaintiffs would settle all disputes through arbitration. Antitrust laws were suspended for the industry.

Washington's industrial policy toward the airplane was a dazzling success. At thirty-five flying schools across the country, the government trained nearly 10,000 pilots and 100,000 support personnel for the Air Corps. Washington invested $350 million to produce 13,894 aircraft and 41,953 engines at home, and spent a further $139 million on European planes and parts. It created a network of airfields, supply and fuel depots, and factories across the country. However, only 2,091 American planes were shipped to Europe, while another 1,040 awaited shipment. Of the forty-five squadrons eventually deployed in Europe, thirty-three were equipped with foreign planes. By the war's end, 175,000 people worked in the aircraft industry, up from 5,000 twenty-one months earlier. When the guns fell silent, the twenty-four firms of America's aircraft industry had the capacity yearly to produce 21,000 airplanes.[27]

Bust followed the boom. After signing the armistice, Washington cancelled its outstanding contracts and tried to sell off its surplus planes, thus swamping a tiny market. The Manufacturers' Aircraft Association tried to promote the industry through lobbying and marketing, but could not prevent its collapse into a few active manufacturers. To worsen matters, in 1920 foreign aircraft producers bought the influence of enough congressmen to investigate a rumored domestic "aircraft trust." Although Congress found no trust, the scare further dampened the industry. The foreign lobbyists also succeeded in derailing a tariff bill that would have protected America's airplane industry. The Manufacturers' Aircraft Association fought back, winning a 1921 suit against the foreign producers for patent infringement. The court ruled not only that the foreigners had to pay royalties but that they could not sell their aircraft in the United States below costs. In 1922, the industry established the Aeronautical Chamber of Commerce, which would supplement the Manufacturers' Aircraft Association in lobbying the federal, state, and local governments for such support as municipal airfields, procurement, weather facilities, and so on. The Chamber included not only aircraft producers, but related industries such as gasoline, tires, machine tools, banks, metal, and others.

Recognizing the need for a viable industry, Washington eventually nurtured it in a variety of ways. In May 1918, the War Department had opened an airmail route between New York and Washington, and over the next eight years expanded it into a grid of routes across the country. The 1925 Air Mail Act retired government from airmail, thus leaving that business to private enterprise. The 1926 Air Commerce Act made the Commerce Department responsible for expanding the network of airports and navigation aids. Under the 1926 Air Corps Act, Congress authorized the Air Corps

Material Division to establish a research and development laboratory and testing facility at what would become Wright Patterson Air Base in Dayton, Ohio. Congress also authorized the navy to purchase 1,614 planes and the army 1,800 planes between 1927 and 1931, at a combined cost of $435,980,000 – about 90 percent of the industry's business.

By the late 1920s, the airplane industry had started to revive after its long postwar depression. Two holding company giants – Curtiss Wright and United Aircraft and Transport – dominated the industry, accounting for 94 percent of all commercial sales, 80 percent of army purchases, and 71 percent of navy purchases from 1927 to 1933. Their commercial airline subsidiaries expanded routes across the country and even the hemisphere. Charles Lindbergh's successful trans-Atlantic flight in 1927 sparked a sales boom as adventurers across the country tried to emulate his feats. The 1927 aircraft sales of $21,162,000 soared to $71,153,000 in 1929. Then the Great Depression sank the aircraft industry as deeply as other economic sectors. Aircraft production plunged from 5,516 in 1929 to 803 in 1932. In 1930, eighteen firms produced 41 aircraft models; by 1935, twelve firms produced 26 models.[28]

Through the early depression, Washington was more concerned with investigating antitrust charges against the industry than bailing it out with procurement programs. In 1933, the Congressional Crane Commission found that aircraft industry holding companies had captured 98 percent of the airmail system alone, along with 90 percent of military purchases of which 92 percent occurred without competitive bids. The 1934 Air Mail Act forced the legal separation of the air transport and aircraft manufacturing industries. The result was the emergence of what would become such independent airline giants as United, TWA, Pan American, Eastern, and others. The 1934 Vinson-Trammel Act limited manufacturers' profits to 10 percent on sales to the navy. In 1939, the profit rate was raised to 12 percent and extended to the army.

In 1935, the White House recognized and acted on the need to revitalize America's aircraft industry. An isolationist Congress, however, undercut Roosevelt's efforts. That year Washington allowed the military to implement another five-year purchasing plan of 2,320 planes for the army and 1,200 for the navy. These government purchases occurred just as global demand surged in response to Japanese, German, and Italian aggression. Aircraft sales boomed from $44 million in 1934 to $150 million in 1939. These boosts to the industry were undercut by the 1935 Neutrality Act, which prevented American manufacturers from selling directly to either side in a war (although ways were found around the restrictions) and established a National Munitions Board, which regulated trade by issuing export licenses. In 1938, America's export sales of $68,209,050 were 45 percent of global sales, surpassing the combined $66,258,542 export sales of Britain, France, Germany, and Italy. In November 1939, Congress repealed the Neutrality Act in favor of a "cash and carry" system. That year, the aircraft industry sat atop $533,000,000 in back orders, of which 70 percent were exports.[29]

By 1940, it was increasingly clear that the United States would sooner or later find itself once again at war. On May 15, 1940, President Roosevelt declared his intention to have the aircraft industry produce 50,000 planes a year. But with only three American producers of engines and thirteen of airframes, the goal seemed impossible. On January 7, 1942, a month after the Japanese attack on Pearl Harbor, the President asked that aircraft production be increased to 125,000 planes a year by 1943.

American aircraft production of 300,317 military aircraft between January 1, 1940 and August 14, 1945 far surpassed Roosevelt's optimistic vision. The 150 different types of aircraft included 417 distinct models, of which the army accounted for 255 models of 97 types in 21 tactical classifications, and the navy for 162 models of 53 types in 17 tactical classifications. By 1943, the number of aircraft workers had risen to 2.102 million from 48,638 in 1939. By 1944, 15 airframe producers cranked out planes at 86 plants. Aircraft production assets had risen from $114 million in 1939 to $3.906 billion by 1944.[30]

Washington's industrial policies were responsible for these dazzling achievements. In April 1942, the War Production Board helped organize the West Coast producers – Boeing, Consolidated Vultee, Douglas, Lockheed, Northrop, North American, and Ryan – into the Aircraft War Production Council. In July, it organized the East Coast producers –

Curtiss Wright, Bell, Pratt & Whitney, General Motors, Grumman, Martin, and others – into a similar council. In April 1943, the two councils were combined into a National Aircraft War Production Council. The production shift from in place ("job shop," "lots," "handmade") to assembly line was revolutionary. Productivity soared and costs dropped. A typical bomber's first assembly took 200,000 man-hours for construction, the 1000th plane, 22,500 man-hours, and the 2000th plane, 13,000 man-hours. Washington financed 92 percent of the industry's expansion and owned 90 percent of total production facilities outright.[31]

Not surprisingly, peace brought a depression to the industry. By December 1945, only sixteen airframe and five engine plants remained open. The number of workers fell from a peak of 2.1 million in 1943 to 519,000 in August 1945 to 138,700 in February 1946. Sales plummeted to $1.2 billion in 1947 from $16.047 billion in 1944.[32] Washington's policies, economic expansion, and the Korean War eventually revived the aircraft industry. In 1948, the President's Air Policy Commission targeted fifteen firms as recipients of an expanded procurement program. But the Korean War was the most important boost to the industry. Congress appropriated $8 billion for 12,000–15,000 aircraft in 1950 alone. The 1950 Defense Production Act allowed manufacturers to amortize a new investment over a five-year period. By January 1951, total employment in the industry had risen to 292,000. After a brief postwar recession, three factors have allowed the aircraft industry to expand steadily from the mid-1950s through to today: continued military procurements, the growth of American and foreign commerical airlines, and the space program.[33]

By the late 1950s, the Pentagon's missile and satellite programs had converted the aircraft industry into the aerospace industry. Washington's interest in missiles, however, dated to World War II and Germany's development of the V-2 rocket. The United States military managed to capture all 525 scientists and V-2 rockets at Germany's Peenemunde and Nordhausen production facilities, and convince many of those scientists to immigrate to the United States to work on nuclear bomb and missile development. America's $2 billion Manhattan Project had successfully tested an atomic bomb on July 16, 1945, and dropped them from B-29 bombers on Hiroshima and Nagasaki in August. Missiles presented an even safer means of delivering an atomic or conventional bomb. The successful Soviet test of an atomic bomb in 1949 spurred the Americans to greater efforts. Throughout the 1950s, the Redstone and Vanguard programs attempted to develop intercontinental ballistic missiles (ICBMs) that could fly through the upper atmosphere.

Unfortunately, those efforts did not prevent the Soviets from beating the United States into space. On October 4, 1957, the Soviets successfully launched the Sputnik satellite atop an ICBM. The United States did not successfully launch its own Explorer I satellite until four months later on January 31, 1958. Later that year, Washington formed the National Aeronautics and Space Administration (NASA) to lead America's efforts to put the first man into space. From 1955 to 1961 alone, Washington spent $4.5 billion on various missile and space programs. The programs' centerpiece was the Mercury program, which mobilized 4,000 firms and 200,000 workers to launch an American into orbit. Once again, the Soviets were faster. On April 12, 1961, Yuri Gagarin was the first human to be shot into space, a mere three weeks before Alan Shepard became the first American in space on May 5.[34]

On May 25, 1961, President Kennedy declared before a televised joint session of Congress that "this nation should commit itself to achieving the goal before the decade is out of landing a man on the moon." Kennedy's dream was fulfilled on July 19, 1969 when American astronauts landed their Apollo 11 spacecraft on the moon. The achievement was extremely expensive. The Apollo moon program cost $100 billion from 1961 to 1969 to put them there. NASA's budget peaked at $21 billion in 1964 when it mobilized 400,000 workers and 5 percent of the nation's scientists for its space programs.[35]

After reaching the moon, America's space program seemed to lose much of its reason for being. An increasing percentage of the electorate maintained that space exploration wasted money that was desperately needed to alleviate a range of worsening socioeconomic problems on Earth. The Mariner probes which reached Mars in the late 1960s and early 1970s revealed a lifeless planet. Any manned voyage to Mars would cost far more than the public was willing to pay, with no discernible payback other than a boost in national prestige. By 1972, when Apollo 17 became the last manned voyage to the moon, NASA's annual budget had dropped to $6 billion. Although President Nixon committed the United States to a space shuttle program in 1972, NASA's budget remained relatively limited. It was able to maintain the space station Skylab in orbit through 1973 and 1974, and launch relatively low-cost projects like the Pioneer I and II probes sent to the solar system's far reaches throughout the decade, and the Viking I and II in the early 1980s.

Meanwhile Washington continued to boost the aircraft division of the aerospace industry. During the 1960s, although Vietnam War procurements swelled the industry's bottom line, the enormous research and development costs of new models pushed all but several firms from the business. Washington has used a variety of means to keep its remaining military aircraft makers solvent. The Pentagon worked with General Electric to develop a turbofan that had four times the power of existing models, and with Boeing, Douglas, and Lockheed to create a huge new military jet transport, the C-5A. All three aircraft makers then tried to apply their experience to a commercial wide-bodied jet. But while Boeing worked on the four-engine 747, Douglas and Lockheed competed over smaller three-engine jets, the DC-10 and L-1011, respectively. That competition wrecked both companies. Douglas lost money on its DC-10 and, along with losses on its DC-9 and DC-11 models, teetered at bankruptcy's brink.

Washington then had to rescue the industry from near collapse. In 1967, it arranged the merger between the Douglas and McDonnell companies to end a ruinous competition that would have probably driven both into bankruptcy. So much for free competition. McDonnell Douglas has yet to recover fully from its losses against Lockheed. Lackluster sales for its L-1011 forced Lockheed to the brink of insolvency. A 1971 government-guaranteed loan of $250 million kept Lockheed alive for another decade until it finally dropped out of the commercial aircraft market in 1981. Europe's Airbus took advantage of the resulting product niche between jumbo and narrow-bodied jets, and established a market with its A300B which it has widened ever since with other models. At times, military procurements alone have saved aircraft producers from bankruptcy – whether or not the purchased aircraft was strategically justifiable or not. In the early 1980s, the Pentagon bought 60 KC 10s, the military version of McDonnell Douglas's DC-10. Without cash infusion, McDonnell Douglas would have had to shut down its DC-10 production line and forgo development of the MD-11.[36]

Washington also aids civilian aircraft makers through a variety of means. Most federal aid to the industry has come indirectly through the subsidization and procurement of military aircraft. In many cases the step from military to civilian aircraft was not great. For example, Boeing's 727 was introduced in 1958 and has sold well ever since. The 727 was developed from the air force's KC-135 tanker. Lockheed sold civilian versions of its C-130, C-141, and C-5A. The Lockheed L-1011, DC-10, and Boeing 747 all capitalized on engines developed for the C-5A. Boeing and McDonnell Douglas are using lightweight composite materials which were originally developed for the B-2 Stealth Bomber program, to be used in their commercial aircraft.[37] Nonetheless, while it has tried to keep its military aircraft makers in the game, Washington has not prevented them from dropping out of making civilian aircraft. Four American corporations – Boeing, Douglas, Convair, and Lockheed – have attempted to manufacture jet aircraft. In 1965, Convair was the first to drop out after the disappointing sales of its 880/990 introduced in 1960.

Washington provides direct aid as well to the commercial aircraft industry via low-interest government-guaranteed loans, procurement, tax write-offs, and research funding. Boeing, for example, receives anywhere from 15 percent to 40 percent of its orders from the government. Washington's largest direct aid to the civilian aircraft industry was the over $1 billion it invested in the Supersonic Transport (SST) project in the late 1960s and early 1970s. Although Washington finally abandoned the project when it realized the SST's potential market was too small ever to be commercially viable, the spin-offs aided the development of Boeing's 757 and 767.

The risks for an established firm in developing a new aircraft are enormous, and if that aircraft does not sell, the result could be bankruptcy. Developing a new jet aircraft costs years and up to $6 billion in research and development, skilled personnel, and equipment. Turning a profit in the industry is increasingly difficult. Through the late 1970s, no corporation had ever made a profit on a jetliner without selling at least 300 of it. During the 1980s, the break-even point rose to 400 jetliners, and by the mid-1990s, it was 600. The reason was the steady rise in labor, technology, and research and development costs. Given just these start-up costs for one aircraft, the costs for a newcomer entering the industry are many times greater. No one corporation or even group of corporations can afford to enter the jet aircraft industry on their own. Government aid remains essential for established and newcomer firms alike.[38]

Through the late 1970s, the federal government also indirectly aided the aircraft industry by regulating the airline industry. With their ticket prices and routes restricted, airlines battled for passengers with quality service which included state-of-the art aircraft. Then, in 1978, the Carter White House deregulated the airline industry.

Deregulation is not the panacea for consumers or producers that advocates tout it to be. An oligopoly of relatively low-priced fares under the regulated industry gave way to an oligopoly of relatively high prices. To succeed in the new market, airline companies aggressively expanded their fleets, routes, and hubs, and moved as many passengers as possible through them while getting as much use as possible from older aircraft. The "hub and spoke" systems succeeded in the short-term – United captured much of Chicago and Denver; TWA, St Louis; Northwest, Minneapolis; American, Dallas; Delta, Atlanta. The airlines charged high prices for these captive markets.

Over the long-term, however, fare wars on competitive routes, overcapacity, and the hub system devastated the industry. The hub system may have captured markets but, in addition to higher prices, it brought many inconveniences to consumers including fewer nonstop flights and long waitovers. It is also expensive to operate. Two-hour morning, afternoon, and evening rushes in which feeder flights reach the hub to disgorge passengers into the larger flights are interspersed with long hours in which few flights take place. In this system, one delayed flight can delay many others.

Thus deregulation concentrated the industry while raising consumer prices for most flights. In 1978, there were twenty-nine major airlines; in 1993, there were only eight. Although the number of miles flown by domestic airlines increased from 200 billion in 1978 to 350 billion in 1993, the recent growth in air miles has plateaued. Meanwhile, the cents earned from each customer per mile have declined from about eight to six cents. American, Delta, and United have doubled their size since deregulation, a result unanticipated and unwanted by the deregulators.[39]

Government policies limited the market shake-out. Liberal bankruptcy laws such as Chapter 11 have allowed airlines such as TWA, Continental, and American West to continue legally to operate without paying their creditors despite ever growing debts. Critics argue that this gives the inefficient airlines an advantage over the stronger ones. While the giants of yesterday like Pan American and Continental are dying off, low-cost carriers flying special routes are thriving. To survive, the remaining giants are increasingly pushing into lucrative foreign markets. To do so, however, they usually have to form a joint venture with a foreign firm. Although, since the mid-1980s, fuel prices have considerably alleviated flying costs, the airline industry continues to shake out its least efficient producers and lose money. The last profitable year for the airline industry was 1988. In the years since then, the airlines' annual losses have shifted between $1.8 billion and $4.5 billion.[40]

While the Reagan and Bush Administrations viewed the airlines' mounting debts with laissez-faire disregard, President Clinton acted to reform the industry. On March 21, 1994, Clinton announced a plan to help the troubled airlines, which included lower-interest loan guarantees, tax relief, lifting of restrictions on foreign ownership of domestic airlines, and negotiated access for domestic airlines into foreign markets. The low-interest loans would help the airlines retire or renovate 2,600 older planes by the year 2000, as required by a 1990 law mandating more fuel-efficient, quieter aircraft. This should prove a much needed financial boost

to Boeing and McDonnell Douglas, which have suffered from
the greater direct subsidies their European rival Airbus receives. The only controversial item in Clinton's package was
the easing of foreign-ownership restrictions to 25 percent
of voting stock and 49 percent of the overall investment.
The financially weaker airlines support it; the stronger ones
criticize it as giving foreign airlines easy access to the domestic market.

As in so many other industries, unfair foreign airline competition cuts deeply into the profits of American firms. Transportation Secretary Frederico Pena explained that "our
domestic carriers don't have the same opportunities to access foreign markets as do foreign carriers accessing domestic
markets."[41] Given America's vast market, Washington has huge
bargaining power in negotiations with other industrial countries over access. Much more than his predecessors, Clinton
has been very skillfull in wielding market power to extract
concessions from foreign rivals and assert American interests.
In 1994, Clinton succeeded in pressuring Britain to grant
greater access to American carriers in return for allowing
British Airways to invest in USAir.

In June 1995, a conflict broke out between the United
States and Japan over air routes among the two and other
countries. Tokyo demanded the renegotiation of a 1952
bilateral treaty which gives American airlines the right to
fly not only to Japan but to destinations beyond. To pressure Washington, Tokyo threatened to prevent Federal Express from flying on recently awarded new routes until the
treaty is renegotiated. Washington argued that international
airline routes should be deregulated in favor of an "open
skies" or free market. It threatened to retaliate against Japanese carriers if Tokyo fulfilled its threat to bar Federal Express. The Japanese complained that a free market would
destroy their national airlines, which could not compete with
the super-efficient American airlines that enjoy vast passen-
ger scale economies with access to combined domestic and
foreign markets.

American carriers already enjoy a 62.5 percent market share
of flights between the two countries while Japanese carriers
have only 32.4 percent (down from 38.5 percent in 1986)
and other foreign carriers 5.1 percent. Japan's claims were

hypocritical given its claims in other trade disputes that its industries enjoyed dominant market shares because they had a competitive advantage. The difference was that Japan's industrial policies allowed its corporations to dominate those other industries while even Tokyo's systematic neomercantilist policies did not succeed in making Japanese airlines global champions. The Japanese had little bargaining power on this issue. On July 20, they agreed to grant Federal Express its previously approved routes in return for an American promise that Japanese carriers would receive more routes to the United States.[42]

Washington also aids the domestic industry by countering the industrial policies of its rivals. Airbus, the European consortium, is the greatest immediate rival to Boeing and McDonnell Douglas. The governments of Britain, France, Germany, and Spain subsidize Airbus in a variety of ways, including $26 billion over the last two decades. The government chipped in an estimated $5.6 billion for the A300 and A310 models and $2.3 billion for the A330 and A340 models. In addition, Bonn spent $3 billion to underwrite a merger between Airbus member MMB and Daimler. Altogether, government aid has made up about 75 percent of Airbus's development costs. Airbus's four partners split the financial and production responsibilities. France's Aerospatialle has a 37.9 percent stake, builds the cockpit and parts of the fuselage, and then assembles the larger planes at Toulouse. Germany's Daimler-Benz Aerospace also owns a 37.9 percent stake, builds fuselage parts, and assembles some smaller planes. British Aerospace has a 20 percent share and builds most of the wings and most of the fuselage. Spain's Construcciones owns 4.2 percent of Airbus and builds the tail's horizontal stabilizers. Each partner's economic health varies widely. In 1995, the French lost $200 million on $10 billion in sales; the Germans lost $2.9 billion on $10.4 billion in sales; the Spanish made $31 million on $888 million in sales; and the British earned $362 million on $8.9 billion in sales.[43]

Washington has periodically protested at Airbus's massive research, development, production, and marketing subsidies. In 1978, the Treasury Department proposed using a countervailing duty to offset Airbus subsidies. The proposal died when Eastern Airlines Chair, Frank Borman, convinced the Carter administration that the duty would force up the price of aircraft and hurt his already financially troubled company and others. Negotiations did, however, begin between American and European representatives in May 1978. The negotiations helped parallel talks in GATT which led to the 1979 Agreement on Trade in Civil Aircraft. The agreement outlawed a variety of trade barriers, export subsidies, quotas, mandatory subcontracting deals, and closed procurement practices. Yet, it did not ban national industrial policies including subsidies. As a result, the global aircraft industry became increasingly integrated as firms formed joint ventures and explored hitherto restricted markets. Through 1991, the agreement saved America's aircraft firms over $1 billion in tariffs and other duties.[44]

Airbus has captured increasing shares of markets traditionally dominated by Boeing. In 1984, it made a major sale to Pan Am. In 1985, it used promises of huge discounts and financing to convince Air India to drop a pending sale by Boeing in 1984. Boeing protested that the deal violated the 1979 Civil Aircraft Treaty which forbade dumped sales. Fearing that to do so might jeopardize its sales in Europe, Boeing stepped back from filing a Section 301 suit against Airbus. Periodic bilateral government talks began in 1986 and continued until an agreement was signed in 1992. The agreement limits direct subsidies to 33 percent of a new aircraft's development costs and indirect subsidies to 4 percent of a firm's annual sales. Airbus has continued to expand. In 1996's first four months, Airbus captured 40.2 percent of new global aircraft orders while Boeing took 66.4 percent and McDonnel Douglas a minuscule 3.4 percent. Airbus's biggest coup was a $2 billion order for 33 jetliners to China.

Overall, in comparing their respective aircraft industrial policies, America's have been more effective than Europe's. America's biggest export earner is aircraft – $17.8 billion alone in 1991. Three huge firms – Boeing and McDonnell Douglas of the United States and Airbus of Europe – spilt the global civilian aircraft market. In 1990, Boeing delivered 379 jet planes to customers while McDonnell Douglas delivered only 142 and Airbus only 95. Since the early 1970s,

Boeing has been the only jet aircraft maker to enjoy a profit. Its 747 has been enormously profitable with Boeing making an average $45 million on each $150 million sale. McDonnell Douglas lost over $1 billion between 1969 and 1989. Despite its huge market share, Airbus has yet to make a profit. Government subsidies keep it alive.[45]

America's aircraft producers face a greater long-term competitive threat from East Asia rather than Europe. The governments of Japan, China, Taiwan, and South Korea all have ambitious aerospace programs. A vital part of their development strategies is to use their market power to play off American and European aerospace producers into selling out their production and technology. That strategy has been highly successful.

By licensing the foreign production of American warplanes, the Pentagon had inadvertently built up these foreign rivals. For example, over the last three decades the Pentagon co-produced with Japan the F-86, F-104, and F-15, giving Japanese corporations realms of technology and production experience. In 1988, Tokyo announced that it would build the FSX, a next-generation fighter jet based on the F-16, despite the fact that it could have bought existing F-16s at one-third the cost. At first, the Pentagon went along with Tokyo. Congressional protests erupted at the give-away of advanced technology and wealth to a rival while the United States remained mired in an array of economic problems. The Pentagon and Tokyo negotiated for months before they signed an agreement splitting the research, development, and production, with 60 percent going to the Japanese and 40 percent to the Americans.[46]

Ironically, in the name of free market competition, Boeing and McDonnell Douglas are selling out to nascent foreign rivals to score more points in their own rivalry. The result of those two giants competing rather than colluding means that wealth, jobs, technology, and markets that could have gone to the United States are diverted to foreign competitors. Smaller American aerospace firms have also given in to the foreign pressure. Pratt & Whitney and General Electric, for example, have sold out technology and production to a Japanese government project to develop a supersonic engine.

Despite being the world's second largest commercial jet producer, McDonnell Douglas has had trouble financing its ambitious development plans. It is currently developing the MD-12, which will compete directly with the Boeing 747. In order to raise enough money to realize the MD-12 and pay off a $2.6 billion debt, in 1991, McDonnell Douglas sold 40 percent of its commercial-aircraft division to the Taiwan Aerospace Corporation for $2 billion. Under the deal, most important parts would be built in Taiwan and the final planes would be assembled in the United States. Taiwan Aerospace Corporation would enjoy not only the profits from the MD-12's development, but also a sales percentage of the MD-11 and MD-80. However, it would have no stake in McDonnell's weapons division, which produces the F-15 fighter, F-18 fighter, Apache helicopter, and Tomahawk missile. Although Taiwan Aerospace had never built an airplane part, let alone an entire plane, it had exactly what McDonnell needed – deep financial pockets, courtesy of the Taiwan government, and access to a skilled, relatively low-wage labor force. The MD-12 will have a cruising range of 9,000 miles, 2,000 more than Boeing's 747.

Boeing's dominant position in the industry has not prevented its leaders from succumbing to Japanese pressure to hand over key technology and production on certain projects. Boeing is co-developing the 777 with a consortium of Japanese aerospace rivals led by Mitsubishi, Fuji, and Kawasaki heavy industries, all of which are lavishly subsidized by Tokyo. MITI's Japanese Aircraft Development Corporation provides what Washington has denied Boeing – direct subsidies and leadership.

Boeing's deal with the Japanese is far more alarming than McDonnell Douglas's with the Taiwanese because Japan's aerospace industry is far more advanced. Tokyo gives massive aid to the industry to help it catch up to and eventually leapfrog the Americans. But Boeing officials argue that they had no choice but to solicit Japanese funds and expertise for the $4 billion project. Not publicly mentioned was Tokyo's threat that if the deal did not go through, the Japanese would turn to Airbus or McDonnell Douglas not just for a similar deal, but to buy their aircraft. Thus, if Boeing had tried to develop the 777 alone, it would have had to raise several times more money and would have lost the lucrative Japanese markets. The Japanese literally had Boeing by its ball-bearings.

Boeing's dilemma is obvious. If it had not surrendered to the Japanese demand, it would have lost sales to Airbus or McDonnell Douglas. But by giving in, Boeing is creating a new competitor that could prove far more voracious than any it now faces. Matt Bates, spokesman for the International Association of Machinists, accused Boeing of "giving away a lot of jobs for future sales, and risking setting itself up to be demolished in future years."[47] Over the long-term, the Faustian deals of Boeing, McDonnell Douglas, and other domestic producers with their Japanese and other Asian rivals will boomerang. Essentially the American firms are selling out their future to pay for the present.

Washington encourages them to do so in several ways. First, it retains antitrust laws written at the turn of the century which prevent domestic firms from colluding while allowing an American firm to ally with a foreign firm to undercut other American firms. Secondly, Washington fails to do what other governments do to develop their aircraft industries – directly subsidize the corporations. When a new jetliner can cost as much as $5 billion, Boeing and McDonnell Douglas must go overseas, cup in hand, to secure enough financing and, increasingly, key skills and technologies. Thirdly, not only has Washington failed to pressure those Asian governments to buy American jetliners off the shelf rather than develop their own more expensive versions, the Pentagon has brokered many of the deals between them and American firms. The United States suffers enormous trade deficits with all of those countries. Aerospace is one of the few industries in which the United States currently enjoys a dominant position. That lead will vanish in the coming century.

In all, Washington has no comprehensive, long-term policy for the aircraft industry. As for other industries, its industrial policy toward civilian aircraft is piecemeal and politically driven. Military rather than civilian needs are the policy's core. Yet, sometimes free market ideals have governed policy. Tyson criticizes Washington for allowing the debilitating rivalry between Douglas and Lockheed which crippled both firms and allowed Airbus an entry through which it has established an ever growing market share. She argues that the "government steadfastly refuses to take on the role of coordinator, even in a market where the players and their competitive strategies were a creation of public policy choices."[48] Instead, Washington's industrial policies toward the industry are becoming less important in keeping it viable. Airline deregulation in 1980 eliminated important incentives for new aircraft purchases. After peaking in the late 1980s, the Pentagon's budget has fallen in real and absolute terms since then, and with it the procurement budget for military aircraft. As with other military equipment, military aircraft once spawned technological "spin-offs," the military now "spins on" technologies from the civilian industry.

While the aircraft industry is starved of finance, Washington continues to launch tens of billions of dollars into space. The reasons for the disparity are embedded in glamor, twisted notions of national security, and entrenched political interests. When it was pitched to him in late 1983, the space station excited Ronald Reagan's Hollywoodish imagination as thoroughly as Star Wars did earlier that year. Reagan launched the "Freedom" space station program in January 1984 with the declaration that the 500-foot, 290-ton craft 250 miles above Earth would help us "follow our dreams to the stars."

Most objective observers refuse to get starry-eyed about the space station. Although it has legions of lobby groups and other enthusiastic boosters, it lacks a mission whose scientific and product developments can justify its enormous costs. As physics professor Robert Pak puts it, "the decision to build a space station . . . had little to do with either science or economics. It was meant to be a visible demonstration of American commitment to superiority in space at a decisive moment of the cold war. With the collapse of the Soviet Union, Freedom is as obsolete as another B-52 bomber base."[49]

Meanwhile, the Russians may have lost out to the Americans in the moon race, but they won in the space station race. What they won is questionable. Although the MIR space station has been continuously operating for seven years now (1996), it has produced little of scientific note. When asked what the Mir astronauts do all day up there, the space program's head replied, "They try to stay alive."[50]

Unfortunately, it would be expensive to cancel the space station outright. Reagan locked the United States into a consortium with Japan, Canada, and nine European countries. While those governments have allayed some of the costs, they are reaping enormous benefits by enjoying access to key American aerospace technology and production techniques which they can apply to their own airline, warplane, and satellite industries. They will not allow the gravy train to stop.

When Reagan initially announced his support for the space station, he claimed the expense would be a relatively modest $8 billion. As with other military and aerospace programs of dubious strategic value, once Congress approved the space station the subsequent cost estimates rose steadily. Although it has been redesigned seven times to reduce costs, and proponents recently claimed it would cost "only" $31.3 billion, a more realistic estimate doubled the cost to $61 billion to build it and another $100 billion to operate it over its 30-year lifetime. Over 17,000 best and brightest people are working on the space station. By 1994, NASA had spent $11 billion on the project. Despite its dubious value, the space station remains enthusiastically supported by a congressional majority. In June 1994, the House voted by 278 to 155 to approve the space station; the Senate approved it by a similar margin.[51]

Unlike the Reagan and Bush Administrations, the Clinton White House has been serious about reducing spending. The space program was an obvious place to cut. In February 1993, President Clinton announced that the space station's scale and design had to be drastically revised in order to halve its costs. NASA engineers and accountants have been exploring different options ever since. In the most recent version, the space station would cost $43 billion to build, be 290 feet wide and 360 feet long, take 85 shuttle missions to assemble, and be manned by only six people. The assembly is scheduled to take place between 1997 and 2002.[52] Russians would join the construction of the space station. The space shuttle would make scores of trips to the Russian station MIR where astronauts would build the 460-ton international space station.

Many knowledgeable observers have questioned NASA's

projected costs as wildly underestimated. The latest General Accounting Office estimate is that the American contribution to the space station's construction alone will be $93.9 billion, of which $50.9 billion would be in shuttle flights. Independent experts estimate the costs to be twice that. And that figure does not include the maintenance costs after the station is built.[53]

Even if the space station should ever be built and operated, it would face enormous dangers. The space shuttle is its lifeline; if a space shuttle blew up, the remainder could be grounded and the space station isolated. Space debris is yet another hazard. The Pentagon tracks around 7,000 objects in orbit ranging in size from a bus to a baseball. Yet, there may be as many as 150,000 pieces of man-made junk orbiting Earth, whose numbers increase by 2 to 5 percent a year. The chances of debris smashing into the station during its building and ten-year lifetime are estimated at one in five. Building a shield could reduce the chances of a catastrophe to one in twenty, but even then would add enormous additional costs to the project.[54]

Ironically, the decision to go ahead with a space station that lacks any real mission gives the space shuttle its first concrete mission. Since its inauguration, the space shuttle program has cost American taxpayers over $80 billion; each shuttle flight costs $1.7 billion (including development costs) and the entire program costs about $6 billion a year. An army of 29,000 highly skilled people is deployed just to ready, launch, and repair the shuttles. Half of NASA's $14 billion budget goes toward maintaining, launching, and recovering its four space shuttles, whose design and technology dates to the early 1970s. Despite this entire industry of experts and equipment, the chances of another accident like the 1986 Challenger disaster in which the space shuttle blew up, are considered at best 1 in 78, compared with a 1 in 2 million chance of an airline disaster.[55]

Has the space shuttle been little more than an expensive and dangerous fireworks display? Adherents justify the shuttle as a means to put satellites into space. Yet, a Delta-2 rocket can put the same satellite into space at one-twentieth the space shuttle's costs. They also argue that the shuttle is essential for building the space station, an argument that might have some weight if they could justify the latter. Finally, they assert that the tie-up between Freedom and MIR would bring better relations between the United States and Russia. But surely that money could be better used dismantling nuclear weapons and safely cleaning and storing nuclear waste.

The political forces which keep the space shuttle and space stations are similar to those which prop up a host of unnecessary weapons, military bases, and units. Like its cousin, the military–industrial complex, the space industrial complex is an iron triangle of NASA and related government bureaucracies, congressional representatives who have projects in their districts, and industrial lobby groups like the Aerospace Industries Association, Council of Defense and Space Industries Association, American Institute of Aeronautics and Astronautics, the National Space Club, and International Association of Machinists and Aerospace Workers. As with the military industrial complex, these political and bureaucratic allies have ensured that the laboratories, launch sites, and tracking stations are distributed through as many congressional districts and states as possible to ensure continued support.

The arguments which emanate from the aerospace industry to maintain the $14 billion worth of annual programs that feed it are just as specious as those from the military–industrial complex. Defenders point to all the consumer-product spin-offs from NASA projects. Most Americans have benefited from teflon, fewer from Tang and the insulation bags for pizza deliveries. But could not have these and other space industry "spin-offs" been developed at far cheaper costs?

Many of the same people who demand the cutting off of welfare for teenage mothers protest at slashing the space program because it would put people out of work. Surely, if anyone can find a job, it would be the highly educated, skilled, intelligent, and creative engineers, technicians, and managers that make up the space program. In all, the space program has drained tens of thousands of America's finest minds from far more productive pursuits.

The space industrial complex has successfully lobbied government for the space shuttle and space station despite the reality that any discoveries made by those programs could never pay back more than a fraction of their operating costs.

Former NASA director James M. Boggs admitted that special rather than national interests caused the space industrial complex to lobby for the space station back in the early 1980s: "The feeling was that unless we get a station, the manned activities would truncate and we'd run out of a mission."[56]

There are alternatives to manned flights and the vast human, industrial, and technological infrastructure which support them. NASA is currently developing a super-light, single-stage rocket that could boost satellites into orbit much cheaper than contemporary rockets and at perhaps 1 percent of the space shuttle's costs. Another way to cut costs is to open military aerospace projects to increased civilian use. For example, the military's global positioning system (GPS) employs 24 Earth-orbiting satellites. By leasing its access to civilian firms the government has generated $2 billion in 1994 alone, a figure that could reach $30 billion by 2005.[57]

Meanwhile, as the military and space industries shrink as a proportion of the economy, the related commercial aircraft industry faces increased difficulties maintaining its lead over foreign rivals. For example, the global market shares for Boeing and McDonnell Douglas declined from 78 percent in 1987 to 67 percent in 1991. America's market share will continue to deteriorate as European and Asian aerospace industries become ever more powerful, largely as a result of their governments' comprehensive industrial policies.[58]

Should Washington do anything about the decline of America's aerospace industry? Economists claim the "magic of the marketplace" will solve all the world's problems and protect all national interests. If aerospace cannot compete then it deserves to go; those resources now in aerospace will be redeployed more effectively elsewhere. That attitude makes a range of unwarranted assumptions, including that the aerospace industries in the United States and elsewhere are shaped by free markets. In reality, governments manage the development of their respective aerospace industries – some governments clearly do a better job of doing so than others. Democratic Representative Jeff Bingaman, who heads a House aerospace subcommittee, argues that the industry "has been declining very dramatically in the last couple of years and it will continue to decline as long as the present circumstances prevail. At some point, our Government can't just go on sitting on its hands and saying, 'Let's leave it to the free market.'"[59]

LEGACY

Was Eisenhower right? Has the United States succumbed to a military and aerospace industrial complex which has sucked the marrow from the nation's economic dynamism? Although its relative and absolute spending levels have shifted over the last half-century, no federal bureaucracy spends more than the Pentagon, which spends only part of the total the United States devotes to the military–industrial complex. An accurate measure must include not just the Defense Department's annual spending but programs from at least thirteen other departments and agencies, including parts of the Energy Department, NASA, the Coast Guard, the Maritime Administration, and the State Department, along with the portion of interest on the national debt attributed to the military, veterans benefits and services, foreign military assistance grants, and the Impact Aid for Education Program.[60]

"So what?" retort those who equate national security with the Pentagon's budget, number of troops, and array of destructive weapons – in other words, the more the better. Others heed Eisenhower's warning that national security is much more than the number of troops, tanks, and missiles a government deploys. National security depends on a nation's economic, institutional, diplomatic, intellectual, scientific, and moral strengths. More specifically, it means the rational analysis of genuine military or economic threats to national interests and the most cost-efficient means of deterring or eliminating those threats.

So, who is right, those who equate national security with the defense budget or those who believe national security rests on a broad array of interrelated domestic and foreign factors?

Many of those same people who favor unlimited defense spending also fervently accept the belief of most economists that the less government, the more growth, and vice versa. Reality does not support that claim. The European governments spend far more as a GNP percentage than the United States. The United States regularly ranks last in education,

infrastructure, industry subsidies, welfare, and social security spending, and tax rates. Yet, after 1945 most European
economies have grown faster than America's. High government spending seems to have enhanced economic growth
in those countries.

However, not all government spending has a net positive
economic effect. While government spending appears to
stimulate growth, different types may vary considerably in
their relative effectiveness. For example, the governments
of the United States and Japan account for similar GNP
percentages. Yet, Japan's economic growth was four times
that of the United States between 1950 and 1973, and about
twice that between 1973 and 1990. How do we explain these
differences?

Defense spending impedes rather than promotes economic
development. Among its allies, the United States has had
the largest military burden as a percentage of GNP over
the last half-century. While American military spending averaged around 6.5 percent over the past five decades, Western
Europe's has averaged around half and Japan's one-seventh
of that. Not surprisingly, the United States has also had the
lowest growth rate.

Why has America's higher military spending resulted in a
lower growth rate? Although military spending creates some
jobs, overall it saps vitality from the economy by draining
skills, laboratories, and money from more productive pursuits. The higher the military spending, the more it tends
to "crowd out" much more productive investments and spending elsewhere in the economy. When the government bor-
rows to finance the military it competes with private investors
for finance, and thus drives up interest rates and the entire
economy suffers. When it raises taxes to pay for more guns,
it takes money from households and businesses and thus
dampens growth. When it prints money, it worsens inflation.

The more a government spends on the military, the lower
that nation's productivity rate. By spending less on the military, the Europeans and Japanese had that much more to
invest in education, infrastructure, and consumer industries.
The United States became mired in a vicious economic cycle of low growth, productivity, investments, savings, and trade
deficits. Meanwhile, the Japanese, Germans, and some other

Europeans mastered virtuous cycles of high growth, productivity, investments, savings, and trade surpluses.

Supporters of high defense spending claim that it creates jobs and growth. That may be true but, in fact, a Pentagon dollar does not stimulate the economy as much as, say, a dollar devoted to schools or highways. Overall, those industries which sell to the Pentagon create fewer jobs than those which sell to consumers. Military spending's net effect is a drag on the economy. Although the military does create some jobs, it destroys more jobs elsewhere. One study found that the impact of shifting $62.9 billion in Pentagon spending would cost 1.5 million jobs in the defense sector but create 3.3 million jobs throughout the civilian economy. Of six job categories, a billion dollars creates the most jobs in education, followed by consumer goods, new public transit, intermediate goods, defense, automobiles, and petroleum refining. Generally, a billion dollars worth of defense spending creates 28,000 jobs while the same amount spent on new public transit yields 32,000, on personal consumption 57,000, and on education 71,000! Given these statistics, politicians genuinely concerned about jobs should have no question about where to invest public funds.

The military and aerospace policies are both driven by extravagant goals that seem to bear little relation to concrete national interests. If, by the Pentagon's own admission, the most probable threats are second-rate powers like Iraq, Iran, and North Korea, why cannot those states' ambitions be contained with a vastly restructured and reduced military backed by creative diplomacy and firm alliances? If NASA's mission is space exploration, why cannot that goal be achieved with unmanned probes and laboratories at a fraction of the costs of manned ventures?

Ironically, even as it fed its own insatiable military–industrial complex, the Kremlin understood that spending too much on the military could be just as dangerous as spending too little. Moscow tried to provoke Washington into diverting so many resources to the Pentagon that it undermined America's economy. They did so by feeding Aldrich Ames, their double agent within the CIA, disinformation claiming that the Soviet military machine was far more powerful than it really was. Even though they suspected the information was tainted, the CIA brass passed on the information to the White House who used it as the basis for their Pentagon budgets. As a result, Washington wasted tens of billions of dollars on weapons systems to counter non-existent threats.

In the post-Cold War era, the Pentagon's budget has become more disconnected than ever from strategies to contain genuine threats. As recently as the 1960s, the Pentagon's budget reflected the ability to fight two and a half wars simultaneously – large World War II-type land wars in Europe and Asia, and a more limited war in the Middle East or elsewhere. Détente with China allowed President Nixon to downsize the Pentagon's mission to fighting one and a half wars simultaneously. He cut the Pentagon's budget accordingly. The Pentagon retained the one-and-a-half-war mission until the Cold War ended. In the 1990s, the Pentagon's mission was dropped to fighting at once two half-wars. Yet, the military budget and forces were reduced only 15 percent and 25 percent, respectively, between 1989 and 1995. How do we explain this?

The reason is simple. Politics rather than pragmatism feeds the military and aerospace industrial complexes. Tens of billions of dollars are annually wasted on weapons systems, bases, and units that have no strategic rationale. Although the Cold War is over, America's military remains oriented toward fighting a massive land war in Central Europe. A restructuring of American forces to fight genuine potential threats could reap scores of billions of dollars more in annual savings. For example, the United States has no need for two more Seawolf submarines costing $3 billion. But 20,000 well-paid workers are affected and their votes could swing a close state election. Projects of dubious worth and enormous costs, like the Seawolf, SDI, B-1 and B-2 bombers, and a range of other weapons of mass destruction, undermine American power by diverting key financial, scientific, technological, and personnel resources from productive, wealth-creating enterprises. Likewise, NASA gets away with annually spending billions of dollars on manned space shuttles and laboratories because it has the political clout to do so. Hundreds of thousands of jobs, including several score representatives and senators, depend on NASA spending as much as possible no matter how wasteful it all is.

Congress and the president frequently give the Pentagon gifts it did not ask for but gladly accepts. Reagan's much ballyhooed 600-ship navy was a central feature of his defense buildup. Where did he get the 600-ship figure? Certainly not from a careful assessment of national risks, interests, and strategies. Six hundred was a nice round figure, much higher than the then 480-ship navy. By the mid-1990s, the navy had shrunk to around 350 ships, about half of Reagan's dream. With no high seas challengers, the navy has more than enough warships and firepower to fulfill its missions. Sometimes the military does not gladly accept political gifts. The navy supported base reductions that went far beyond the 1991 Base Realignment and Closure Commission recommendations. Those extra bases bleed money from the navy's budget that is needed for training and supplies.

Virtually every new weapons or space system costs more and performs less than was promised in the bid. "Cost creep" accounts partly for the higher price tags. Contractors are notorious for grossly underestimating their costs and then "goldbricking" the project once their bid is approved. A nightmarish labyrinth of regulations further drives up procurements costs in time and money. Pentagon specifications for weapons, equipment, uniforms, food, fuel, and every item it buys exceed 35,000 pages. Although defense contractors bid for Pentagon orders, once a lucky contractor is chosen it then enjoys a monopoly over that system which may be used for decades. Despite all the regulations, Pentagon procurement choice may rest on dubious foundations. The Pentagon may pick a bid even though the weapon or equipment may exist only on a blueprint. The military contractors are not accountable for their cost overruns or performance failures. The Pentagon penalizes taxpayers rather than contractors. Like many other huge corporations, contractors frequently take advantage of tax loopholes and pay no or little taxes. Meanwhile, they are annually subsidized by about $100 billion in taxpayer dollars. Not surprisingly, the average weapons system costs twice the original estimate.

Even after all the downsizing of the 1990s, Pentagon dollars still account for nearly one-quarter of the nation's public and private R&D investments, and about 10 percent of all manufacturing. Defense industries demand a highly skilled research, development, and assembly workforce. Unfortunately, with a finite number of such workers in the economy, the more the Pentagon demands, the less are available for other industries. Pentagon spending thus drains "brains" from the rest of the economy. Ironically, when politicians save an unnecessary military base or weapons system from the budget axe, they save the jobs of people who would have the least trouble finding employment elsewhere.

And what of the 1.6 million personnel in uniform? They are consumers rather than producers. Like any other workers, they do spend or invest their paychecks. However, for all their activity, whether it be doing calisthenics, shuffling papers in offices, shoveling food onto plates, flying high-ranking generals around the world, or whatever, they do not create anything – they simply redistribute wealth produced by others.

The relative effects of military spending on the economy have changed over time. When troops marched or rode horses into battle and fought with muskets and swords, the costs of conversion from civilian to military production and back again were relatively low. As weapons have become more specialized and technologically sophisticated, the conversion costs have risen astronomically. Likewise, a farmer could be given a musket and uniform, marched off to war, and then, after the fighting ended, if he survived, marched back to his plow. While the contemporary military is filled with maintenance jobs that could be done just as easily by the private sector (somehow most of those favoring privatization exclude the Pentagon), most jobs have no equivalent. Discharged soldiers usually require extensive retraining before they can find a civilian job.

When microelectronics technology was relatively new, the military spun off its technology to the civilian sector. Today, the reverse is true – the military gets most of its technology from consumer industries. Rather than spin off, the Pentagon now spins on. As military technology became more complex and the specifications tightened, advances slowed. Certain communication systems, for example, must be built strong enough to withstand a nuclear blast. Consumer technologies, on the other hand, are encumbered only by what will sell.

Spin-on would not be a problem except for the fact that America's consumer electronics industry was wiped out by the Japanese during the 1960s and 1970s, while many segments of its computer-chip industry were similarly destroyed during the 1980s. American firms may be able to produce a camera so powerful that it can record writing on a piece of paper lying on the ground from 150 miles above in space, but it is Japanese manufacturers which have captured the global camera trade, thus generating tens of billions of dollars in wealth annually for themselves. The Pentagon is increasingly dependent on foreign sources for some of the most vital innards of its weapons, surveillance, and communication equipment.

Given these realities, why has the military–industrial complex proved so difficult to reform? The complex has grown ever more politically and economically powerful throughout the twentieth century. The more entrenched political economic interests become, the more difficult they are to uproot.

For nearly 150 years following the Revolution, Americans distrusted the military and tried to maintain as minimal an army and navy as possible. This tradition continued even after the United States became the world's largest industrial power and acquired a small overseas empire around the century's turn, and after the United States fought in World War I. But a decade of Great Depression, followed by four years of World War and a half-century of Cold War revolutionized American attitudes toward the military. The suspicion with which most Americans once viewed a standing army has given way to sentimental adulation and a blind support for everything the Pentagon does for "national security." The result is systematic corruption, inefficiency, and waste throughout the military–industrial complex.

No bureaucracy wastes more of the taxpayers' money than the Pentagon. In 1988, Robert Costello, the Pentagon's procurement officer, estimated that the Defense Department wasted between 20 percent and 30 percent, or $50 billion annually, on buying goods and services. Why does the Pentagon waste $50 billion annually of the taxpayers' money just in procurement? Studies consistently conclude that at least a quarter of the Pentagon's budget is wasted. Many weapons are not merely useless, they are downright danger-ous to America's soldiers. Yet, most Americans seem inured to these tragic costs or to the general predominance of a vast military–industrial complex in their political, economic, social, and cultural lives. A majority of Americans have come to equate the level of defense spending with national secu-rity. The more the United States spends on defense, the greater its national security, they argue. Every penny that circulates within the complex is justified by at least one in-terest group as essential to national security, while count-less other Americans unquestionably accept such assertions.

These attitudes explain the silence that greeted two re-cent revelations of massive Pentagon corruption. A three-year investigation by the General Accounting Office (GAO) revealed in June 1993 that throughout the 1980s the Penta-gon had systematically lied to Congress about the costs, abilities of, and needs for $350 billion of weapons systems. More specifically, the GAO report found "dubious support for claims of their high performance, insufficient and often unrealistic testing, understated cost, incomplete or unrep-resentative reporting, lack of systematic comparison against the systems they were to replace, and unconvincing rationales for their development in the first place."[61] Caspar Weinberger, the Defense Secretary at that time, denied all this, yet ad-mitted that, "we used a worst-case analysis. You should al-ways use a worst-case analysis in this business." On March 5, 1994, the *New York Times* reported that a $1.3 billion mili-tary communications satellite had failed after only one month in space. The satellite was the first of six designed to main-tain communications amidst a nuclear war whose possibility was near nil even before the Cold War's end. The total cost of this "Milstar" program is $27 billion. The story was buried on page nine. Even if it had been featured on the front page, it would have been unlikely to stir more than a fatal-istic shrug from the vast majority of readers.[62]

Only three Defense Secretaries have tried to reform this system – all three have failed. In the 1960s, Robert McNamara demanded that contractors would be held to their bids. Of four weapons systems developed under the new system, all failed to meet their cost or performance promises. The Pentagon ended up bailing out the four. During the early

1970s, Deputy Secretary David Packard required contractors to build a prototype before the Pentagon decided. Under Packard, the Pentagon adopted the A-10 and F-16, two of its most successful war weapons. But the Pentagon happily reverted to its old ways after Packard left. Defense Secretary William Perry has had some successes in cutting some of the procurement waste during the Clinton Administration, but tens of billions of dollars of wasted programs and practices persist that should be eliminated.

Procurement reforms boil down to

> three simple principles: new weapons must grow out of realistic threat estimates and proven technology; contracts must be awarded only after competitive prototyping; and contractors who deliver weapons that work as promised, at a reasonable cost, should receive rewards in the shape of higher profits and future contracts, while contractors who fail to perform should be penalized, not bailed out.[63]

Simple and obvious as these fiscally conservative reforms may seem, they are political nonstarters at any time, particularly with a Republican-controlled Congress.

Two of America's best weapons sytems, the Sidewinder missile and the F-16, were built outside the military–industrial complex. The Sidewinder was developed by the missile engineer William McLean, in his garage in the late 1940s; he built the missile from junk-yard scrap. The air force deployed the first Sidewinders in 1956 for $3,000 each. Since then it has bought over 195,000. The current price is $50,000. The Sidewinder is a deadly air-to-air missile. The F-16 was designed in the early 1970s by two fighter pilots and an engineer who wanted a smaller, cheaper, faster, and deadlier fighter-jet than currently existed. General Dynamics produced the first F-16s and they did indeed prove to outgun and outfly the air force's F-15. The Pentagon adopted them but loaded down subsequent versions with more armor, night-vision radar, and ground-attack weapons that the F-15 already had. The F-16's weight and expense rose; its combat deadliness dropped. Originally produced for $3 million each, an F-16 now costs $10.3 million. The air force has bought 785 F-16s.

Meanwhile, hundreds of billions of taxpayer dollars have been wasted on unworkable weapons systems with no strategic rationale. One of the more notorious of these was the B-1 bomber, which President Carter canceled, arguing that it was a waste of taxpayers' money given that existing B-52s could do the same job with a bigger payload, and the B-2 Stealth bomber would be available within a decade. The B-1 was obsolete while it was still a blueprint. Carter laid the B-1 in its grave but lost office before he could bury it. Ideological and political imperatives resurrected the B-1. Not surprisingly, with B-1 components produced in 48 of the 50 states, Democrats as well as Republicans continued to fight for the B-1. In the 1980 election, Ronnie Reagan promised to bring back the B-1 from the dead because he believed in a "strong defense." Reagan won. To date, the 96 B-1 bombers are grounded because an unfixable array of mechanical and electronic flaws make it unsafe to fly. The direct loss to America's taxpayers – $28 billion. The indirect cost may be twice that.[64]

The B-2 Stealth bomber was designed to penetrate Soviet airspace undetected and destroy mobile missiles sites. Unfortunately, the B-2 is unstable in flight and easily detected by radar. The 20 B-2 bombers that have been produced have yet to pass their flight tests. With the Soviet Union gone, the B-2s lack a mission. Perhaps they are better off without a mission because Soviet air defenses would have wiped them out long before they reached their targets. The B-2s cost the taxpayers $44 billion, or three times the machines' collective weight in gold. As part of their "strong defense" stance, congressional Republicans are trying to appropriate $16 billion for 20 more B-2s.

Although each was sold to Congress and the public as the next-generation strategic bomber, both the B-1 and B-2 proved inferior to the B-52 which was originally built in the early 1950s. Since then there have been eight improved versions of the B-52. In 1993, the Pentagon had a bomber fleet of 148 B-52s which could drop conventional and nuclear bombs, sea mines, cluster bombs, and fire cruise missiles.

Yet, the Pentagon's desire to discard the B-52 in favor of the B-1 and B-2 was not surprising. When it comes to weapons, the Pentagon consistently values extravagance and glitz over

workability and necessity.[65] For example, the A-10 Thunder-
bolt was the most effective anti-tank aircraft ever designed.
Slow moving and heavily armored, its seven 30-millimeter
cannons could wipe out entire armored columns. Yet, the
Pentagon killed the A-10 and replaced it with the high-tech,
supersonic A-16s, which have proved much easier to shoot
down and less able to destroy enemy tanks. And regardless
of whether a bomber works or not, in an age of guided
missiles and satellites, there is little justification for manned
bomber, fighter, or reconnaissance aircraft. All of those
functions could be accomplished at a fraction of the cost
and more effectively with other machines. But the military's
"white scarf" or romantic war culture demands otherwise.

Pentagon extravagance is certainly not confined to air force
projects. The M-1 Abrams tank burns three to eight gallons
of gas for every mile it lumbers forward. One armored division requires 600,000 gallons a day. The M-1 was designed
to replace the M-60 tank and confront the Soviet's newest
tank, the T-80. The Pentagon had hyped the T-80 as a kind
of supertank that would devastate America's M-60. Only the
M-1 could stand up to the T-80, they solemnly swore. When
a T-80 was finally captured by the Israelis in 1982, it proved
to be no more than an improved version of the T-72, which
had been developed two decades before, and which the M-60
could match.

In 1995, Congress approved a $266.7 billion budget for
the following year, $9 billion more than the Pentagon had
requested. The budget included more money for B-2 bombers,
V-22 Osprey marine vertical-take off transport planes, Apache
helicopters, CVN-76 carriers, attack submarines, FA-18 navy
fighters, F-22 air force fighters, Seawolf submarines, LHD-7
amphibious assault ships, C-17A transport planes, and other
weapons systems that the Pentagon did not want or could
not justify strategically. The long-term costs of these wasteful weapons systems alone was $391.4 billion. Cost overruns
will double that figure. Meanwhile, the United States keeps
100,000 soldiers in both Europe and Asia. Of its $267 bil-
lion budget, the Pentagon diverted $80 billion to NATO.
The combined budgets of NATO's other members was only
$147.6 billion. The Pentagon's budget is ten times greater
than Russia's and twenty-seven times the combined $9.64

billion budget of America's vaguely possible enemies, Cuba, Libya, Syria, Iraq, Iran, and North Korea. The tentative 1997 fiscal year budget would spend $14 billion more than the Pentagon requested.[66]

Politics has once again triumphed over strategy. The House National Security Committee contains representatives from 31 states of which 26 divided some $500 million in new military construction projects. Senator Trent Lott, the Republican whip, convinced the Senate Armed Services Committee to appropriate $1.3 billion to build the unwanted LHD-7 assault ship in his state. The F-22 is partially built in House Speaker Newt Gingerich's district. House Minority Leader Richard Gephardt's district will build part of the C-17A and FA-18. Not all Republicans went along with this expense. Senator John McCain, a former air force pilot, rejected the B-2 bomber as "a relic of the Cold War . . . that could cost the American people $36 billion over the next ten years. The simple fact is that we don't need more strategic bombers to meet the likely threats of the future."[67]

As the world's only military superpower, the United States is locked into an arms race against itself. And it is losing.

5 Doctors and Drugs: The Medical–Industrial Complex

It is believed by many that America has the world's best health care system. But by what measure? By three key criteria – costs, access, and results – America's health care system is abysmal, the worst among the democratic industrial countries. In fact, no nation anywhere pays more per person for health care and has an unhealthier population.

From 1980 to 1990, health care costs rose 4.4 percent annually, nearly three times faster than the average consumer price index increases of 1.7 percent. In 1993, the United States health care bill was $884 billion, the equivalent of 13.9 percent of GNP and $3,299 for each of the 268 million residents. Health care costs may consume 20 percent of the economy by 2010 and 25 percent by 2030.[1]

These costs far exceed those of other democratic industrial countries. In 1992, while Americans diverted 13.3 percent of their national income to paying for health care, the Japanese paid only 6.8 percent of their GNP, Swedes 8.8 percent, the French 9.1 percent, Britons 6.6 percent, Germans 9.1 percent, and Canadians 9.9 percent. The average annual health care cost in twenty-one other democratic industrial countries was $1,603; in the United States, $2,932.[2]

While health costs have risen in all the democratic industrial countries, the United States has been the least effective in controlling costs. Between 1960 and 1991, America's health care costs rose by 2.53 times from 5.3 percent to 13.4 percent of GNP while Britain's rose by 1.7 times from 3.9 percent to 6.6 percent, Germany's by 1.77 times from 4.8 percent to 8.5 percent, Canada's by 1.82 times from 5.5 percent to 10.0 percent, and Japan's by 2.2 times from 3.0 percent to 8.3 percent.[3]

While nearly everyone in those other countries is covered by health insurance, about 17 percent or nearly 40 million

193

Americans have no access to health insurance. Given how many Americans lack adequate health care, it comes as no surprise to learn that among the 25 countries of the Organization for Economic Cooperation and Development (OECD) the United States ranks 20th in infant mortality, 17th in male life expectancy, and 16th in female life expectancy.

How did America get such an inefficient, expensive health care system? How have the other democratic industrial countries managed to provide inexpensive health care to all their citizens and surpass the United States in life expectancy and child mortality?

In his Pulitzer Prize-winning book *The Social Transformation of American Medicine*, Paul Starr argues that the answer lies in the policies shaped by the "social privilege, economic power, and political influence" of the medical industrial complex.[4] Despite the Hypocratic Oath doctors are supposed to make, the profession's economic interests have prevailed over public interests. Put simply, in America's health care system, the profits of the providers come first, the needs of patients second.

Public health issues are largely determined by a vast medical–industrial complex[5] composed of the American Medical Association (AMA), insurance corporations, hospital chains, drug and equipment makers, the Department of Health and Welfare (HEW), and politicians who receive weighty financial gifts from the industry. Representatives of the medical industrial complex have fought and usually defeated every substantial reform bill to appear in Congress while successfully pushing through bills that serve their own interests.

Federal policies are responsible for simultaneously encouraging and restraining the medical industrial complex. The result is that America's health care system is neither truly private nor public, but a strange, expensive, and inefficient hybrid of both. Washington's policies have strengthened the medical industrial complex through three broad means: direct subsidies, favorable tax treatment of insurance and health care expenditures, and government programs such as Medicare, social security, and Medicaid. Susan Feigenbaum summarizes the process:

In 1985 more than 190 million Americans benefited from health insurance subsidies resulting from the tax deductability of premiums and the tax exclusion for employer-paid health premiums; another 27.5 million received assistance through the Medicaid program. Yet another 30 million individuals benefited from Medicare insurance coverage, and an untold number received health services from federal, state, and local care givers. Finally, a long-standing government commitment to subsidize hospital capital costs – through grants, tax exempt bonds, and government backed debt instruments – has arguably reduced the private cost of hospital care and thereby improved access.[6]

Yet, it is the health care providers themselves rather than the sick which have primarily benefited from this system.

The medical industrial complex's power is peculiarly American. In no other country has the medical establishment been so successful in serving its own interests to the detriment of public health. In other national systems, the needy rather than the providers come first. No other nationality allows the market and private ownership of the medical industrial complex to play a greater role in determining the quality, access, and cost of health care than Americans. Nowhere else are insurance companies, doctors' associations, drug and medical equipment corporations, and hospitals – the medical industrial complex – more powerful in shaping national health policy.

PUBLIC POLICY AND THE RISE OF THE MEDICAL INDUSTRIAL COMPLEX

American doctors have not always enjoyed the power they now have – the medical industrial complex did not begin to emerge until the late nineteenth century. Until then, as the editors of the *Medical Record* lamented in 1869, medicine was "the most despised of all the professions which liberally-educated men are expected to make."[7] These attitudes were not peculiar to Americans. Throughout history, patients in most cultures have reviled their doctors. And with good reason. Before the scientific revolution of the late nineteenth century, doctors relied more on faith than on drugs to regain the patient's health. At best, their drugs were useless; usually they did more harm than good.

Throughout the colonial era, governments attempted to regulate the medical industry. In 1633, Massachusetts became the first colony to forbid doctors from overcharging their patients; Virginia followed suit in 1639. Eventually all colonies passed laws restricting doctors' fees. In 1760, New York City required doctors to receive a license before practicing medicine. In 1765, Philadelphia chartered the College of Philadelphia, the first medical school in America. Most other cities and colonies eventually set up their own licensing boards and colleges.

These laws and schools helped only the few who actually relied on doctors. Most Americans relied on their own simple remedies to treat illnesses. William Buchan's *Domestic Medicine* was published in Philadelphia in 1768. In its thirty editions, it gave readers the latest advice on the causes and treatments of disease, thus encouraging people to doctor themselves. People widely believed that disease reflected in part or whole the patient's moral disequilibrium. In other words, "Health came from God, not doctors."[8] Faith and moral rectitude were believed to be the best medicines. The idea of healing oneself meshed nicely with America's libertarian culture.

During the 1760s, American doctors began trying to professionalize themselves, to at once raise medical standards and market exclusiveness. They faced a long, grueling uphill struggle. In 1766, New Jersey doctors formed the first medical association. Doctors in other colonies soon formed their own associations. During this era, no one was more influential in encouraging the trade's professionalization than Benjamin Rush who maintained that all diseases resulted from an imbalance of bodily "humeurs," which could be purged by blood-letting. American medicine combined the latest European theories with native American herbs, with the latter battling to overcome disasters inflicted by the former.

Doctors were prominent among the colonial elite. For example, among the first 100 members of the New Jersey Medical Society, 17 became members of Congress or the state legislature. Four doctors – Benjamin Rush, Josiah Bartlett, Lyman Hall, and Matthew Thornton – signed the Declaration of Independence. Twenty-six doctors were members of the Continental Congress.[9] Many of America's early doctors also stepped behind a pulpit every Sunday. Yet, doctors were far from representing a professional class. Of the 3,500 to 4,000 practicing doctors on the Revolution's eve, only about 400 of them enjoyed any formal medical training, of which about half received degrees.[10]

The medical profession's status and numbers jumped following the American Revolution. In the late eighteenth century, medical faculties were establishd at the University of Pennsylvania, Harvard, King's College (Columbia), and Dartmouth. From 1790 to 1850, the number of licensed doctors increased from 5,000 to 40,000, while the number of people per doctor dropped from 950 to 600.[11] The vast majority of these doctors learned their trade as apprentices; medical schools accounted for less than 10 percent of doctors. Nonetheless, by 1850, 42 medical schools educated and graduated doctors. Student fees financed these schools. The unsalaried professors received a cut of each of their students' fees. Students learned through lectures rather than practice on genuine patients. Terms lasted three or four months; students graduated after two years.

During this era, doctors united to squeeze women out of their traditional role in ministering to the sick and delivering babies. During the early nineteenth century, starting first among the urban middle class, doctors armed with forceps and medical degrees elbowed aside midwives to birth an increasing proportion of the nation's babies. In 1815 Philadelphia, for example, the city directory listed as midwives 23 men and 21 women; by 1819, 42 men and only 13 women delivered babies. This trend spread rapidly through America's cities then towns and finally rural regions.[12]

Women fought back. Among the few successes of the women's rights movement's first wave in the 1840s was to secure a few openings in the medical field. In 1848, the New England Medical College opened to become the world's first exclusive women's medical school. Other women's colleges appeared throughout the nineteenth century while some male bastions began admitting women. By 1900, there were 17 women's medical colleges, while women represented about 10 percent of the coeducational medical schools and composed 5.6 percent of all doctors.[13]

The first doctrinal split among doctors occurred with the rise of Samuel Thomas in the 1820s. Thomas essentially married the ideas of William Buchan that people could and should doctor themselves with Benjamin Rush's that there was only one disease (bad humor) and one cure (purging). Through his charisma, pamphlets, and a devoted following, Thomas espoused simple health remedies built around a notion of perspiring "colds" from the body with peppers and steam baths, while condemning "mineral" drug cures. Thomasism reflected and reinforced the era's ever more popular Jacksonian democracy, which called for sweeping away such aristocratic privileges as property and religious qualifications for voting and public office, and classical education in Latin and Greek in colleges. Many states and cities responded by eliminating licensing for doctors, and with it much of the success the medical profession had made a half-century earlier in monopolizing their field. But the states also did away with the fee restrictions that had hobbled doctors' incomes since the colonial era.

During the early nineteenth century, other medical sects like the eclectics and homeopaths emerged to challenge the mainstream profession. The eclectics took many Thomasian ideas while using plants for drugs and allowing women to practice. The homeopaths believed that disease had a psychological rather than physical cause, and could be cured by giving the patient drugs which produced the same symptoms as the disease itself. In the 1890s, other "sects" such as the osteopaths and Christian Scientists would emerge.

In 1841, mainstream doctors fought back by forming the American Medical Association (AMA) to assert their common interests. The AMA battled first against the "sectarians" by lobbying state legislatures and medical colleges to impose licenses and raise education standards. States and schools were reluctant to do so, however, for fear that if they imposed higher standards potential students and doctors would simply go elsewhere. Others used social Darwinian arguments to condemn licensing as a restraint of trade, cartelization of medicine, and inhibition on medical research.

It was not until 1877 that Illinois became the first state to license practitioners. One by one, other states followed. These regulations

> developed incrementally. First, a minimal statute was en-
> acted requiring only a diploma; then the principle was
> established that diplomas could be examined and candi-
> dates rejected if the school they had attended was judged
> inadequate; and, finally, all candidates were required to
> present an acceptable diploma and to pass an indepen-
> dent state examination. By 1901 twenty-five states and the
> District of Columbia were in this last category, while only
> two states were in the first. No jurisdiction was without a
> licensing statute of some sort.[14]

Opponents challenged state licenses in the courts. The Supreme Court unanimously upheld the state regulation of the medical field in its 1888 *Dent* v. *West Virginia* decision. The Supreme Court expanded this decision in the 1898 *Hawker* v. *New York*, in which it noted that for doctors, "charac-ter is as important as knowledge," and thus states could use both as criteria in licensing.

The AMA also countered sectarians by forbidding its mem-bers from consulting with them, and went so far as to expel the New York Medical Association when it voted in 1882 to allow such consultations. Some dissidents voluntarily left the AMA. In 1886, a faction which rejected outright the AMA's political and ethical agenda split off to form the Association of American Physicians. Other doctors may well have agreed with the AMA and enjoyed its success yet did not join in order to save paying the membership dues. The AMA maintained its hard line at a price. In 1900, only 8,000 doctors were AMA members while 33,000 were members of other medical associations and 77,000 were completely unaffiliated.

The watershed in the AMA's national power occurred in 1901 when it drew up a new constitution whereby the House of Delegates would be reduced to 150 members, to be period-ically reappointed among the states; and delegates had to be members of an affiliated state medical association, which in turn had to be comprised of county medical associations.

These new requirements caused membership to explode to 70,000, or half the nation's doctors, by 1910.

Meanwhile, the number of medical colleges rose rapidly from 51 to 75 between 1850 to 1870, then to 100 by 1880, 133 by 1890, and 160 with 25,138 students by 1900. The number of physicians rose 153 percent between 1870 and 1910 while the nation's population increased by 138 percent. Even at this more recent date, few doctors had received more than an apprenticeship before they open a business. Status and income among doctors varied considerably according to their skills, education, family background, and location. Reflecting on his practice in the 1870s, one doctor observed that

> the rank and file of the profession were – as far as general education went – little, if any, above the level of their clientele. And the clientele not only felt this, but knew it. Hence the medical man had to be more than modest, he had to be circumspect, even deferential, in facing ignorance, absurd pretensions, and ill manners – especially where they abounded most, among a certain class of the self-made, uncultured wealth.[15]

The leader in promoting medical school reforms was Charles Eliot of Harvard University; the AMA merely cheered from the sidelines. Upon becoming Harvard President in 1869, Eliot completely revamped the standards of admission, curriculum, and graduation. Although enrollment initially dropped, it surpassed its previous height within a decade. During the 1890s, other medical schools began emulating Harvard's reforms. Founded in 1893, Baltimore's Johns Hopkins' medical school was free of the traditional outlooks of other schools, and quickly became a leader in research and treatment of medical problems.

In 1904, the AMA established the Council on Medical Education to evaluate the nation's 160 existing medical schools and promote reforms. When its survey was completed in 1906, the Council rated 82 schools Class A, or first class, 46 Class B, or redeemable, and 32 Class C, or beyond the pale. To avoid animosity, the AMA chose not to publish the report. Instead, it invited the Carnegie Foundation for the

Advancement of Teaching to conduct a similar survey. Thomas Flexner was charged with making the survey, and conducted an even more vigorous evaluation of the nation's medical schools. When it was published in 1910, the Flexner Report or Bulletin Number Four blasted most of the schools for insufficient or non-existing laboratories and libraries, and low standards, and proposed comprehensive reforms.

The Flexner Report accelerated a weeding out of medical colleges that was already well under way, with the number dropping from 162 in 1906 to 131 in 1910 as states raised their licensing requirements. In 1912, the Federation of State Boards formed and embraced the AMA's standards. In the survivors the curriculum was broadened, class sizes were reduced, hands-on training in laboratories and clinics increased, and stringent entrance requirements were imposed. Internship programs became increasingly popular; by 1912, 80 percent of graduates became interns before entering their own practice. The number of schools further dropped to 92 with 3,536 graduates by 1915. By 1922, when 38 states required two or more college years of preliminary work before acceptance to medical school, the number of schools had fallen to 81 with 2,529 graduates.

What the nation's doctors gained in professionalism, they lost in numbers and diversity. An adverse effect of the reforms was to produce a shortage of doctors which persisted until the 1980s. Tougher entrance requirements often meant that blacks, Jews, and women were excluded. Aspiring black doctors had to concentrate their hopes on Howard and Meharry Universities. Doctors had always been underrepresented in rural regions; the new standards further reduced the proportion of rural doctors in the population. Alternative medicine also suffered. By 1931, non-traditionalists comprised only 5.1 percent of all doctors.[16]

The technological advances of the late nineteenth-century revolutionized medicine in many ways, including the doctor–patient relationship. Like it or not, patients are dependent on their doctors; as medicine has become more sophisticated, patients have become more dependent. Unless the doctor displays gross negligence, most people will give him or her the benefit of the doubt. This authority evolved with medical technology. In preindustrial America, people largely relied on themselves for medicine. Families and communities treated their own members. A midwife might be called to help deliver the baby but generally people doctored themselves. People viewed doctors with skepticism at best, and frequently contempt. Doctors had to be relatively humble or else lose their patients.

The interrelated forces of scientific and technological advances, industrialization, and urbanization at once improved people's lives and eroded the patient's autonomy. For example, the spread of telephones starting in the 1870s and automobiles in the 1890s, gave doctors the unprecedented ability to communicate and meet with their patients. As medicine advanced and degrees proliferated among practitioners, the traditional humbleness among most doctors gave way to a self-assurance that often bordered on arrogance. D. W. Cathell's manual *The Physician Himself,* reprinted numerous times after it first appeared in 1881, called on doctors to cultivate distance and an air of mystery between themselves and their patients.[17] Nearly all Americans have gradually become prisoners of specialists and institutions – and their attitudes.

The same scientific advances that enabled doctors to better practice their trade pushed governments to take responsibility for improving public health. Scientific advances revealed that many diseases traveled through bad water and food, and inoculations were developed to prevent a lengthening list of diseases. During the 1870s, as researchers discovered the importance of hygiene and antiseptics in combating infection, political pressure grew on local, state, and federal governments to improve public hygiene.

Louisiana formed the nation's first state board of health in 1855, but it had little effect on quelling disease or inspiring emulators. After its creation in 1869, New York City's Metropolitan Board of Health made highly effective and well-publicized inroads against diseases which had ravished the population. Other cities and states formed health boards modeled after New York's. In March 1879, Congress established a National Board of Health.

The AMA fought hard against any public health initiatives. Its greatest victory occurred in 1883 when it pressured Congress into terminating the National Board of Health.

Reformers, however, were better organized at the local than the national level. One by one, city governments began purifying public water, better disposing of garbage, mass-inoculating school children, and requiring warehouses, meat-packers, and restaurants to invest in refrigeration and hygiene. States passed workmen compensation laws. These regulations allowed people to live longer, healthier lives.

Although the AMA opposed this government threat to reduce their army of clients – or "socialized medicine" as they labeled it then as now – they did actually lobby for regulation in at least one area. A prime AMA target at the century's turn was the pharmaceutical industry. Doctors, progressives, and muckraking journalists had long railed against the "snake-oil" manufacturers which promised miracle drugs. An investigative report by Samuel Adams in the October 1905 issue of the popular magazine *Collier's* charged 264 companies and individuals with willfully selling useless or harmful medicines. The AMA distributed 150,000 copies of Adams's article "The Great American Fraud," and established a Council on Pharmacy and Chemistry to set standards and test drugs.

The AMA's long-standing campaign combined with Adams's article and the previous year's publication of Upton Sinclair's novel *The Jungle*, which blasted the meat-packing industry for corrupt, unsanitary conditions, to incite a public outcry that pressured Congress into passing the 1906 Pure Food and Drug Act.

For decades, the AMA fought a losing battle against the creeping "socialized medicine" not just of government but of business as well. The swelling labor union movement demanded from corporate heads health care along with better pay and safety. In 1897, about half a million workers were union members, a number that expanded to 2 million by 1910 and 5 million by 1920. Industry-wide strikes periodically disrupted the railroad, steel, and mining industries, among others. Governmental and newspaper reports increasingly sympathized with some union demands, particularly worker safety. An increasing number of gruesome accidents had accompanied America's industrialization. A 1900 Interstate Commerce Commission study reported that accidents injured one of every 28 railroad workers and killed one of every 399. In response to growing union and public pressure, state legislatures began passing workmen compensation laws. Owners grudgingly conceded to the new regulations and public pressure. Increasing numbers of industrial firms began paying for some of the health care costs of their employees. They did so to attract reliable labor and deter liability suits for injuries on the job. Firms provided doctors and victims relief funds to cover the direct (medical) and indirect (income loss) costs of accidents.

Ironically, the AMA fought longer than the corporate leaders against these reforms. The AMA battled against these reforms in the courts, arguing that corporations could not be licensed to practice medicine. Courts in some states agreed and struck down the company medical services. Reformers replied by pressuring the state Houses into passing laws explicitly allowing the practice. By 1930, company medical services covered 530,000 railroad, 540,000 mining and logging workers, and hundreds of thousands of workers in other industries. Not only industries but an increasing number of national fraternal associations adopted medical plans, against which the AMA protested vainly. As early as 1914, 179 societies provided some sort of health care to their 7.7 members.

Yet another threat to AMA interests emerged with the hospital complexes pioneered by the Mayo family in Rochester, Minnesota, in the 1880s. By 1929, the Mayo Clinic had become a vast medical complex employing 386 doctors and dentists, 175 research fellows, and 895 laboratory technicians, nurses, and other workers, in 288 examination rooms, 21 sprawling laboratories enclosed in a fifteen-story building.[18]

The Mayo Clinic represented a revolutionary transformation of American hospitals. America's first "hospitals" were almshouses for the homeless who could not help themselves, including the sick, orphans, the insane, and the aged. In 1752, Philadelphia founded Pennsylvania Hospital as the first general hospital dedicated to helping the sick alone. In 1771, New York City chartered the New York Hospital, but it did not open until 1791. The nation's third general hospital opened in Boston in 1821. By the mid-nineteenth century, most of the nation's cities had general hospitals. Private charities run by Catholic, Protestant, and Jewish groups formed many hospitals. The Civil War spawned advances in hospital administration. By 1865, the Union Army had built a 130,000 bed system with a mortality rate of only 8 percent. Union hospital administrators incorporated many of the ideas and procedures pioneered by Florence Nightingale during the Crimean War a decade earlier. In 1873, nursing emerged as a profession with the establishment of nursing schools in New York, Boston, and New Haven. By 1900, there were 432 nursing schools across the United States and 1,129 by 1910. These new nursing schools barely kept pace with an explosion in the number of hospitals, from about 170 in 1870 to over 4,000 in 1910. By the late nineteenth century, increasing numbers of hospitals were run as businesses rather than charities, and became centers of medical research affiliated with medical schools. Hospital income became as diverse as their practices. By 1922, general hospitals received 65.2 percent of their income from patients, 17.7 percent from public money, 5.7 percent from donations, 3.6 percent from endowments, and 7.8 percent from other sources. As with corporate and public medical reforms, while ever more professionally and scientifically run hospitals allowed Americans to enjoy better health, they diminished the control doctors had over the process and profits.[19]

Despite these defeats, the AMA did succeed in preventing the "socialized medicine" sweeping across Europe from infecting the United States. Although, by 1914, America's economy was larger and more prosperous than that of Germany, Britain, and France combined, it was the odd man out in health coverage. Germany created a national health insurance system as early as 1883, Austria in 1888, Hungary and Sweden in 1891, Denmark in 1892, Norway in 1909, Serbia in 1911, Britain in 1911, Russia and Switzerland in 1912, and the Netherlands in 1913. These national care programs varied greatly, but generally were first instituted to help the poor and then gradually expanded to encompass everyone.

Washington refused to emulate other industrial countries and create a national health system. As early as 1904, the Socialist Party espoused the creation of a national health program. In 1906, the American Association for Labor Legislation (AALL) joined the crusade. The movement climaxed in 1912 when former president Theodore Roosevelt abandoned the Republican Party to run for president as an independent candidate who called for, among other progressive causes, national health insurance. Amidst the growing support for national health insurance, the AMA and National Association of Manufacturers (NAM) flirted with the AALL scheme.

Roosevelt's defeat emboldened the AMA and NAM to announce that from now they adamantly opposed any national health insurance. Surprisingly, labor unions were also opposed. Samuel Gompers, the head of the American Federation of Labor (AFL), insisted that corporations rather than the state should provide health care and pensions for workers. Gompers reasoned that national health and retirement insurance would weaken the loyalty of workers to the unions. With virtually all interest groups opposed, national health insurance would have had little chance of passage even if Roosevelt had been elected. During the 1910s, opponents scuttled reform bills proposed not only in Congress, but in California, New York, Ohio, Pennsylvania, and Illinois as well. These defeats killed the national health insurance movement; the 1917 Russian Revolution and subsequent "red scare" in the United States would bury it for another two decades. The best that reformers could do was to pressure Congress into passing the 1921 Shepherd-Towner Act, which gave matching funds to states which provided prenatal and child health centers. The AMA succeeded in getting Congress to kill the program in 1927.

Contrary to economic theory, the free market did not supply the demand for health insurance. Until the 1930s, aside from the corporate health plans, no medical care was covered by insurance. Around 1900, however, some insurance firms did begin offering insurance against specific diseases, which they sold at premium prices only to the very wealthy and healthy. However, prior to the 1930s, insurance firms did not offer health insurance because they feared that the sickly would be more likely to apply and demand more care thus prompting doctors and hospitals to raise fees. At the time, household insurance marketing and collection was largely door-to-door, a very labor-extensive and expensive undertaking. In all, health insurance seemed a money losing concept for insurance firms.

This conundrum was overcome by the rise of group insurance plans. In 1928, General Motors contracted Metropolitan Life to cover 180,000 workers. In 1929, 1,250 school teachers contracted with Baylor University Hospital in Dallas to provide up to twenty-one days of hospitalization annually for a monthly premium of fifty cents. This was the first arrangement of what would become the Blue Cross plans which hospital associations promoted during the Great Depression. Blue Cross plans were offered to all firms within certain districts, a scheme called "community rating." Blue Shield plans emerged around this time whereby groups of patients could insure with physicians. Private insurance companies soon got in on the act since community rating spread the risks, but undermined the system by selling to firms with healthier workforces. The cost of Blue Cross programs rose as they took in firms which could not get lower-cost insurance elsewhere. By 1940, the thirty-nine Blue Cross plans had enrolled 6 million while private insurance had 3.7 million.[20]

Ironically, the mass poverty of the 1930s provided little more fertile political ground for the passage of national health insurance than the prosperity of the 1920s. Free enterprise had caused, then proved incapable of overcoming, the Great Depression. The collection of government programs known as the New Deal pumped jobs and money into the hands of millions of Americans. While national health insurance was on Roosevelt's list of reforms, it had become a secondary issue.

After launching a dozen programs designed to create jobs and stimulate the economy, Roosevelt focused on providing social security for retirees. In June 1934, Roosevelt created a Committee on Economic Security and empowered it to investigate and propose reforms for the problem of retiree income and health care. The AMA, NAM, and labor groups immediately voiced opposition. In October, fearing that a linkage between health insurance and social security would sink the latter, the American Association for Social Security urged Roosevelt to shelve the former. The President complied. The subsequent Social Security Act of 1935 provided not only retirement income for all Americans aged 65 years and older, but workman's compensation as well. Social security was financed by payroll deductions.

The health care lobby continued to push for national health insurance. In July 1938, a coalition of labor, farm, and progressive health care groups convened the National Health

Conference, whose purpose was to rally support for national health insurance. Since polls had first asked about social security, in 1935, they indicated that as many as three of four Americans favored some sort of national health insurance, although only one of three preferred it over affordable private insurance.[21] Sensing he had a hot issue, Roosevelt at first enthusiastically embraced the National Health Conference's goals and wanted to make national health insurance a prominent issue in that year's presidential campaign. But he backed away from the issue as polls indicated a conservative backlash was rising against the New Deal. Conservative Republican and southern Democrats swept the November election. Swimming against the political tide, New York Senator Robert Wagner introduced a national health insurance bill in February 1939. Roosevelt refused to endorse the Wagner bill, and said he only favored a tenet promoting more hospital construction. The Wagner bill died along with a Roosevelt bill on hospital construction.

Undaunted, Wagner joined in 1943 with Montana Senator James Murray and Michigan Representative John Dingell to propose an even more sweeping national health insurance bill. In February 1944, to drum up support for his bill, Wagner organized the Social Security Charter Committee composed of progressive labor, health, and farm representatives. Later that year, Roosevelt gave one last half-hearted plug for national health insurance when he asked Congress to include it in a bill promoting an "economic bill of rights." The bill did not pass and Wagner's bill remained bottled up in committee.

The insurance industry, allied with the AMA and other medical lobby groups, not only fought off the attempt to nationalize it, but actually expanded its power during World War II. In 1944, the Supreme Court ruled that insurance as interstate commerce was subject to antitrust laws. The insurance industry rallied a majority in Congress to pass the McCarran–Ferguson Act in 1945 exempting them from antitrust laws. Although Congress originally intended to allow health insurance only a three-year reprieve from antitrust laws, courts ever since have interpreted an ambiguous clause as giving the industry unlimited relief. The industry claims that it must pool data in order to determine rates. The trouble is that the rates are not competitive. The insurance corporations fix rates, restrict coverage, divvy up markets, and require consumers to buy drugs from their affiliated producers. With Washington having conceded the power to regulate health insurance, the states must do the job themselves. At best, the states' management is lax; it varies widely from one state to the next. Today, a few huge corporations – Aetna, Cigna, Metropolitan Life, Travelers, and Prudential – dominate the system.

As after World War I, the return to prosperity and "red scare" following World War II politically sank any prospects for the passage of national health insurance. Shortly after taking office in April 1945, President Harry Truman unveiled his own health care plan but, like his predecessor, got nowhere with the issue. The AMA claimed that passage of Truman's plan would make doctors "slaves" to "socialized medicine."

The best Truman could get was the 1946 Hospital Survey and Construction Act, better known as the Hill–Burton Act, which provided Federal funds to help expand the nation's hospitals and their facilities. Between 1946 and 1970, the program invested $3.7 billion which included 30 percent of all hospital construction, while generating an additional $9.1 billion in matching state and local funds. Altogether Hill–Burton helped construct over 400,000 hospital beds. In addition, the government encouraged the financing of hospitals by allowing their construction and maintenance through tax-exempt revenue bonds. By allowing hospitals to deduct all interest and depreciation costs, the government encouraged them to expand their services whether or not demand existed. As a result, a glut of hospital beds emerged in the 1960s when the total number peaked at 1.7 million or 8.6 per head of the population in 1965. Although the number has since declined steadily, the glut continues as the average stay has dropped even faster.[22]

Yet another important Truman contribution to health care was passage of the 1946 GI Bill, which has since funded the education of thousands of doctors and hundreds of thousands of other Americans in other professions. By 1965, Washington underwrote half the cost of the nation's medical schools.

Republicans took the Senate in 1946 and killed any chance of Truman's comprehensive plan being enacted. The Republicans did, however, push through the 1947 Taft-Hartley Bill, which at once outlawed union-based welfare funds and made a firm's health insurance payments tax-deductible. The bill followed crippling strikes by the United Mine Workers of America (UMWA) led by John Lewis, and President Truman's seizure of the mines in 1946. During the labor-scarce 1940s, firms were happy to provide such benefits to retain skilled workers, and with such provisions tax-deductible, the number of workers covered by company insurance rose from 2.7 million in 1948 to 12 million workers and 17 million dependants, or about one-fourth of all private insurance. By the late 1940s, the employer-based health insurance system was firmly rooted. By 1958, over 80 percent of all full-time workers had some form of health insurance.[23]

Other innovations arose from local governments and businesses. In 1943, New York's Mayor Fiorello La Guardia appointed a committee to investigate a prepayment insurance scheme for city workers. In 1947, La Guardia's efforts bore fruit when New York City passed the Health Insurance Plan (HIP), which allied with Blue Cross. Other cities began adopting their own HIP–Blue Cross plans. Meanwhile, in Portland, Oregon, and Oakland, California, Henry Kaiser set up a group insurance plan that included 500,000 people by 1955. An AMA boycott of Kaiser ended in 1951 when Washington ruled it was an illegal restraint of trade. By 1953, commercial insurance covered 29 percent of all Americans, Blue Cross 27 percent, and other group plans 7 percent.[24]

Throughout the twentieth century, the federal government has developed the pharmaceutical industry through an ever expanding array of agencies, programs, and funds. The Agriculture Department has traditionally led the industrial policies for drug research and development. Since the 1906 Food and Drug Act, the Agriculture Department's Chemistry Bureau has conducted an ever expanding range of pharmacological and toxicological studies. Many of these studies led to the development of new drugs. Other agencies have emerged to contribute to these developments. Congress passed the 1902 Biologics Control Act to regulate serums and vaccines, and directed the Hygienic Laboratory of the Marine Hospital Service in New York to implement the law. In 1912, the Marine Hospital Service was renamed the US Public Health Service, and in 1930 the Hygienic Laboratory became the National Institute of Health (NIH). In 1937, Congress expanded the NIH's duties by creating and attaching to it the National Cancer Institute, and authorized the Public Health Service to provide grants for private researchers. In 1938, the NIH moved to a privately donated estate in Bethesda, Maryland. Its laboratories have developed many new vaccines and serums which have saved or bettered countless lives.

Despite the Public Health Service's expansion, its budget was only $3.8 million in 1938 compared with the Agriculture Department's $26.3 million. In 1941, Roosevelt created the Office of Scientific Research and Development (OSRD). During the war, the OSRD's Medical Research Committee invested $15 million in 450 contracts with universities and 150 with hospitals, research institutes, and clinics, which altogether employed 5,500 scientists and technicians. These government agencies work closely with private foundations like the American Cancer Society and March of Dimes. By 1945, funds from governments, universities, and foundations contributed $25 million to the research and development of new drugs, an enormous boost to the $40 million that pharmaceutical firms invested that year.[25]

The powers of these agencies expanded quickly following the war. In 1948, Congress renamed the NIH the National Institutes of Health and added to it five new institutes; two years later, in 1950, Congress established the National Science Foundation. From 1941 to 1951, the total federal budget for medical research rose by twenty-five times from $3 million to $76 million, while total national expenditures rose ten-fold from $18 million to $181 million. In other words, by 1951, Washington contributed 40 percent of the nation's investments in medical research.[26]

During the 1960s, the Kennedy and Johnson Administrations inaugurated new programs and institutions, along with more spending for older programs. In 1963, Congress succeeded in passing the Health Professions Educational Act over shrill AMA protests. The Act provides federal grants to medical schools to allow them to expand their student body and provide scholarships for poor and minority students. These federal training policies more than doubled the ranks of medical school graduates, and boosted many times the number of specialists in different areas. From 1965 to 1980, federal grants helped boost the nation's medical schools from 88 to 126, and the number of graduates from 7,409 to 15,135. The 1965 Immigration Act and its revision in 1976 inadvertently further boosted the nation's number of doctors by removing nationality restrictions on immigrants and favoring those with professions. By the 1970s, there was a glut of specialists – at least in urban areas.[27]

But the biggest expansion of federal involvement in public health occurred on July 1, 1965, when Congress passed a bill creating the Medicare and Medicaid programs. Medicare provides both hospital and physician insurance for everyone 65 years or older. It includes two components, a Part A coverage of hospital patients and Part B coverage of outpatients. Medicare is not means-tested; everyone 65 years or older is eligible for Medicare regardless of their wealth. Medicaid is a joint federal–state program which provides health insurance for the poor or disabled. Each state runs its own Medicaid program within federal guidelines and with matching federal grants, although Washington's contribution rises for poorer states to the height of 77 percent for Mississippi. Those eligible for Medicaid include those on welfare. While Medicare standards are set by Washington, Medicaid's are set by the states. Both systems provide limited coverage. Medicare has required an ever higher deduction for hospital care and provides no coverage for long-term care; altogether it provides only one-half of the elderly's medical bills. Medicaid covers only about one-third of the nation's poor.

Medicare and Medicaid took a half-dozen years from their inception to passage. A version of the Act was originally introduced in 1958 by Rhode Island Representative Aimee Forand. Although Forand's modest bill – it only expanded social security coverage for the aged – was shelved, it inspired a series of committee hearings and other bills which addressed public health issues. The most prominent of these was the Medicare bill introduced by Oklahoma Senator Robert Kerr and Arkansas Representative Wilber Mills. Kennedy espoused the bill but lacked the congressional votes to push it through. The 1964 Democratic sweep of Congress gave Johnson the opportunity to make it the keystone of his Great Society program.

Economic theory would predict that the proliferation of doctors, hospitals, research institutes, insurance firms, and government subsidies would drive down costs. Instead costs soared, from $198 to $336 for every American between 1965 and 1970 alone, while the federal medical budget rose from $10.8 billion to $27.8 billion.[28] In July 1969, President Nixon declared a health crisis and called for measures to prevent "a breakdown in our medical system." A consensus emerged across the political spectrum that America's health care system was the democratic industrial world's worst. A January 1970 issue of *Fortune* magazine echoed the views of most analysts:

> Much of U.S. medical care, particularly the everyday business of preventing and treating routine illnesses, is inferior in quality, wastefully dispensed, and inequitably financed. . . . Whether poor or not, most Americans are badly served by the obsolete, overstrained medical system that has grown up around them helter-skelter . . . the time has come for radical change.

And who was primarily responsible for the crisis? According to *Fortune*, "The doctors created the system. They run it. And they are the most formidable obstacle to its improvement.[29]

Incremental rather than radical change eventually came, but that did little to arrest the ever rising costs and comparatively abysmal health standards for Americans. Senator Edward Kennedy and Michigan Representative Martha Griffiths introduced a national health insurance bill in 1970 but it remained bottled up in committee. While most politicians agreed that a radical overhaul of the medical industrial complex was necessary, it would be more expensive in the short-run and the nation was already experiencing a financial crisis from the costs of the Vietnam War and Great Society.

Meanwhile in 1971, the Nixon Administration sponsored a bill that encouraged the rise of health maintenance organizations (HMOs) to alleviate health care's growing costs.

The White House predicted the bill would expand the nation's HMOs from 30 in 1971 to 1,700 by 1976, which would enroll 90 percent of the population by 1980. Congress passed the bill in 1973. Under the bill, the federal government would provide start-up grants to HMOs and require all firms with twenty-five or more employees to offer an HMO as an insurance option. The bill marked an important health care reform victory over the medical industrial complex, which had long opposed HMOs as eroding the existing highly profitable fee-for-service system. Unfortunately, the number of HMOs established fell far short of the White House's hopes. Between 1973 and 1981 when the Reagan Administration killed the grant program, Washington invested $145 million in grants and $219 million in loans to seed 115 HMOs, matching $348 million in private funds.[30]

Two other bills passed in 1974 that helped reform the system. The National Health Planning and Resource Development Act required the states to establish State Health Planning and Development Agencies and Statewide Health Coordinating Councils. In addition, the bill created a Bureau of Health Planning and Development and a National Health Planning Advisory Council at the federal level to oversee the state institutions. The purpose of these new agencies was to coordinate investments by local hospitals in order to deter duplication of efforts and spread institutions where they were most needed. The Employee Retirement Income Security Act provided an enormous incentive for businesses to provide health care insurance by allowing their self-funded programs to escape state insurance regulations.

The health crisis deepened despite these programs. Within days of taking office in August 1974, President Ford called for national health insurance. However, in his January 1975 State of the Union speech he reversed his attitude, arguing that national health insurance would worsen inflation. In 1975, Congress did pass the Employment Security and Retirement Act, which regulates employee benefit plans.

National health insurance advocates took heart when Jimmy Carter entered the White House in 1977. Surely, they reasoned, Carter would embrace Kennedy's bill and together they would push it through the Democratic-controlled Congress. But the White House viewed Kennedy's plan as a political and economic disaster. Instead, the Carter Administration proposed a bill which required businesses to provide minimal health insurance for their employees, expanded public coverage for the poor, and created a federal corporation which would provide low-cost insurance for the entire population. While Kennedy and Carter deadlocked over their respective visions, in 1978, Representatives David Stockman and Richard Gephardt introduced a health care reform bill which would have imposed modest cost-controls, but it was tabled in committee. Unable to compromise, in May 1979, Kennedy introduced his bill in Congress; Carter submitted his the following month. Congress ultimately rejected both bills.

By the 1980s, the nation's health care system was clearly locked into a chronic and worsening financial crisis. Medicare and Medicaid costs spiraled to twice the inflation rate. With the government paying over 40 percent of the nation's health care bill, it was clear that Washington had the power to reform the system if only it had the will. State and local medical costs rose as well, from $8 billion in 1970 to $24 billion in 1980. In 1950, health care consumed 4.4 percent of GNP; in 1980, 11.7 percent. Health care costs increased an average 5.9 percent annually during that time; in 32 of those 35 years, it exceeded the inflation rate. Between 1950 and 1985, health care costs had soared from $12.7 billion to $425 billion, or from $1 billion a month to $1 billion a day![31]

Consistent with its "market-magic" beliefs, the Reagan White House denied there even was a problem. The only reform of the Reagan era came from Congress; Reagan reluctantly signed it into law. On April 1, 1983, Congress partly addressed the growing health care crisis by passing the Medicare Prospective Payment Service (PPS) bill. Taking effect a half-year later, the bill imposed price caps on 468 diagnosis-related groups (DRGs). Feigenbaum writes that the

> price of each DRG is independent of hospital specific costs and characteristics, but is adjusted to reflect local wage rates, location (urban/suburban), and teaching intensity. In effect the DRG system has replaced a cost-based reimbursement system, which imposed no financial risk on the hospital, with an indemnity payment per admission. Since

hospitals cannot recoup any additional charges from the Medicare patient, this new mode of payment renders the hospital the sole risk bearer should patient costs deviate from the prospective payment.[32]

Since they receive no Medicare payments for charges beyond the cap, hospitals had an incentive to bring down costs below the cap. The lower the costs, the higher the hospital's profit. But the incentives are for hospitals, not doctors who continue to demand and receive high salaries. The Federal DRG policy was a major reason for the subsequent reduction in hospital stays. Yet costs continued to rise.

The only other health policy passed during the 1980s was the Medicare Catastrophic Act of 1988, which extended social security coverage to families suffering a bankrupting medical crisis. Congress repealed the act the following year.

THE BATTLE FOR HEALTH CARE REFORM

Health care re-emerged as a salient issue in American politics during 1993 and 1994 when a half-dozen reform bills entered and eventually died in Congress. Traditionally, most Americans viewed health care as a welfare issue which mostly concerned the poor. During the 1980s, however, health care costs soared and employers began cutting back or eliminating their insurance for employees. As the middle class's real income deteriorated and their health care costs rose, increasing numbers began clamoring for reform. As Starr puts it, "health insurance had changed from a problem that affects 'them' to one that affects 'us.' That not only widened the potential constituency for reform; it also converted health insurance from a poverty issue to a general problem of economic prosperity."[33]

Despite its ever rising costs, gross inefficiencies, and fraud, health care remained on the policy back-burner throughout the 1980s. Then, those who had long advocated health care reform received an enormous boost when in 1991 Harris Wolford, a Democrat running for a Pennsylvania Senate seat, embraced reform as the keystone of his campaign. At one point Wolford was forty points in the polls behind his opponent, former Attorney General Richard Thornburgh. Yet, largely by hammering away at the need for health care reform, Wolford won a resounding victory, thus demonstrating the issue's political power.

By the 1992 election, health care reform had risen to the front political burner. The public and media demanded to know each candidate's reform plan. Democratic front-runner Bill Clinton asserted that health care reform would be a primary objective of his presidency. Trying to steal the thunder from his rivals, on February 6, President Bush unveiled a plan to provide tax credits for those who buy health care insurance. Congress did not take up his proposal.

During the campaign, Clinton rejected both the pure-market and single-payer approaches. On September 26, having won the nomination, Clinton announced his "managed competition" plan whereby employers could choose either to buy insurance for their employees or to pay higher taxes ("play or pay"), the government would cover the uninsured, small businesses could buy discounted insurance, and a panel would set national health-spending limits. Clinton acquired the idea for managed competition from medical historian Paul Starr whose book *The Logic of Health Care Reform* appeared amidst the campaign. Robert Reich, who would become Labor Secretary, and Ira Magaziner, who would head the group drawing up Clinton's health care reform, read the book and encouraged Clinton to embrace managed competition. Some criticized the pay or play scheme because "the public program would tend to attract employers not only with above-average risks but also with below-average wages. Endemically underfinanced, the government program would almost certainly become a fiscal albatross and a source of inferior coverage."[34]

Shortly after entering the White House, Clinton named Magaziner to head and his wife to chair a task force which would prepare the health care reform bill. The effort was divided into over thirty task forces which explored different problems of the complex issue and proposed solutions. The group received extensive advice from a diverse range of sources, including the Departments of Health and Human Services (HHS), Labor, Treasury, and Defense, along with the Office of Management and Budget (OMB) and Council of Economic Advisors, the National Governors Association, and various health care experts. The effort received a boost on March 8 when the Chamber of Commerce endorsed his "managed competition" concept as the best way to control costs.

Yet, the task force was criticized for at once trying to be secret and relatively exclusive while at the same time trying to introduce as many perspectives as possible. Those excluded such as the insurance industry and AMA howled for inclusion. Meanwhile internal memos were continually leaked to the press. The effort was further stymied when Mrs Clinton was diverted by lawsuits over her role in the task force and her father's death. The result was confusion and resentment over the direction the effort seemed to be taking. Nonetheless, by May 1993, the task force had completed its research and presented its proposals. A new team took over, this one composed largely of representatives from the HHS, Treasury, OMB, and Council of Economic Advisors, who would crunch the numbers and write up the specific bill.

As details of the Clinton bill were leaked, the medical industrial complex, particularly the insurance corporations, launched preemptive and highly effective attacks. On September 8, the insurance industry unveiled its "Harold and Louise" television advertisement in which a middle-class couple denounced Clinton's proposal as "big government." Analysts would later point to the commercials as an important reason for the eroding public support not only for Clinton's program but for all reform proposals.

On September 22, Clinton unveiled his Health Security Act before a joint session of Congress. His plan's centerpiece was regional "health alliances" or purchasing groups to which businesses and households would belong. Corporate health alliances would be allowed for all of those with 5,000 or more employees. Employers would provide insurance to all employees working twenty or more hours, and pay 80 percent of their insurance premiums, but would not have to pay costs above 7.9 percent of their payroll costs. Individuals would pay up to 20 percent of their premiums. The government would subsidize small businesses. Universal coverage would be achieved by 1999.

Firms would have to provide at least three choices to their employees, a fee-for-service, HMO, or preferred-provider network. Each package would have to provide minimum coverage for doctor and hospital bills, prescription drugs, and some mental health and substance-abuse care. Insurance firms would have to accept all who wished to sign up. Penalties for preexisting conditions would be banned. People could not only take their health insurance from one firm to the next, but the coverage would continue even if the employer went bankrupt, the employee lost his or her job, moved to another state, or lost a spouse from death or divorce. Malpractice suits would be reduced by their first passing through mediation and, if still unresolved, the complaint had to be approved by a doctor before going to court. Lawyers' fees would be limited to no more than one-third of the award. Within these broad confines, states would be even freer than they currently are in experimenting with different methods of providing care and cost cutting. To help further control costs, a National Health Board would set standards for the pricing of services and approve the operations of the health care alliances.

The program would be paid for by savings of $238 billion in reduced Medicare and Medicaid payments between 1995 and 2000, along with new taxes of $175 billion on tobacco and large corporations that avoided the regional purchasing alliances. After deducting for the increased subsidies for the uninsured, the net cut in the projected Federal deficit would be about $58 billion. For the nation, health care costs would rise less quickly because of the huge savings providers would reap in reduced administrative costs and the insured in economies of scale. Employers would pay about $27 billion in lower costs between 1995 and 2000; state and local governments could save as much as $65 billion during those five years. Overall, the health care bureaucracy would be trimmed rather than fattened. Yet, health care costs would continue to rise, albeit at a slower rate, from 14.3 percent of GNP costs in 1993 to 16.9 percent by the year 2000, well below the projected costs of 17.5 percent.

Clinton tried to sell his plan as a compromise between a single-payer system that socialized medicine and cosmetic reforms that would not restrain health care's ever swelling costs. He argued that employer mandates were the best means of providing insurance because most employers already provide such benefits. A system in which all businesses paid for insurance would be much fairer and the costs cheaper than in the current system where only some paid, and thus bore the burden of costs. The health care alliances would bring down costs and improve service through economies of scale and their power to negotiate with insurance firms and hospitals. He emphasized that, unlike a single-payer system, his plan would reform rather than eliminate the private insurance industry.

Opponents argued that employer mandates would impose enormous and unnecessary costs on all businesses, bankrupting thousands and rendering all less competitive in an ever more competitive world. Unemployment would rise, the growth rate would fall, they predicted. Predictably, those opposed to any reforms stepped up their attacks.

More disturbing to Clinton was an increasing number of congressional Democrats who endorsed plans other than his. On October 6, Democratic Representative Jim Cooper unveiled his own reform plan that would not include the employer mandates. Democratic Senator John Breaux introduced a similar bill on October 21. When Clinton submitted his bill to both Houses of Congress on November 20, his supporters were a distinct minority.

All along, Clinton was faced with a tough decision over whether or not to compromise with alternative plans. He announced his decision on January 25, 1994, during his State of the Union message. While his bill's details were negotiable, he promised to veto any bill that did not include universal coverage. A week later, the pressure for health care reform rose higher when the 50 governors unanimously called on Congress to pass a bill that year, although they divided over employer mandates.

From the time he first proposed health care reform until its final defeat, Clinton lost along the way numerous key potential congressional and industrial allies. The Cooper and Breaux plans were the first serious defections. Then, between February 2 and 4, 1993, the White House suffered a series of powerful blows when the Business Roundtable endorsed the Cooper plan and the Chamber of Commerce and National Association of Manufacturers rejected the Clinton plan. Clinton was hurt again on May 31 when House

Ways and Means Chairman Dan Rostenkowski was indicted on 17 criminal charges and had to relinquish his chairmanship.

Clinton's bill itself was scattered in various congressional committees. It was not until March 15 that the first significant action on the bill took place when the House Ways and Means voted for its segment of the bill. Other committees began debating and voting on their fragments. In June, three House committees approved a bill based on the president's. But on June 28, the House Committee on Energy and Commerce announced that it had deadlocked over employer mandates. On July 2, the Senate Finance Committee passed a bill that did not require employer mandates and pushed back 95 percent coverage until 2002.

By the spring of 1994, there were four health care reform bills either working their way through or stalled somewhere in Congress. The Congressional Budget Office (CBO) issued a comparative assessment of three of them in May. The Clinton plan would save America money by cutting $150 billion from the expected rise in health spending to a cumulative $2.220 trillion between 1995 and 2004. During those years, the budget deficit would increase by $126 billion, but might well decrease thereafter. The Cooper plan would generate less savings than Clinton's plan, only $30–50 billion by 2004, while increasing the deficit by $301 billion. Cooper would subsidize the purchases of health insurance by the poor and encourage purchasing cooperatives. The McDermott single-payer bill would initially cost the budget an additional $59 billion by 1997, but would save $114–175 billion by 2004. The plan would supplant private with public insurance; everyone would be covered. Of the three plans, the single-payer was clearly the most cost-effective, followed by Clinton's and then Cooper's.[35]

A fourth bill, sponsored by Republican Senator John Chaffee, called for voluntary purchasing cooperatives before 2005, and a requirement for all firms to provide minimal insurance thereafter. The Cooper and Chaffee plans were similar. The trouble with those plans was that if they were implemented health care costs would actually rise as insurance firms cherry-picked the healthy instead of providing for all. The voluntary alliances would mostly include those firms with less healthy workforces. Without the economies of scale that universal coverage provides, bureaucracy and costs would expand rather than contract.

The public overwhelmingly supported reform, but did not understand any of the proposals and was sensitive to the medical industrial complex's accusations that the reforms would bring big government rather than savings. A *New York Times* poll conducted on July 14–17, 1994, revealed that 69 percent of Americans were disappointed and only 24 percent pleased with the health care system. Health care had tied with crime as the most important problem facing the nation for 19 percent of the public. Americans supported the key tenets of Clinton's health care bill, with 49 percent agreeing that employers should be required to pay most of the health insurance costs for their workers, while 40 percent thought employers should simply make plans available to their workers, who would pay for it. Nearly four of five Americans (79 percent) thought it was "very important" that everyone receive health insurance, 17 percent thought it was "somewhat important," and only 3 percent thought it was "not very important." Although most agreed with Clinton's goals, a slight majority thought he should bow to political realities in the health care battle. A little more than half (53 percent) of the public agreed that Clinton should compromise on his goal of insuring 95 percent of Americans; 42 percent thought he should not compromise. And the vast majority of Americans (80 percent) presciently believed that Congress would not pass a health care bill that year, while only 19 percent believed it would.[36]

Bowing to the political realities in Congress and public opinion, Clinton announced on July 19 his willingness to compromise. Ten days later, the House Democratic leaders announced a plan which would, like Clinton's, require employers to pay 80 percent of costs. In addition, their plan would extend Medicare to cover the uninsured. Federal subsidies would help small businesses cover their employees. On August 2, Mitchell proposed his own health care plan, which would cover 95 percent of Americans by 2000 through subsidies and voluntary contributions. Two days later, Clinton endorsed the Mitchell plan.

The Senate did not begin its debate on health care until

August 9. The debate in the House, however, was delayed by Clinton's crime-prevention bill. When debate finally did begin it was complicated by a bipartisan compromise bill which would simply subsidize the efforts of the working poor to buy insurance. On August 17, the House leaders announced that the Congressional Budget Office had yet to complete its analysis. Given these various delays, the House leaders did not know when the debate could begin. Then, on August 25, Congress recessed until September 12.

By this time, it was clear that Clinton's bill was dead. Negotiations among congressional Democrats began over a quick compromise bill that they hoped might pass. On September 26, Mitchell announced that this effort too had failed and that there would be no health care reform in 1994.

The Clinton health care bill died for many reasons. An important reason for its defeat was the way it was composed. By drawing up the bill behind closed doors, the White House failed to generate congressional support for the bill before it emerged. By refusing to compromise until the last moment, the White House lost any chance for a bipartisan bill that might well have passed. Half of a reform loaf might well have been better than none. At least some check might have been made in health care's soaring costs. As in so many other issues, politics rather than national interests prevailed. Once Clinton made the health bill a partisan issue, Republicans and his Democratic enemies ignored the bill's merits and made it a referendum on the president himself. The Democratic Party itself was split into four different factions, three of which rallied behind either the Clinton, Cooper, or McDermott plans, which represented an unbridgeable spectrum of health care systems, and a fourth faction wanted no reforms at all.

The longer the White House delayed in getting a bill into Congress, the more time its opponents had to organize, poison the public's mind against it, and defeat it. The bill's merits were difficult to explain; its demerits easy to exaggerate. The bill itself – 1,400 pages – allowed its opponents to cry "big government." John Motley, Vice President of the National Federation of Independent Businesses, asserted that the White House had "seriously overreached and developed a proposal that was too large and too expensive, that gave too big a role to the Government and that simply could not pass."[37] Yet, "big government" was just a political bogeyman. Under the Clinton plan, health care costs would be borne mostly by business rather than society; government expenditures would have actually dropped.

Yet, those factors might not have been decisive without the concerted, continual attacks of special interest groups such as insurance, hospitals, and drug corporations, all of whose profits would be hurt by the bill. The "Harold and Louise" ads did a brilliant job of discrediting Clinton's bill, not with rational, in-depth arguments, but simply by sowing fear. Senate minority leader Bob Dole and House minority leader Newt Gingrich wielded every tactic they could muster to delay and finally derail the bill.

President Clinton, Senate majority leader George Mitchell, and House majority leader Richard Gephart did a poor job of justifying the bill and rallying support. They crowded the congressional agenda with too many issues rather than concentrating on passing health care. For a crucial month in late summer, the health care issue was shelved as Clinton's crime bill took the spotlight. As Senator Ted Kennedy put it, "Time was our principal enemy, and time just ran out, with the Republican's blind obstructionism and gridlock."[38] All along, the public sent mixed messages. An overwhelming majority wanted health care reform that covered every American – but they did not want to pay for it or increase government regulations.

The health care crisis may have been simply too complex and vast for any one plan to address within the context of America's political culture and system. The single-payer plan was by far the most cost-effective, but was politically dead on arrival. Negative advertising destroyed Clinton's plan in the minds of increasing numbers of Americans. Democratic Party disunity left Clinton groping helplessly for support that would never materialize. Republican Party unity was the rock on which the Clinton plan finally broke apart.

After the Republican Party captured both congressional Houses in November 1994, the health care battle was fought through the war of the budget. Although both the Republicans and the White House proposed budgets that would balance the finances within seven years, the details of each

plan differed significantly. Among other budget cuts elsewhere, the Republicans proposed slashing $270 billion from
Medicare, $163 billion from Medicaid, and $36.2 billion from
school lunches, food stamps, and day-care center meals from
the anticipated growth in those respective health care budgets
over the next seven years. Americans overwhelmingly rejected
these proposals. An October 1995 *New York Times*/CBS poll
revealed that 57 percent of Americans opposed the Republican plan and only 26 percent favored it. How did the
Republicans choose the politically unpopular goal of chop-
ping $270 from Medicare? After deciding to cut taxes by
$245 billion, they added up all their budget items and found
they were still $270 billion short of reaching a balanced budget
by 2002. Hence, the Medicare figure.

The Republicans also tried to "reform" health care with a
bill based on an AMA wish list that included waiving most
antitrust, liability, and financial requirements for doctors'
groups; essentially doctors would be even freer than they
already are to set their own professional standards and police themselves. Proponents argued that it would allow market magic to reform the health care system. Critics charged
that it would unleash severe conflicts of interests that would
raise both financial and health costs to patients. Under
Clinton's veto threat, the Republican leaders decided not
to submit these bills to a vote.

Neither party was willing to overhaul one of the most
wasteful institutions in America's health care system – the
Veterans Health Administration (VHA). During the midst
of the budget debate when other health care institutions
found their budgets slashed, the Democrats and Republicans alike proposed increasing the VHA's budget. While the
Clinton White House has shrunk the federal workforce by 8
percent since 1992, the VHA's personnel has increased by
1.4 percent. In 1996, the VHA will spend $16.6 billion to
care for 2.6 million veterans. Private or other public hospitals could provide the same medical care that veterans receive in the VHA hospitals. Politics rather than expanded
need explain why neither party even speaks of reforming
the VHA, let alone privatizing it – most congressional districts have VHA facilities, all have large populations of veterans. As with most well-organized interest groups, when it

comes to veterans, fiscal toughness gives way to patronage.

Just when it seemed as if serious health care reform was impossible with a Republican Congress, in May 1996 a bipartisan Senate bill that allowed individuals to carry their insurance between jobs, sponsored by Republican Nancy Kasselbaum and Democrat Ted Kennedy, passed both Houses. President Clinton signed the bill into law. It was one small step in a long journey to rescue the system from inequities, inefficiencies, and, ultimately, bankruptcy.

GUARDING THE STATUS QUO

America's health care system suffers from a chronic and ever worsening crisis. The system is nearly the worst among democratic industrial nations. Americans pay far more and receive far poorer care than citizens in other democratic industrial countries. While other societies provide universal health care, one of seven Americans is uninsured. Despite all the money poured into the medical industrial complex, Americans have a higher infant mortality rate and lower life expectancy than most other citizens of democratic industrial countries. In 1995, America's medical industrial complex consumed $1 trillion or 14 percent of the economy, or about twice as much per person as the OECD average. These health care costs will rise as America's society ages. If current demographic rates hold, by the year 2040 18 percent of males and 24 percent of females will be over age 65. The more money the nation spends on health care, the less it has to invest in research and development, build infrastructure, educate children, re-train adults, and fight crime, among a myriad of other pressing needs.

America's medical system is far more expensive and less efficient than those of other industrial democracies because it has too little rather than too much regulation. Elsewhere governments control prices, allocate technologies, doctors, equipment, and beds where they are needed to minimize redundancies, and encourage the training of primary care rather than specialist doctors. Almost 80 percent of American doctors are specialists compared with 20 to 40 percent of European doctors.

The essence of the health care crisis is that it is an employer-based rather than state-based system. American employers are burdened with enormous and rising costs that their overseas rivals do not have. From 1948 to 1990, business spending on health care soared an average 15.6 percent annually to now account for more than 8 percent of payroll costs. In 1965, businesses paid $6.5 billion in health insurance for their workers; by 1990, their contribution had soared to $186.2 billion! In 1970, the average Fortune 500 firm had twelve employees for every retiree; in 1990, it had only three.[39]

American business executives certainly recognize a national health crisis. A 1990 Gallup poll found that 91 percent of chief executive officers at Fortune 500 firms believed the health care system required fundamental changes or a complete reconstruction. An even more extensive 1990 survey of 2,000 executives revealed that 62.7 percent thought that the rising cost of health care was the most serious problem they faced, followed by government regulations (45.9 percent), worker productivity (40.7 percent), environmental issues (30.6 percent), the quality of work produced (19.0 percent), and foreign competition (13.0 percent).[40]

Those businesses which provide health care for their workers face ever greater costs that drag down their competitiveness in an increasingly competitive world. The more a firm must pay for health care, the less money it has to invest in research and development, manufacturing, and marketing. Ironically, not so long ago, corporations thought it made more economic sense to increase health care rather than salaries for their workers. Health care contributions were tax-free for the firms and workers alike, and seemed to make workers more dependent on the firm. Today, corporations are trapped between the health care promises they have made to their workers and rising costs. Increasing numbers have responded by trying to cut back benefits. The result is worsening relations between labor and management. In 1986, only 18 percent of strikes were related to health care cutbacks; by 1989, 78 percent were.[41]

As if spending 14 percent of the nation's wealth on health care were not bad enough, the system imposes enormous other burdens on America's economy and society. Fearing they might lose their health insurance, increasing numbers of Americans refuse to change jobs for better but more risky enterprises. This "job lock" phenomenon makes the economy run far less efficiently. The forty million people without coverage lack a genuine choice; either health insurance is simply too expensive for them or they have a "preexisting condition" whereby the insurance firms deny them coverage. Unable to afford the checkups that can detect and treat health problems before they become too serious, the uninsured are forced by the current system to seek emergency care only when the problem has become a crisis and treatment's costs have become exorbitant. Society eventually picks up the tab.

A related problem with employer-based health care is that it is inherently unequal. The tax exemption for employer premiums and tax deductibility of private insurance tends to favor those with higher incomes who would like to reduce the impact of their higher tax brackets. Fortune 500 firms obviously can afford better health care systems than smaller firms. The administrative costs of insurance consume only 5 percent of the total health care costs for firms with 10,000 or more workers, and 40 percent of the costs for firms with less than five workers.[42] Many firms cannot afford to provide any care at all. Businesses provide health insurance to only about two-thirds of all Americans under age 65, and the coverage varies considerably among businesses. Taxpayers are ultimately stuck with the bill and pay much more than their counterparts elsewhere. America's health care system thus hurts the economy twice, once because employers bear most of the burden and secondly because the total cost is twice that of most other industrial countries.

If these were the system's only problems, they would be serious enough. But an array of other problems plague America's health care system. Although no country anywhere allows the private sector to play a greater role in providing for its citizens, America's health care system responds little to market forces. For example, despite a glut of hospitals and doctors, prices paradoxically continue to go up rather than down.

The number of patients admitted to hospitals fell from 36 million in 1981 to 31 million in 1991, a drop of more than 14 percent, while the average stay fell from 7.6 days to 7.2 days. Did prices also drop to reflect the decreased demand? Hardly. During the same decade, hospital staff increased from 3 million to 3.5 million, a 17 percent increase. Health care prices rose about 45 percent. Hospitals paid for the salaries of those extra workers by passing the costs on to consumers. Rather than compete through lower prices, hospitals try to attract more customers by providing the latest medical technologies. As a result, many cities have more services than are necessary. American hospitals own two-thirds of the world's magnetic resonance machines and half of the CAT scan machines. About 850 hospitals perform open-heart surgery; only half do more than the minimal number required by the Federal Health Care Financing Administration. More than elsewhere, American patients risk having their hearts opened by inexperienced surgeons. Prices at hospitals thus do not fall when their beds, CAT scans, and doctors are underused; they may well rise to make up the revenue shortfall.[43]

Likewise there is a national glut of most types of physicians. Between 1985 and 1995, the ratio of doctors to population dropped from one for every 450 to one for every 380. Yet, as with the growing number of hospital beds, the swelling ranks of doctors did not reduce prices. Again, Washington is largely responsible. The federal policy of promoting specialists caused a glut by the 1990s. About 80 percent of doctors are specialists rather than general practitioners. Specialization can lead to conflicts of interest. The more specialities a doctor performs, the more he or she may be inclined to charge them to a patient whether they are necessary or not. Interests may conflict. Doctors who performed their own radiological tests, for example, charged more for the tests and ordered such tests four times more often than those who referred patients elsewhere.[44]

Although America's health care system is mostly privately owned, its costs are not determined by market principles of supply and demand. Hospitals and doctors, along with insurance and drug corporations, form a tightly knit oligopoly known as the medical industrial complex. The medical industrial complex is the most powerful player in shaping health care issues and policies. Within the medical industrial complex, there are over 80 medical speciality groups, each of which uses its money and influence to get Washington and the state Houses to enact favorable laws. The medical industrial complex has succeeded in killing any government attempts to provide the public with comparative prices among hospitals and physicians, or comparative skills of doctors, including malpractice suits.

The most powerful constituent within the medical industrial complex is the American Medical Association (AMA), founded in 1846 and today composed of 290,000 members or 41 percent of the nation's doctors. While the overall membership is larger than ever, the AMA's percentage of doctors is down from the 1970s when fees were raised and specialist groups became more assertive. Nonetheless, the AMA wields enormous financial power. During the 1992 elections, it distributed $2,950,138 to various candidates, the second largest amount contributed by an industrial association. While the AMA has done a brilliant job of promoting its financial interests, it has wretchedly enforced its own Hypocratic oath. Ralph Nader's "Health Research Group" revealed that of 13,012 doctors disciplined by federal or state regulatory agencies, the AMA allowed more than two-thirds to retain their licenses.[45]

As in any other business, members of the medical industrial complex applaud some regulations and deplore others. Doctors fought hard for their government-sanctioned monopoly over drug prescriptions and the license to practice. While those monopolies might well be for the public good they clearly violate market principles. The AMA remains adamantly opposed to mandatory health care spending limits. The AMA insists on self-regulation. Unfortunately, self-regulation does not work. For example, in prescribing various remedies, doctors essentially purchase services for their patients, a clear conflict of interest. The tendency for doctors is to order the most expensive procedures rather than cost-cutting preventive medical measures.

Who pays directly for health care? Washington pays 32 percent, state and local governments 10 percent, insurance firms 32 percent, and patients about 26 percent. The federal government's financial contribution rose from 28 percent to 32 percent between 1990 and 1993 alone. Although the government plays an increasing role in financing health care, it is the private insurance companies, hospitals, drug companies, and doctors that control America's health care system and its costs. In contrast to the 42 percent that government contributes to health care in the United States, Britain's government in 1990 paid 84 percent, the governments of West Germany and Canada each paid 73 percent, and of the Netherlands 72 percent. Most analysts would agree that the "serious weaknesses of the American system are rooted in its decentralized structure; the advantages of European systems are rooted in their centralized funding control."[46]

Contrary to economic theory, the private sector has failed miserably to provide health insurance which is more efficient and inexpensive than that provided by the governments of all other democratic industrial countries. The Health Insurance Association of America is as powerful as the AMA in asserting its interests and blocking reforms. The largest insurance corporations are the 82 nonprofit automonous Blue Cross and Blue Shield Plans which provide about one-third of all physician insurance coverage to one-quarter of the population. Ironically, Blue Cross and Blue Shield are regulated much more than for profit-insurance firms.

What is the price of good health? Most consider good health priceless and would pay anything to retain it. Either insurance firms or the government pay for nine-tenths of hospital bills and three-quarters of doctors fees. By paying few direct costs of their health care, most Americans have few incentives to shop around for the lowest fees. Even if they wanted to, consumers do not pressure their doctors, dentists, and hospitals to lower costs because they usually have no understanding of the value of what they are buying. After all, how much is good health, or even an excruciating, terminal survival worth? Even if they did question prices, as individuals they have no power before health institutions – even the neighborhood clinic. In most situations requiring medical care, consumers are charged when they are least able to make rational decisions, negotiate, or shop around for a cheaper price. Essentially, an accident or disease victim is at the mercy of whatever institution he or she uses. Patients rarely know just what treatment is necessary and what its costs should be. And even someone who just needs a check-up will not find much fee difference from one doctor to the next. Hospitals and doctors are not in the habit of posting their fees.

Health care has been provided by a hodgepodge of institutions including voluntary and public hospitals founded to aid the destitute, company hospitals, general private fee-for-service hospitals, and inumerable private physicians. About 70 percent of all hospital care is provided by private, non-profit organizations, about 20 percent by state and local governments, and only 10 percent by private profit-seeking firms. Of course, regardless of where they work, doctors seek and generally receive the highest possible salaries and fees. The infusion of Federal funds through Medicaid and Medicare encouraged the creation of investor-owned hospital chains, of which the four largest, the Hospital Corporation of America (HCA), American Medical International (AMI), Humana, and National Medical Enterprises (NME), account for about half of all the nation's for-profit hospital beds. The chains allow for economies of scale in facilities, finance, and personnel. However, these chains, and private hospitals in general, have been criticized for cherry-picking the patients with the best insurance and minimal health problems, thus increasing the financial and care burden for the non-profit hospitals.

Fraud burns more than 10 percent of annual health care costs. With a national health bill of $884 billion in 1994, fraud cost $88 billion. Perhaps as much as 30 percent of all surgery done in the United States is completely unnecessary. The traditional fee-for-service system encourages abuse. In the fee-for-service sector, there were an average 960 days of hospital care per thousand people compared with only 460 for those covered by prepaid group health plans. Hospitals and doctors' offices are notorious for padding bills with charges for services that often never occurred. While the average hospital stay in the United States is comparable to that in other democratic industrial countries, America's high costs come partly from the battery of often medically unnecessary tests that patients are forced to take. Doctors order the tests to help protect themselves from possible malpractice suits or simply to generate income from expensive and often underused equipment. These costs are passed on to patients and taxpayers. Fraud is easy in as fragmented, bureaucratized, inefficient, and largely "self-regulated" a health care system as America's.[47]

One of the most important reasons for America's exorbitant health care costs is the exorbitant prices that the pharmaceutical industry charges customers. Like Dr Frankenstein, Washington created an industrial monster which it cannot control. The pharmaceutical industry would be far less powerful and internationally competitive today if federal government had not targeted it for development by a variety of means. The National Institute of Health (NIH) is responsible for identifying new treatments, technologies, and drugs, and encouraging the medical industry to adopt them. Its laboratories develop drugs and then grant exclusive licenses to pharmaceutical corporations to manufacture and market them. Since 1955, Washington has provided the decisive financing for 34 of the 37 anti-cancer drugs developed under the auspices of the National Cancer Institute.[48]

Although the NIH does use criteria such as the firms' relative abilities to manufacture and market drugs, it does not determine the drugs' price. Since 1989, the NIH has inserted a standard clause in its contracts admonishing the firm to charge a "fair price" for the drug. The clause is a meaningless gesture since NIH does not try to determine what a fair price is, let alone enforce one.

Many are critical of this government give-away to the pharmaceutical corporations. Health economist Peter Arno argues: "A monopoly is not a gift. It is a social privilege. We confer it for the sole aim of stimulating innovation. But if the innovation is created by government scientists and paid for by the taxpayer, then where is the innovation."[49] Arno argues that at the very least, the corporations that receive the government gifts should open their books and allow economists to determine the drug's fair price. Others argue that rather than worry about lower drug prices, Washington should get a better return on its investments by auctioning off the license or charging higher royalties.

With the government's encouragement, the drug corporations shamelessly gouge consumers. One of the worst horror stories of price gouging involves the anti-cancer drug levamisole, discovered and developed by federal scientists before it was given to the company, Johnson & Johnson. The drug was originally developed to treat worm infestation in sheep and only later was discovered to be effective against colon cancer. Johnson & Johnson charge one hundred times more to the human cancer victims than to sheepowners – $6 a dose for humans, six cents for sheep. Levamisole costs cancer patients $1,200 a year.[50]

One key reason for the high infant mortality rate in the United States is the high price of childhood vaccines. Between 1977 and 1992, the price of giving a child all the recommended vaccines rose 1,000 percent! To give some prominent examples, the whooping cough vaccine soared from 19 cents to $10.04, the polio vaccine from $1 to $9.91; the measles, mumps, and rubella vaccine from $6.01 to $17.88, and the whooping cough, diphtheria, and tetanus vaccine from 19 cents to $8.92.[51]

The drug industry claims that the higher costs result from higher taxes, lawsuits, regulations, liability costs, and development expenses for new drugs. Although all of those reasons are true, the most important is the monopoly power that developers have over their drugs. When a corporation receives a patent for a new drug, it has about fifteen years to sell the product at any price it wishes. Corporations will often license their patents to others, which theoretically does allow for some competition. But producers usually follow the price leader in the oligopoly. Pharmaceutical firms are not required to open their books to the public to allow an understanding of how they price their products. Drug prices elsewhere are much lower than in the United States. In France, for example, the oral polio vaccine costs only $1, one-tenth the price in the United States.

In 1993, fearing the imposition of stronger federal measures, the Pharmaceutical Manufacturers Association (PMA) told President Clinton that it would limit price increases to the level of inflation. Even if the PMA was able to fulfill its promise, it would not prevent manufacturers from charging as much as they wanted for new drugs. The PMA was adamantly opposed to any government price controls over drugs, arguing that this would limit the funds available for the research and development of new drugs.

America's "market" system is much more inefficient than the "socialist" systems of its competitors. Administrative costs consume 25 percent of America's system and only 10 percent in Canada. Even within the United States the government is more efficient than the private sector – insurance corporation overhead is 14 percent, three times greater than that of the federal Medicare and Medicaid programs. Drug manufacturers spend 20 percent – $10 billion in 1992 – of their revenue on marketing. That price, of course, is passed on to consumers.[52]

As in other economic sectors, the medical industrial complex's power, and national health policy, are shaped profoundly by American values and traditions. Decentralization of political power, private ownership, and markets – in other words, Social Darwinism – are core cultural values. Yet these cultural values that Americans celebrate simply do not exist in a modern world of massive institutions, psychological and social manipulation through the mass media, and the ever greater interdependence and complexity of issues. Culture can be the most powerful barrier to reform. A single-payer system may be the most cost-efficient and fair system yet devised, but is a nonstarter within American political culture.

Yet, American values have changed in the past and undoubtedly will continue to do so in the future. Today, most Americans accept Washington's social security and Medicare programs for those over 65 years old. Yet those programs were revolutionary concepts when they were introduced in 1935 and 1965, respectively. Given the ever-worsening health care crisis, Americans are harshly critical of the medical industrial complex. A 1990 poll revealed that 90 percent of Americans thought the health care system needed to be fundamentally changed or even rebuilt.[53] The medical industrial complex, however, can neutralize this overwhelming public support for systematic reform simply by having "Harry and Louise" wave the red banners of "big government" and "socialized medicine."

The public's attitude toward the health care crisis is similar to its attitude toward the national debt crisis. Although public opinion polls reveal a growing awareness of the worsening crisis, that concern does not flare into a political pressure for reform powerful enough to overcome the entrenched interests of the medical industrial complex. Although the health care crisis did rank among the top concerns in the early 1990s, after the failure of Clinton's reform package in 1994 it dissolved as a pressing issue for most Americans.

Most Americans lack the requisite knowledge and interest with which to comprehend the health care crisis and propose reforms. The attention spans of most Americans are notoriously short and easily distracted by sensationalism rather than substance. Most people adopt the same "out of sight, out of mind" attitude toward the health care crisis that they do toward the national debt problem. Only the appearance of a doctor or hospital bill seems to shake the apathy.

As in so many other issues, Americans tend to display contradictory opinions about the health care system. Most Americans tend to be unconcerned about health care's growing costs as a percentage of the economy. If anything, they believe the United States spends too little rather than too much on health care. Polls consistently show that majorities favor national health insurance and more spending but less regulation and government. People like their own doctor while denigrating doctors in general for overcharging and selfishness, an attitude similar to their feelings about legislators. They favor reform for the system while maintaining their own arrangements, albeit at lower costs.[54]

Paul Starr explores and dismisses two common accounts for America's high health care costs – malpractice suits and an aging population.[55] Malpractice suits are far more common in the United States than elsewhere and do push up costs. However, malpractice suits are less than 1 percent of total health care costs, a percentage that has remained constant for some time. Obviously, the healthier one's patients, the less chance some among them will have reason to sue for malpractice. If doctors were really concerned about deterring malpractice suits, they would spend more time in early prevention rather than treatment of diseases. Likewise, an aging population is not a significant reason for the health care crisis. As people grow older, their medical needs rise. America's aging population has raised costs, but only by an average 0.3 percent annually between 1946 and 1986. Among the democratic industrial countries, America's population ranks 17th in average age, well behind say Britain, Sweden, and Germany whose health care costs are half or less that of the United States.

INTO THE TWENTY-FIRST CENTURY

So what is the future for health care in the United States? Will the crisis worsen as costs spiral ever higher while one of every seven Americans lacks any insurance and American health standards remain among the lowest of the democratic industrial countries? Any successful reform effort must overcome two interrelated and daunting barriers that have killed previous attempts.

Perhaps the most important hurdle is cultural. American myths celebrating free enterprise and demonizing government immediately warp the debate over health care just as they do any other industrial policy issue. Health care is a perfect example of an industry where the government is more efficient than the private sector. The administrative costs for Medicare are about 3 percent of total costs while those for private insurers are 13 percent of total costs. All other democratic industrial countries have government-run systems which cover virtually all their citizens at an average cost half that of the United States.[56] Ideological blinders prevent most Americans from comprehending these simple realities. The medical industrial complex can kill any comprehensive reform proposal by smearing it as "socialized medicine."

And then there is the political hurdle. One central reason the health care crisis has steadily worsened over the decades is that politicians prefer to duck the crisis and divert the public's attention to issues more easily simplified to sound bites. The medical industrial complex has enormous financial, media, and political power to manipulate politicians against attempting any systematic reforms. With a Republican-controlled Congress, comprehensive health care reform is dead for the foreseeable future. The Republicans want to cut costs by reducing Medicare and Medicaid expenditures. That will simply raise the costs for those who can afford to pay while largely removing coverage for millions of poor Americans. Cutting government spending without imposing accompanying reforms will worsen rather than alleviate the crisis.

And yet America's health care system has been incrementally changing for the better despite these related cultural and political barriers. For example, as recently as 1988, 72.6 percent of Americans used a traditional fee-for-service for their health care while 17.3 percent used health maintenance systems (HMOs), and 10.1 percent used other types of managed care such as Preferred Provider Organizations (PPOs). By 1993, the proportion of Americans using a fee-for-service system had been cut in half to 38.1 percent, while those using health maintenance or other managed care had risen to 20.5 percent and 41.5 percent, respectively.[57] HMOs and PPOs reduce the reliance on hospitals by stressing preventive medicine. In all, HMO and PPO patients are 40 percent less likely to require hospital care than fee-for-service patients. The downside of HMOs and PPOs is that they tend to attract healthier, younger people while leaving those with worse health problems to the traditional system. And although HMOs and PPOs have recently become increasingly important, pay-for-service remains the most prominent and costly form of payment.

The fear of reform may have temporarily caused those running the system to find temporary savings. In 1993, health care costs rose only 7.8 percent, the smallest increase since 1986 when it rose 7.2 percent. The previous smallest increase was in 1961.[58] While the fear of reform may have been the immediate cause for cost cutting, the federal program of DRGs since 1983 has reduced the incentives for hospitals to encourage long stays. Technological advances have also cut back the costs and stay lengths for many kinds of surgery while allowing home care for many chronic ailments. In addition, the rise in deductibility premiums has encouraged many patients to forgo or shorten hospital stays.

There are reforms that can significantly cut costs yet avoid the "socialized medicine" stigma of a single-payer system. Many reformers advocate a global budgeting system whereby ceilings are placed on the system's total costs, but administrators are free to cut or increase funds and programs anywhere within the budget's confines. Because profits come from cost cutting rather than volume, global budgeting encourages hospitals and doctors to be more efficient and use their services more sparingly. It is thus different from price controls where the prices of specific procedures are rigidly set. Price controls encourage hospitals and doctors to impose more procedures on patients whether they need them or not, in order to reap more profits.[59] And then there is the example of Hawaii. Ironically, Clinton did not utilize the experience of a state with a health care system very similar to what he was trying to pass. In 1975, Hawaii's government passed a bill that required all businesses to provide health insurance for any employees who worked twenty or more hours a week. Workers contribute only 1.5 percent of their paychecks to insurance, an amount so low that most employers do not bother to collect.

The results have been remarkable. Health insurance covers about 96 percent of Hawaiians. Hawaii is either at or near the top in low infant-mortality rates, longevity, and a low rate of early deaths from cancer, heart, and lung disease. The American Public Health Association and National Life Insurance Company have rated Hawaii as having the nation's best health. Health insurance premiums are about 30 percent lower in Hawaii than in the other states, while the cost of living is among the nation's highest. The system generates enormous savings by emphasizing primary care. For example, Hawaii has the nation's lowest breast-cancer death rate because of its determination to detect early and root out diseases before they spread. Hawaiians live free of the fear that their health insurance can be canceled if they switch jobs or acquire a debilitating disease. When asked whether they are satisfied with their health care services, 82 percent of Hawaiians and 61 percent of other Americans agreed; only 18 percent of Hawaiians and 39 percent of other Americans said no. While some businesses and doctors may complain about costs, few have moved away. The employer mandates did not bankrupt businesses as opponents claimed they would. Hawaii's unemployment rate is among the nation's lowest.[60]

Will the United States eventually adopt comprehensive reforms that can arrest the nation's ever worsening health care problems? Unfortunately, a reform of any kind rarely succeeds in America's fragmented political system and free market political culture unless it is preceded by crisis. While there is no question that America's health care is in crisis, its nature is chronic and insidious rather than immediate and devastating. The medical industrial complex will undoubtedly continue to protect its vested interests to the detriment of the nation's interests well into the twenty-first century.

And that is true too for all the other complexes of special political economic interests that shape Washington's industrial policies and constrain American power and prosperity.

Notes

Notes to the Introduction

1. Chalmers Johnson, *The Industrial Policy Debate* (San Francisco, Cal.: Institute of Contemporary Studies, 1984), p. 2.
2. Stuart Bruchey, *Enterprise: The Dynamic Economy of a Free People* (Cambridge, Mass.: Harvard University Press, 1990), p. 208.
3. B. Guy Peters, *American Public Policy: Promise and Performance* (Chatham, NJ: Chatham House, 1993), pp. 174–5.
4. Adam Smith, *Wealth of Nations* (New York: Dutton, 1964).
5. David Ricardo, *The Principles of Political Economy and Taxation* (London: Dent, 1973). For contemporary neoclassical economists, see: Milton Friedman, *Capitalism and Freedom* (Chicago: University of Chicago Press, 1962); Jagdish Bhagwati, *Lectures: International Trade* (Cambridge, Mass.: MIT Press, 1983); Jagdish Bhagwati, *Protectionism* (Cambridge, Mass.: MIT Press, 1988); Jagdish Bhagwati and Hugh Patrick (eds), *Aggressive Unilateralism* (Ann Arbor, Mich.: University of Michigan Press, 1990); Jagdish Bhagwati, *The World Trading System at Risk* (Princeton, NJ: Princeton University Press, 1991).
6. Quoted in Stephen Bailey, *Congress Makes a Law* (New York: Columbia University Press, 1950), p. 6.
7. John Maynard Keynes, *The General Theory of Employment, Interest, and Money* (New York: Harcourt, Brace, 1936).
8. Robert Kuttner, "Economists Really Should Get Out More Often," *Business Week*, April 24, 1989; Clyde Prestowitz, Alan Tonelson, and Robert Jerome, "The Last Gasp of GATTism," *Harvard Business Review*, March–April 1991, p. 134; Laura D'Andrea Tyson, *Who's Bashing Whom? Trade Conflict in High-Technology Industries* (Washington, DC: Institute for International Economics, 1992), p. 3.
9. John Frendreis and Raymond Tatalovich, *The Modern Presidency and Economic Policy* (Itasca, IL.: F. E. Peacock Press, 1994), p. 170.
10. Robert B. Reich, *The Next American Frontier* (New York: Times Books, 1983), p. 233.
11. Johnson, *Industrial Policy*, p. 8.
12. Quoted in Johnson, ibid., p. 18.
13. Martin and Susan Tolchin, *Selling our Security: The Erosion of America's Assets* (New York: Alfred A. Knopf, 1992).
14. For discussions of strategic trade theory, see: Paul Krugman, "New Theories of Trade among Industrial Countries," *American Economic Review*, **73**, May 1983; R. W. Jones (ed.), *International Trade: Surveys of Theory and Policy* (Amsterdam: North-Holland, 1986); Klaus Stegemann, "Policy Rivalry among Industrial States: What Can We Learn from Models of Strategic Trade Policy," *International Organization*, **43**: 1 (Winter 1989); Helen V. Milner and David B. Yoffie,

241

"Between Free Trade and Protectionism: Strategic Trade Policy and a Theory of Corporate Trade Demands," *International Organization*, **43**: 2 (Spring 1989), pp. 239–73.

15. Tyson, *Who's Bashing Whom?* (Washington, DC: Institute for International Economics, 1992), p. 250.

16. "Report and Recommendations of the Senate Republican Task Force on Industrial Competitiveness and International Trade," March 16, 1983, p. 1.

17. US Congress, House Energy and Commerce Committee," Report on HR 4360, reprinted as *House Report* 98–697, part 2, p. 23, quoted in Robert W. Russell, "Congress and the Proposed Industrial Policy Structures," in Claude Barfield and William Schambra (eds), *The Politics of Industrial Policy* (Washington, DC: American Enterprise, 1986), pp. 319, 324.

Notes to Chapter 1: Steel and Automobiles

1. Paul A. Tiffany, *The Decline of American Steel: How Management, Labor, and Government Went Wrong* (New York: Oxford University Press, 1988), p. 117.

2. William T. Hogan, *Economic History of the Iron and Steel Industry in the United States*, 5 vols (Lexington, Mass.: Lexington Books, 1971); Kenneth Warren, *The American Steel Industry, 1950–1970, A Geographical Interpretation* (London: Oxford University Press, 1973); Robert W. Crandall, *The US Steel Industry in Recurrent Crisis* (Washington, DC: Brookings, 1981); Donald F. Barnett and Louis Schorsch, *Steel, Upheaval in a Basic Industry* (Cambridge, Mass.: Ballinger, 1983); William Scheurman, *The Steel Crisis: The Economics and Politics of a Declining Industry* (Westport, CT: Greenwood Press, 1986).

3. "Impromptu Remarks of the President," in *AISI Yearbook, 1925* (New York: AISI, 1925), p. 222.

4. Tiffany, *Decline of American Steel*, p. 85.

5. Edward N. Hurley, "Cooperation and Efficiency in Developing our Foreign Trade," in *AISI Yearbook, 1916* (New York: AISI, 1916), p. 192.

6. Gerald T. White, *Billions for Defense: Government Financing by the Defense Plant Corporation during World War II* (University of Alabama Press, 1980); Richard A. Lauderbaugh, *American Steel Makers and the Coming of the Second World War* (Ann Arbor, Mich.: University of Michigan Research Press, 1980), pp. 123–4. In 1945, Washington sold off its steel plants to private industry at a fraction of its costs.

7. AISI, *Annual Statistical Report* (cited years); Duncan Burn, *The Steel Industry, 1939–1959* (Cambridge: Cambridge University Press, 1961), p. 132.

8. AISI, *Annual Statistical Report* (cited years).

9. *The Statistical History of the United States: From Colonial Times to the*

Present (New York: Basic Books, 1976; Series D 970–85), p. 179.
10. US Senate, 90th Congr., 1st Sess., Committee on Finance, Committee Print, *Steel Imports* (Washington, DC: Government Printing Office, 1967), pp. 299–304; Gerald Manners, *The Changing World Market for Iron Ore, 1950–1980* (Baltimore: Johns Hopkins Press, 1971), p. 99. See also, Robert A. Pollard, *European Security and the Origins of the Cold War, 1945–1950* (New York: Columbia University Press, 1985); William Lockwood, *The Economic Development of Japan* (Princeton, NJ: Princeton University Press, 1954), pp. 64–77; Chalmers Johnson, *MITI and the Japanese Miracle: The Growth of Industrial Policy, 1925–1975* (Stanford: Stanford University Press, 1982); William S. Borden, *The Pacific Alliance: United States Foreign Economic Policy and Trade Recovery, 1947–1955* (Madison, Wis.: University of Wisconsin Press, 1984), pp. 176–87; David A. Baldwin, *Foreign Aid and American Foreign Policy* (New York: Praeger, 1966).
11. AISI, *Annual Statistical Report* (cited years).
12. Otto Eckstein and Gary Fromm, "Steel and Postwar Inflation," Study Paper No. 2, US Congress, JEC, 86th Congr., 1st Sess., *Materials Prepared in Connection with the Study of Employment, Growth, and Prices Levels* (Washington, DC: Governing Printing Office, 1959); Bureau of Labor Statistics, US Congress, JEC, 88th Congr., 1st Sess., Hearings, *Steel Prices, Unit Costs, and Foreign Competition* (Washington, DC: Government Printing Office, 1963), p. 35.
13. Walter Adams, "The Steel Industry," in Walter Adams (ed.), *The Structure of American Industry*, 5th edn (New York: Macmillan, 1977), p. 110.
14. Walter Adams and J. B. Dirlam, "Big Steel, Invention and Innovation," *Quarterly Journal of Economics*, **80** (May 1966), pp. 167–89; Edwin Mansfield, *Industrial Research and Technological Innovation* (New York: W. W. Norton, 1968), pp. 83–108; Tiffany, *Decline of American Steel*, p. 133.
15. US Steel Corporation, *Steel and Inflation, Fact vs. Fiction* (New York: US Steel Corporation, 1958), pp. 181–5; Manners, *Changing World Market for Iron Ore*, pp. 24–5.
16. US Congress, JEC, 88th Congress, 1st Sess., Hearings, *Steel Prices, Unit Costs, Profits, and Foreign Competition* (Washington, DC: Government Printing Office, 1963), PP. 124–5.
17. Robert Crandall, "Investment and Productivity Growth in the Steel Industry: Some Implications for Industrial Policy," in Walter H. Goldberg (ed.), *Ailing Steel: The Transatlantic Quarrel* (New York: St Martin's Press, 1986), p. 193.
18. Tiffany, *Decline of American Steel*, p. 116.
19. AISI, *Annual Statistical Reports* (1965), p. 8.
20. AISI, *Annual Statistical Reports* (1970); Barnett and Schorsch, *Steel, Upheaval in a Basic Industry*.
21. Thomas R. Howell et al., *Steel and the State: Government's Intervention and Steel's Structural Crisis* (Boulder, Colo.: Westview Press, 1988), pp. 502–3.
22. Howell, ibid., p. 503.

23. John Holusha, "Why American Steel is Big Again," *New York Times*, July 21, 1994.

24. Jonathan Hinks, "A Comeback for Big Steel in the US," *New York Times*, March 31, 1992; John Holusha, "Steel Mini-Mills could Bring Boon or Blood Bath," *New York Times*, May 30, 1995; John Holusha, "Big Steelmakers Shape Up," *New York Times*, April 16, 1996.

25. John Rae, *The American Automobile Industry* (Boston: Twayne, 1984), pp. 18, 17.

26. US Federal Trade Commission, *Report on the Motor Vehicle Industry* (Washington, DC: Government Printing Office, 1939), pp. 29, 632.

27. Mira Wilkins, "Multinational Automobile Enterprises and Regulation: An Historical Overview," in Douglas H. Ginsberg and William J. Abernathy (eds), *Government, Technology, and the Future of the American Automobile* (New York: McGraw-Hill, 1980), pp. 224–8.

28. Robert Thomas, *An Analysis of the Pattern of Growth in the Automobile Industry* (New York: Ayer, 1977), p. 324; see also, Rae, *American Automobile Industry*, pp. 61, 63, 69; Harold C. Katz, *The Decline of Competition in the Autombile Industry, 1920–1940* (New York: Arno Press, 1977).

29. Sydney Fine, *The Automobile under the Blue Label* (Ann Arbor, Mich.: University of Michigan Press, 1963), p. 19.

30. *Freedom's Arsenal: The Story of the Automotive Council for War Production* (Detroit: Automobile Manufacturers Association, 1950), p. 193.

31. Rae, *American Automobile Industry*, p. 96.

32. See William Nester, *Japanese Industrial Targeting: The Neomercantilist Path to Economic Superpower* (New York: St Martin's Press, 1991), pp. 99–118.

33. Rae, *American Automobile Industy*, p. 134.

34. Mitsuo Matsushita and Lawrence Repeta, "Restricting the Supply of Japanese Automobiles: Sovereign Collusion?" *Case Western Reserve Journal of International Law*, **14** (Winter 1982), p. 49.

35. Alfred D. Chandler and Stuart Bruchey (eds), *Giant Enterprise: Ford, General Motors, and the Automobile Industry* (New York: Arno Press, 1980).

36. Harold C. Katz, *Shifting Gears: Changing Labor Relations in the US Automobile Industry* (Cambridge, Mass.: MIT Press, 1985).

37. Steve Lohr, "Ford and Chrysler Outpace Japanese in Reducing Costs," *New York Times*, June 18, 1992; "Hourly Wages at the Big Three: Facts and Figures," *New York Times*, April 21, 1996.

38. Keith Bradsher, "Return of an Issue: Protectionism," *New York Times*, June 15, 1992; Andrew Pollack, "Japan's Share of US Car Market Rose in '94," *New York Times*, January 6, 1995.

39. Andrew Pollack, "Japan Gives US Cars a Second Look," *New York Times*, June 21, 1994.

40. Martin Tolchin, "Auto Makers Ask White House for Broad Range of Help," *New York Times*, April 28, 1993.

41. Matthew L. Wald, "Washington Joins Big Three Auto Venture," *New York Times*, September 29, 1993.

42. Tiffany, *Decline in American Steel*, pp. 186–7, 190. See also, Robert W. Crandall, *The US Steel Industry in Recurrent Crisis* (Washington, DC: Brookings Institute, 1981).

43. Quoted in Davis Dyer, Malcom Salter and Alan Webber, *Changing Alliances* (Boston: Harvard Business School Press, 1987), p. 187. See also, Avinash Dixit, "Optimal Trade and Industrial Policy for the US Automobile Industry," in Robert Feenstra (ed.), *Empirical Methods for International Trade* (Cambridge, Mass.: MIT Press, 1988), pp. 141–65.
44. Quoted in Dyer et al., *Changing Alliances*, p. 217.

Notes to Chapter 2: Banks and Stocks

1. Unless otherwise indicated, statistics come from Margaret Myers, *A Financial History of the United States* (New York: Columbia University Press, 1970), p. 23; See also, John Kenneth Galbraith, *A Short History of Financial Euphoria* (New York: Whittle Books, 1994).
2. *Historical Statistics of the United States*, p. 773.
3. Myers, *A Financial History of the United States*, p. 124.
4. Ibid., p. 118.
5. Ibid., pp. 118–19.
6. Ibid., p. 120.
7. Ibid., p. 165.
8. Ibid., p. 175.
9. Ibid., p. 200.
10. Ibid., p. 344.
11. Ibid., pp. 384–7.
12. Christine Pavel and John McElravey, "Globalization in the Financial Services Industry," *Economic Perspectives* (Chicago: Federal Reserve Board of Chicago, May 1990), p. 8.
13. Joseph Nocera, *A Piece of the Action: How the Middle Class Joined the Money Class* (New York: Simon and Schuster, 1994), p. 446.
14. Andrew Pollack, "Venture Capital Loses its Vigor," *New York Times*, October 8, 1989.
15. Peter Dombrowski, "The Impact of Domestic Financial Reregulation on International Competitiveness: The American Case," Paper presented at the American Political Science Association Annual Meeting, August 1991.
16. Robert Pear, "IRS Audits Rising for Foreign Banks doing US Business," *New York Times*, June 12, 1990.
17. "Bonfire of the S&Ls," *Newsweek*, May 21, 1990.
18. Peter Passell, "$500 Billion Here, $500 Billion There," *New York Times*, February 12, 1992.
19. Steven Greenhouse, "US Caps Amount of Interest Offered by Weakest Banks," *New York Times*, May 21, 1992.
20. "Bonfire of the S&Ls," *Newsweek*, May 21, 1990, p. 24.
21. Steven Labaton, "Congress Takes Up Banking Bills," *New York Times*, November 14, 1992.
22. Clifford Krauss, "House Panel Backs Clinton Student Loan Plan," *New York Times*, May 13, 1993; Adam Clymer, "New US Program of

Student Loans Clears Key Panel," *New York Times*, June 10, 1993; Catherine S. Manegold, "US has High Hopes for New Student Loan Plan," *New York Times*, September 19, 1994.

Notes to Chapter 3: Chips and Networks

1. Sidney Winter, "Knowledge and Competence as Strategic Assets," in David Teece (ed.), *The Competitive Challenge* (Cambridge, Mass.: Ballinger, 1987), pp. 159–84; Michael Borrus, *Competing for Control: America's Stake in Microelectronics* (Cambridge, Mass.: Ballinger, 1988); Thomas Howell et al., *The Microelectronics Race: The Impact of Government Policy on International Competition* (Boulder, Col.: Westview Press, 1988); Jean-Claude Derian, *America's Struggle for Leadership in Technology* (Cambridge, Mass.: MIT Press, 1990); David Mowery and Nathan Rosenberg, "New Developments in US Technology Policy: Implications of Competitiveness and International Trade Policy," *California Management Review*, **32**: 1 (Fall 1989), pp. 107–24; Richard Nelson, "US Technological Leadership: Where did it Come From and Where did it go?" *Research Policy*, **19**, pp. 117–32; Richard Levin, "The Semiconductor Industry," in Richard R. Nelson (ed.), *Government and Technical Progress: A Cross-Industry Analysis* (New York: Pergamon, 1982).

2. Kenneth Flamm, *Creating the Computer: Government, Industry, and High Technology* (Washington, DC: Brookings Institute, 1988), pp. 16, 18; Norman J. Asher and Leland D. Strom, "The Role of the Department of Defense in the Development of Integrated Circuits," IDA Paper P-1271 (Arlington, VA: Institute for Defense Analyses, 1977).

3. Dieter Ernst and David O'Connor, *Competing in the Electronics Industry – The Experience of Newly Industrializing Economies* (London: Pinter, 1992), p. 27.

4. Flamm, *Creating the Computer*, p. 40; James Pennick et al., *The Politics of American Science: 1939 to the Present* (Cambridge, Mass.: MIT Press, 1972), p. 100.

5. Flamm, *Creating the Computer*, p. 78.

6. Rexmond C. Cochrance, *Measures for Progress: A History of the National Bureau of Standards* (Washington, DC: US Department of Commerce, Government Printing Office, 1966), p. 497.

7. Estimates vary from $4 billion to $12 billion. See Claude Baum, *The System Builders* (Santa Monica: Systems Development Corporation, 1981), pp. 12–13.

8. Franklin M. Fisher, James W. McKie, and Richard B. Mancke, *IBM and the US Data Processing Industry: An Economic History* (New York: Praeger, 1983), p. 23; Kenneth Flamm, *Targeting the Computer: Government Support and International Competition* (Washington, DC: Brookings, 1987), pp. 96–7.

9. Marie Anchordoguy, "Mastering the Market: Japanese Government Targeting of the Computer Industry," *International Organization*, **42**: 3

(Summer 1988), pp. 509–43; Marie Anchordoguy, *Computers Inc: Japan's Challenge to IBM* (Cambridge, Mass.: Harvard University Press, 1989).

10. B. R. Inman and Daniel F. Burton, "Technology and Competitiveness: The New Policy Frontier," *Foreign Affairs*, **69**: 2 (Spring 1989), p. 117.

11. Kozo Yamamura and Jan Vandenberg, "Japan's Rapid Growth Policy on Trial: The Television Case," in Gary Saxonhouse and Kozo Yamamura (eds), *Law and Trade Issues of the Japanese Economy* (Seattle: University of Washington, 1986); Richard Rosenbloom and Michael Cusamano, "Technological Pioneering and Competitive Advantage: The Birth of the VCR Industry," *California Management Review*, **29**: 4 (Summer 1987), pp. 51–76.

12. Eben Shapiro, "Zenith Bets the Store on New TV," *New York Times*, March 10, 1990; Barnaby Feder, "Last US TV Maker will Sell Control to Koreans," *New York Times*, July 18, 1995.

13. Thomas Howell, Brent L. Bartlett, and Warren Davis, *Creating Advantage: Semiconductors and Government Industrial Policy in the 1990s* (Santa Clara: Semiconductor Industry Association, 1992); Laura D'Andrea Tyson, *Who's Bashing Whom? Trade Conflict in High Technology Industries* (Washington, DC: Institute for International Economics, 1992), chapter 4; Michael Borrus, James Millstein, and John Zysman, "US–Japanese Competition in the Semiconductor Industry," *Policy Papers in International Affairs*, 17 (Berkeley: Institute for International Studies, University of California, 1983).

14. Borrus, "US–Japanese Competition," p. 38.

15. Tyson, *Who's Bashing Whom?* p. 101.

16. Clyde Farnsworth, "Report Warns of Decline of US Electronics Industry," *New York Times*, June 9, 1990.

17. "Uncle Sam's Helping Hand," *The Economist*, April 2, 1994, pp. 77–9.

18. Robert Baldwin and Paul Krugman, "Market Access and International Competition: A Simulation Study of 16K Random Access Memories," in Robert C. Feenstra (ed.), *Empirical Methods for International Trade* (Cambridge, Mass.: MIT Press, 1988), pp. 171–97.

19. Tyson, *Who's Bashing Whom?* p. 113.

20. Tyson, ibid., p. 109.

21. John Markoff, "New War for Chip Makers," *International Herald Tribune*, April 16, 1995; "Uncle Sam's Helping Hand," *The Economist*, April 2, 1994, pp. 77–9.

22. US Department of Commerce, Bureau of Export Administration, Office of Industrial Resource Administration, 1991.

23. Tyson, *Who's Bashing Whom?* p. 146.

24. Defense Science Board Task Force, *Foreign Ownership and Control of US Industry* (Washington, DC: Defense Science Board, June 1990); Defense Science Board Task Force, *Foreign Ownership and Control of US Industry*, released by the Office of Congressman Mel Levine (D-CA), May 13, 1991; US General Accounting Office, National Security and International Affairs Division, *US Business Access to Certain Foreign State-of-the-Art Technology* (Washington, DC: US General

Accounting Office, September 1991); National Advisory Committee on Semiconductors, *Toward a National Semiconductor Strategy: Regaining Markets in High-Volume Electronics* (Washington, DC: National Advisory Committee on Electronics, 1991).

25. Linda H. Spencer, *Foreign Investment in the United States: Unemcumbered Access* (Washington, DC: Economic Strategy Institute, 1991); Linda H. Spencer, "High Technology Acquisitions: Summary Charts, October 1988–April 1992" (Washington, DC: Economic Strategy Institute, 1992).

26. Office of the US Trade Representative, *Procedures to Introduce Supercomputers* (Washington, DC: Government Printing Office, 1990).

27. John R. Rice, *HDTV: The Politics, Policies, and Economics of Tommorrow's Television* (New York: Union Square Press, 1990); Cynthia Beltz, *High-Tech Maneuvers: Industrial Policy Lessons of HDTV* (Washington, DC: AEI Press, 1991); Jeffrey Hart and Laura D'Andrea Tyson, "Responding to the Challenge of HDTV," *California Management Review,* **31**: 4 (Summer 1989), pp. 132–45; Edmund Andrews, "Quest for Sharper TV Likely to Bring More TV Instead," *New York Times,* July 10, 1995.

28. Tyson, *Who's Bashing Whom?* p. 142.

29. Michael Borrus and Jeffrey Hart, "Display's the Thing: The Real Stakes in the Conflict over High-Resolution Display," *BRIE Working Papers,* 52 (Berkeley, CA: Berkeley Roundtable on the International Economy, 1992); John Holusha, "Flat Monitors' Bargain Prices are Hampering US Producers," *New York Times,* May 29, 1995.

30. William Broad, "Clinton to Promote High Technology, with Gore in Charge," *New York Times,* November 10, 1992.

31. John Markoff, "Building the Electronic Superhighway," *New York Times,* January 24, 1993.

32. Eric von Hippel, *The Sources of Innovation* (New York: Oxford University Press, 1988).

33. Deborah Spar and Ray Vernon, *Beyond Globalism: Remaking American Foreign Economic Policy* (New York: Free Press, 1989); Anne Krueger, "Theory and Practice of Commercial Policy, 1945–1990," *NBER Working Papers,* 3569 (Cambridge, Mass.: National Bureau of Economic Research, 1991).

34. Dataquest.

35. "Another Losing Battle with Japan?" *New York Times,* March 1, 1992.

36. For an in-depth study, see, William Nester, *American Power, the New World Order, and the Japanese Challenge* (New York: St Martin's Press, 1993).

37. Charles H. Ferguson and Charles R. Morris, *Computer Wars: How the West can Win in a Post-IBM World* (New York: Times Books, 1993).

Notes to Chapter 4: Weapons and Spaceships

1. Dwight Eisenhower, Speech before the American Society for Newspaper Editors, on April 16, 1953,

2. Adam Smith, *The Wealth of Nations* (New York: Modern Library, 1937), p. 315.
3. Dwight D. Eisenhower, "Spending into Trouble," *Saturday Evening Post*, May 18, 1963, p. 18.
4. Among prominent books on the subject, see: C. Wright Mills, *The Power Elite* (New York: Oxford University Press, 1956); Walter Millis, *Arms and Men: A Study in American Military History* (New York: Putnam, 1956); Samuel Huntington, *The Soldier and State: The Theory and Practice of Civil–Military Relations* (Cambridge, Mass.: Belknap Press, 1957); Morris Janowitz, *The Professional Soldier: A Social and Political Portrait* (New York: Putnam, 1960); Carroll W. Pursell (ed.), *The Military-Industrial Complex* (New York: Harper & Row, 1972); Sam C. Sarkesian (ed.), *The Military-Industrial Complex: A Reassessment* (Beverly Hills, Calif.: Sage, 1972); Steven Rosen (ed.), *Testing the Theory of the Military–Industrial Complex* (Lexington, Mass.: D. C. Heath, 1973); Stuart H. Loory, *Defeated: Inside America's Military Machine* (New York: Random House, 1973); Robert K. Griffith, *The Military–Industrial Complex: A Historical Perspective* (New York: Praeger, 1980); Gordon Adams, *The Iron Triangle: The Politics of Defense Contracting* (New York: Council of Economic Priorities, 1981); Ann Markusen et al., *The Rise of the Gunbelt: The Military Remapping of Industrial America* (New York: Oxford University Press, 1991).
5. "Preliminary Report of the Special Committee on Investigation of the Munitions Industry," *Senate Report*, 74th Congr., 1st Sess., No. 944, Part I (Serial 9881), pp. 220–1.
6. Smaller War Plants Corporation, "Economic Concentration and World War II," 79th Congr., 2nd Sess., S. Doc. 206 (1946), pp. 21, 54.
7. Harlan K. Ullman, *In Irons: US Military Might in the New Century* (Washington, DC: National Defense University, 1995), pp. 169, 34.
8. Russell Weigley, *The American Way of War: A History of the United States Military Strategy and Policy* (New York: Macmillan, 1973), pp. 378–81, 394.
9. Ullman, *In Irons*, pp. 28, 169.
10. Ibid., pp. 28, 169, 34.
11. Ibid.
12. Ibid.
13. Ibid.
14. Matthew Wald, "Today's Drama: Twilight of the Nukes," *New York Times*, July 16, 1995; Peter Passell, "Economic Scene: A Lot of Money Spent on Nuclear Arms was Wasted, Studies Show," *New York Times*, September 14, 1995.
15. Colonel Harry Summers, "A Bankrupt Military Strategy: Our Military Assets No Longer Cover our Foreign Policy Liabilities," *Atlantic Monthly*, June 1989, p. 36.
16. Jack Beaty, "The Exorbitant Anachronism," *Atlantic Monthly*, June 1989, p. 41.
17. Tom Gervasi, *The Myth of Soviet Military Supremacy* (New York: Harper & Row, 1987).
18. Strobe Talbott, "Rethinking the Red Menance," *Time*, January 1, 1990, pp. 66.

19. Ullman, *In Irons*, pp. 28, 169; David Rosenbaum, "Arms Makers and Military Face a Wrenching New Era," *New York Times*, August 4, 1991.

20. Eric Schmitt, "A Job-Oriented Defense: Protecting the Work Place," *New York Times*, September 2, 1993.

21. Adam Clymer, "Without Being Asked, House Votes Extra $1.2 Billion for Pentagon," *New York Times*, May 27, 1993.

22. Edmund L. Andrews, "Clinton's Technology Plan would Redirect Billions from Military Research," *New York Times*, February 23, 1994.

23. "Still No Policy on Arms Sales," *New York Times*, April 3, 1994.

24. William D. Hartung, *And Weapons for All: How America's Multi-Billion Dollar Arms Trade Warps our Foreign Policy and Subverts Democracy at Home* (New York: HarperCollins, 1994); William D. Hartung, "The Phantom Profits of the War Trade," *New York Times*, March 6, 1994.

25. Steven Greenhouse, "Study says Big Cities Don't Get Fair Share of Military Spending," *New York Times*, May 11, 1992.

26. Eric Schmitt, "A Mission Accomplished: In Deciding Which Military Bases to Close, the Commission was a Fortress against Politics," *New York Times*, June 28, 1993; Ullman, *In Irons*, pp. 158–60; Tim Weiner, "Decrying Base Closing Plan as an 'Outrage,' the President Gives a Grudging Go-Ahead," *New York Times*, July 13, 1995.

27. Harry Mingos, "Birth of an Industry," in G. R. Simonson (ed.), *The History of the American Aircraft Industry* (Cambridge, Mass.: MIT Press, 1968), pp. 43–4.

28. Elsbeth E. Freudenthal, "The Aviation Business in the 1930s," in Simonson, *History of American Aircraft Industry*, pp. 73, 85; Ann Markusen et al., *Rise of the Gunbelt*, p. 33.

29. Ibid., pp. 99–100, 106, 113.

30. Reginald Cleveland and Frank Graham, "Aviation Manufacturing Today in America," in Markusen et al., *Rise of the Gunbelt*, p. 146.

31. The Aircraft Industries Association of America, "Aircraft Manufacturing in the United States," in Simonson, *History of the American Aircraft Industry*, pp. 163, 165.

32. William Glenn Cunningham, "The Aircraft Industry in 1950," in Simonson, *History of the American Aircraft Industry*, pp. 182, 185.

33. John S. Day, "Aircraft Production in the Korea War," in Simonson, *History of the American Aircraft Industry*, p. 209.

34. Leonard Silk, "Outer Space: The Impact on the American Economy," in Simonson, *History of the American Aircraft Industry*, p. 24.

35. Michael Michaud, *Reaching for the High Frontier: The American Pro-Space Movement, 1972–1984)*, p. 12; Mary Holman, *The Political Economy of the Space Program* (Palo Alto, Calif.: Pacific Books, 1974), and *The Decision to Go to the Moon: Project Apollo and the National Interest* (Chicago: University of Chicago Press, 1970). For a highly readable account of the early space program, see Tom Wolfe, *The Right Stuff* (New York: Farrar, Straus, & Giroux, 1979).

36. Laura Tyson, *Who's Bashing Whom? Trade Conflict in High-Technology Industries* (Washington, DC: Institute for International Economics, 1992), p. 170.

37. S. L. Carrol, "The Market for Commercial Aircraft," in R. E. Caves

and M. J. Roberts (eds), *Regulating the Market* (Cambridge, Mass.: Ballinger, 1975), pp. 145–69.

38. David Mowery and Nathan Rosenberg, "The Commercial Aircraft Industry," in Richard Nelson (ed.), *Government and Technical Progress: A Cross-Industry Analysis* (New York: Pergamon Press, 1982), pp. 101–61.

39. Agis Salpurkas, "Hurt in Expansion, Airlines Pull Back and May Cut Hubs," *New York Times*, April 1, 1993.

40. Martin Tolchin, "Clinton Considers Measures to Help Troubled Airlines," *New York Times*, March 21, 1994.

41. Ibid.

42. Andrew Pollack, "Wait! Isn't This Backward? Roles Reversed in US–Japan Dispute on Airlines," *New York Times*, June 20, 1995.

43. Office of Technology Assessment, *Competing Economies: America, Europe, and the Pacific Rim* (Washington, DC: Government Printing Office, October 1991); Testimony of J. Michael Farren, Under Secretary of Commerce for International Trade, before the Joint Economic Committee, February 27, 1992; John Tagliabue, "Airbus Tries to Fly in a New Formation," *New York Times*, May 2, 1996.

44. Tyson, *Who's Bashing Whom?* p. 200.

45. Richard Stevenson, "Gain for McDonnell Douglas Raises Fear of US Loss," *New York Times*, November 20, 1991; Tyson, *Who's Bashing Whom?* pp. 185, 190.

46. Jeff Shear, *The Keys to the Kingdom: The FSX Deal and the Selling of America's Future* (New York: Doubleday, 1994).

47. John Mintz, "Boeing Bets its New 777 will Leave European Airbus in the Dust," *Herald Tribune*, March 28, 1995.

48. Tyson, *Who's Bashing Whom?* p. 192.

49. Robert L. Pak, "Pork Barrel in Low-Earth Orbit," *New York Times*, April 18, 1993.

50. Ibid.

51. William Broad, "Shuttle Program's Cost Fuels Effort to Streamline," *New York Times*, March 22, 1993; Warren Leary, "Clinton Plans to Ask Congress to Approve Smaller, Cheaper Space Station," *New York Times*, June 18, 1993.

52. William Broad, "Space Station Faces Danger from Flotsam," *New York Times*, June 27, 1994.

53. William Broad, "Space Linkup with $100 Billion Future," *New York Times*, June 29, 1995.

54. William Broad, "Space Station Faces Danger from Flotsam," *New York Times*, June 27, 1994.

55. William Broad, "Question on Eve of a Shuttle Flight: Is It Worth It?" *New York Times*, October 21, 1992; William Broad, "High Costs for Shuttles Limit their Future Use," *New York Times*, May 9, 1992.

56. William Broad, "How the $8 Billion Space Station Became a $120 Billion Showpiece," *New York Times*, June 10, 1990.

57. Theodore H. Moran and David C. Mowery, "Aerospace and National Security in an Era of Globalization," *CCC Working Papers*, 91–2 (Berkeley: Center for Research and Management, University of

California, 1991); Warren Leary, "Civilian Uses are Proposed for Satellites," *New York Times*, May 31, 1995.

58. Richard Stevenson, "Will Aerospace be the Next Casualty?" *New York Times*, March 15, 1992.

59. Ibid.

60. Robert W. DeGrasses, *Military Expansions, Economic Decline: The Impact of Military Spending on US Economic Performance* (New York: M. E. Sharpe, 1983), pp. 223–9. See also, Marion Anderson, Jeb Brugmann and George Erickcek, "The Price of the Pentagon: The Industrial and Commercial Impact of the 1981 Military Budget" (Lansing, Mich.: Employment Research Associates, 1982); John Zysman, "US Power, Trade, and Technology," *International Affairs*, **67**: 1 (1991), pp. 81–106; Richard Stubbing and Richard Mendel, "How to Save $50 Billion a Year," *Atlantic Monthly*, June 1989, p. 53; J. A. Stockfish, *Plowshares Into Swords: Managing the Defense Establishment* (New York: Mason and Lipscomb, 1973).

61. Tim Weiner, "Military Accused of Lies over Arms," *New York Times*, June 28, 1993.

62. Tim Weiner, "After Month's Orbit, War Satellite has Power Loss," *New York Times*, March 5, 1994.

63. Richard A. Stubbing and Richard Mendel, "How to Save $50 Billion a Year," *Atlantic Monthly*, June 1989, p. 58.

64. Gordon Adams, "The B-1: Bomber for All Seasons?" *Council on Economic Priorities Newsletter*, February 1982.

65. The following examples come from, Peter Cary and Bruce B. Auster, "Best and Worst Weapons," *Newsweek*, July 10, 1989.

66. "The Pentagon Jackpot," *New York Times*, July 10, 1995; Seymour Melman, "Preparing for War against Ourselves," *New York Times*, June 26, 1995.

67. Eric Schmitt, "GOP would Give Pentagon Money it Didn't Request," *New York Times*, July 4, 1995.

Notes to Chapter 5: Doctors and Drugs

1. "Cost of Health Care in the United States is Continuing to Grow," *New York Times*, November 27, 1994; Sally Sonnefeld et al., "Projections of National Health Expenditures through the Year 2000," *Health Care Financing Review*, **13**: 1 (1991).

2. Paul Spector, "Failure by the Numbers," *New York Times*, September 24, 1994.

3. Peter Passell, "Health Care's Fever: Not So High to Some," *New York Times*, May 16, 1993.

4. Paul Starr, *The Social Transformation of American Medicine* (New York: Basic Books, 1982).

5. The term was popularized by Arnold S. Relman, "The New Medical-Industrial Complex," *New England Journal of Medicine*, **303** (October 23, 1980), pp. 963–70.

6. Susan Feigenbaum, "Risk Bearing in Health Care Finance," in Carl Schramm (ed.), *Health Care and its Costs: Can the US Afford Adequate Health Care?* (New York: W. W. Norton, 1987), p. 132.

7. "American versus European Medical Science," *Medical Record,* 4 (May 15, 1869), p. 133.

8. Keith Thomas, *Religion and the Decline of Magic* (New York: Scribner, 1971).

9. Starr, *Social Transformation of American Medicine,* p. 83.

10. Samuel Haber, "The Professions and Higher Education in America," in *Higher Education and the Labor Market,* (ed.) Margaret Gordon (New York: McGraw-Hill, 1974).

11. US Bureau of the Census, *Historical Statistics of the United States, Colonial Times to 1970* (Washington, DC: Department of Commerce, 1975), p. 76; William Barlow and David O. Powell, "To Find a Stand: New England Physicians on the Western and Southern Frontier, 1790–1840," *Bulletin of the History of Medicine,* 54 (Fall 1980), p. 386.

12. Catherine M. Scholten, "On the Importance of the Obstetrick Art: Changing Customs of Childbirth in America, 1760 to 1825," *William and Mary Quarterly* (Summer 1977), pp. 427–45.

13. Mary Walsh, *"Doctors Wanted; No Women need Apply,"* (New Haven, CT: Yale University Press, 1977), p. 176.

14. Starr, *Social Transformation of American Medicine,* p. 104.

15. Arpad Gerster, Recollections of a New York Surgeon (New York: Paul B. Hoeber, 1929), p. 43; US Bureau of the Census, *Historical Statistics,* p. 76.

16. Starr, *Social Transformation of American Medicine,* p. 118.

17. D. W. Cathell, *The Physician Himself* (Philadelphia: F. A. Davis, 1890).

18. Starr, *Social Transformation of American Medicine,* pp. 201, 209, 211.

19. Jo Ann Ashley, *Hospitals, Paternalism, and the Role of the Nurse* (New York: Teachers College Press, 1976), p. 2; US Bureau of the Census, *Hospitals and Dispensaries* (1923), p. 4.

20. Herman and Anne Somers, *Doctors, Patients, and Health Insurance* (Washington, DC: Brookings Institute, 1961), p. 548.

21. Michael Schiltz, *Public Attitudes Toward a Social Security 1935–1965* (Washington, DC: US Government Printing Office, 1970), pp. 123–50.

22. Judith and Lester Lave, *The Hospital Construction Act: An Evaluation of the Hill-Burton Program, 1948–1973* (Washington, DC: American Enterprise Institute, 1974); Steven Renn, "The Structure and Financing of the Health Care Delivery System of the 1980s," in Carl J. Schramm (ed.), *Health Care and its Costs: Can the US Afford Adequate Health Care?* (New York: W. W. Norton, 1987), pp. 10–11.

23. Odin Anderson and Jacob Feldman, *Family Medical Costs and Voluntary Health Insurance: A Nationwide Survey* (New York: McGraw-Hill, 1956), p. 11.

24. Odin Anderson, Patricia Collette, and Jacob Feldman, *Changes in Family Medical Expenditures and Voluntary Health Insurance: A Five Year Survey* (Cambridge, Mass.: Harvard University Press, 1963), pp. 8–9.

25. Stephen Strickland, *Politics, Science, and Dread Disease: A Short History of United States Medical Research Policy* (Cambridge, Mass.: Harvard

University Press, 1972), pp. 1–14; Ralph C. Williams, *The United States Public Health Service, 1798–1950* (Richmond, VA: Whittet and Shepperson, 1951); Richard A. Rettig, *Cancer Crusade: The Story of the National Cancer Act of 1971* (Princeton, NJ: Princeton University Press, 1977); Richard Shryock, *American Medical Research* (New York: Commonwealth Fund, 1947), pp. 135–6.

26. Kenneth M. Endicott and Ernest M. Allen, "The Growth of Medical Research 1941–1953 and the Role of the Public Health Service Research Grants," *Science,* **118** (September 25, 1953), p. 337.

27. "Medical Education in the United States, 1979–1980," *Journal of American Medical Association* **244** (December 26, 1980), p. 2813.

28. Victor Fuchs, *Who Shall Live?* (New York: Basic Books, 1974), pp. 92–5.

29. "It's Time to Operate," *Fortune,* **81** (January 1970), p. 79; Dan Cordtz, "Change Begins in the Doctor's Office," *Fortune,* **81** (January 1970), p. 84.

30. Renn, "Structuring and Finance of Health Care in the 1980s," p. 36.

31. Renn, ibid., p. 45.

32. Feigenbaum, "Risk Bearing in Health Care Finance," p. 137.

33. Paul Starr, *The Logic of Health Care Reform: Why and How the President's Plan Will Work* (New York: Whittle Books, 1994), p. xxxvi.

34. Ibid.

35. "The C.B.O. on Three Health Proposals," *New York Times,* May 9, 1994.

36. "Americans' Attitudes on Health Care," *New York Times,* July 29, 1994.

37. "Why Health Care Fizzled: Too Little Time and Too Much Politics," *New York Times,* September 27, 1994.

38. "Why Health Care Fizzled," *New York Times,* September 27, 1994.

39. Katherine R. Levit and Cathy A. Cowan, "Businesses, Households, and Governments: Health Care Costs, 1990," *Health Care Financing Review,* **13**: 2 (1991); Roger Taylor and Bonnie Newton, "Can Managed Care Reduce Employers' Retiree Medical Liability," *Benefits Quarterly,* **7**: 4 (1991); Starr, *Logic of Health Care Reform,* pp. 11, 4.

40. The Wyatt Company, *Management USA – Leading a Changing Work Force* (Washington, DC: Wyatt Company, 1990).

41. Service Employees International Union, *Labor and Management: On a Collision Course Over Health Care* (AFL–CIO, Department of Public Policy, February 1990).

42. Starr, *Logic of Health Care Reform,* p. 58.

43. David Rosenbaum, "Economic Outlaw: American Health Care," *New York Times,* October 25, 1994; Philip R. Lee and Richard D. Lamm, "Europe's Medical Model," *New York Times,* March 1, 1993.

44. David Rosenbaum, "Economic Outlaw: American Health Care," *New York Times,* October 25, 1994.

45. Barnaby J. Feder, "Medical Group Battles to be Heard over Others on Health-Care Changes," *New York Times,* June 11, 1993; Philip J. Hilts, "Most Doctors with Violations Keep their License," *New York Times,* March 29, 1996.

46. Robert G. Evans and Morris L. Barer, "The American Predicament,"

in *Health Care Systems in Transition* (Paris: OECD, 1990), p. 84; "Cost of Health Care in the United States is Continuing to Grow," *New York Times*, November 27, 1994; George Schieber, Jean-Pierre Poullier, and Leslie Greenwald, "Health Care Systems in Twenty-four Countries," *Health Affairs*, **10**: 3 (1991).

47. Warren E. Leary, "National Effort is Urged to Fight Worsening Fraud in Medical Bills," *New York Times*, May 7, 1992; "Cost of Health Care in the United States is Continuing to Grow," *New York Times*, November 27, 1994. Starr, *Logic of Health Care Reform*, pp. 24, 25.

48. Gina Kolata, "US is Asked to Control Prices of Drugs it Develops," New Yorks Times, April 25, 1993.

49. Ibid.

50. Ibid.

51. Elisabeth Rosenthal, "Claims and Counterclaims on Vaccine Costs Generate Heat but Little Light," *New York Times*, March 15, 1993.

52. Paul Spector, "Failure, by the Numbers," *New York Times*, September 24, 1994.

53. Robert Blendon et al., "Satisfaction with Health Care in Ten Nations," *Health Affairs*, **9**: 2 (1990).

54. R. J. Blendon and D. E. Altman, "Public Attitudes about Health Care Costs: A Lesson in National Schizophrenia," *New England Journal of Medicine*, **311** (1984), pp. 613–16; L. J. Freshnock, *Physicians and Public Attitudes on Health Care Issues* (Chicago: American Medical Association, 1984).

55. Starr, *Logic of Health Care Reform*, pp. 20–2.

56. Ibid., p. 58.

57. Milt Freudenheim, "To Economists Managed Care is No Cure-all," *New York Times*, September 6, 1994.

58. "Cost of Health Care in the United States is Continuing to Grow," *New York Times*, November 27, 1994.

59. K. Davis and D. Rowland, *Medicare Policy: New Directions for Health and Long-Term Care* (Baltimore: Johns Hopkins University Press, 1986).

60. Adam Clymer, "Hawaii is a Health Care Lab as Employers Buy Insurance," *New York Times*, May 3, 1994.

Bibliography

Abramovitz, Moses and Paul A. David, "Reinterpreting Economic Growth: Parables and Realities," *American Economic Review*, **63** (1973).

Adams, Donald, "American Neutrality and Prosperity, 1793–1808: A Reconsideration," *Journal of Economic History*, **40** (1980), 713–38.

Adams, Gordon, *The Iron Triangle: The Politics of Defense Contracting* (New York: Council of Economic Priorities, 1981).

Adams, Gordon, "The B-1: Bomber for all Seasons?" *Council on Economic Priorities Newsletter*, February 1982.

Adams, Walter and J. B. Dirlam, "Big Steel, Invention and Innovation," *Quarterly Journal of Economics*, **80** (May 1966), 167–89.

Adams, Walter, "The Steel Industry," in Walter Adams (ed.), *The Structure of American Industry*, 5th edn (New York: Macmillan, 1977).

Aitken, Hugh G. J. (ed.), *The State and Economic Growth* (New York: Social Science Research Council, 1959).

Albro, Martin, *Enterprise Denied: Origin of the Decline of American Railroads* (New York: Columbia University Press, 1971).

Almond, Gabriel and Sidney Verba, *The Civic Culture* (Boston: Little, Brown, 1965).

Anchordoguy, Marie, "Mastering the Market: Japanese Government Targeting of the Computer Industry," *International Organization*, **42**, no. 3 (Summer 1988), 509–43.

Anchordoguy, Marie, *Computers, Inc.: Japan's Challenge to IBM* (Cambridge, MA: Harvard University Press, 1989).

Anderson, Marion, Jeb Brugmann and George Erickcek, *The Price of the Pentagon: The Industrial and Commercial Impact of the 1981 Military Budget* (Lansing, Mich.: Employment Research Associates, 1982).

Anderson, Odin and Jacob Feldman, *Family Medical Costs and Voluntary Health Insurance: A Nationwide Survey* (New York: McGraw-Hill, 1956).

Anderson, Odin, Patricia Collette, and Jacob Feldman, *Changes in Family Medical Expenditures and Voluntary Health Insurance: A Five-Year Survey* (Cambridge, Mass.: Harvard University, 1963).

Andreano, Ralph (ed.), *The Economic Impact of the American Civil War* (Boston: Schenkman, 1967).

Asher, Norman and Leland D. Strom, "The Role of the Department of Defense in the Development of Integrated Circuits," IDA Paper P-1271 (Arlington, VA: Institute for Defense Analyses, 1977).

Ashley, Jo Ann, *Hospitals, Paternalism, and the Role of the Nurse* (New York: Teachers College Press, 1976).

Atack, Jeremy and Jan Brueckner, "Steel Rails and American Railroads, 1867–1880: A Reply to Harley," *Explorations in American History*, **20** (1983), pp. 258–62.

Atack, Jeremy and Fred Bateman, *To Their own Soil: Agriculture in the Antebellum North* (Ames: Iowa State University Press, 1987).

Atkins, Hugh, *Did Slavery Pay? Readings in the Economics of Black Slavery in the United States* (Boston: Houghton Mifflin, 1971).

Baack, Bennett and Edward Ray, "The Political Economy of Tariff Policy: A Case Study of the United States," *Explorations in Economic History*, 44 (1984), pp. 73–93.

Bailey, Stephen, *Congress Makes a Law* (New York: Columbia University Press, 1950).

Bailyn, Bernard, *Ideological Origins of the American Revolution* (Cambridge: Harvard University Press, 1967).

Bailyn, Bernard, *Voyagers to the West: A Passage in the Peopling of America on the Eve of the Revolution* (New York: Alfred A. Knopf, 1986).

Baldwin, David A., *Foreign Aid and American Foreign Policy* (New York: Praeger, 1966).

Baldwin, Robert, *The Political Economy of US Import Policy* (Cambridge: MIT Press, 1986).

Baldwin, Robert and Paul Krugman, "Market Access and International Competition: A Simulation Study of 16K Random Access Memories," in Robert C. Feenstra (ed.), *Empirical Methods for International Trade* (Cambridge, MA: MIT Press, 1988), pp. 171–97.

Barber, James, *Presidential Character* (Englewood Cliffs, NJ: Prentice Hall, 1985).

Barfield, Claude E. and William A. Schambra (eds), *The Politics of Industrial Policy* (Washington, DC: American Enterprise Institute for Public Policy Research, 1986).

Barlow, William and David O. Powell, "To Find a Stand: New England Physicians on the Western and Southern Frontier, 1790–1840," *Bulletin of the History of Medicine*, 54 (Fall 1980).

Barnett, Donald F. and Louis Schorsch, *Steel: Upheaval in a Basic Industry* (Cambridge, MA: Ballinger, 1983).

Bartlett, Donald, and James B. Steele, *America: What Went Wrong?* (Kansas City: Universal Press Syndicate Company, 1992).

Bartley, Robert, *The Seven Fat Years* (New York: The Free Press, 1992).

Bateman, Fred and Thomas Weiss, "Comparative Regional Development in Antebellum Manufacturing," *Journal of Economic History*, 35 (1975), pp. 182–208.

Baum, Claude, *The System Builders* (Santa Monica: Systems Development Corporation, 1981).

Bautier, Robert-Henri, *The Economic Development of Medieval Europe* (New York: Harcourt, Brace, Jovanovich, 1971).

Bayard, Thomas O. and Kimberly Ann Elliott, *Reciprocity and Retaliation: An Evaluation of Aggressive Trade Policies* (Washington, DC: Institute of International Economics, 1992).

Beard, Charles, *An Economic Interpretation of the Constitution* (New York: Macmillan, 1913).

Beard, Charles and Mary, *The Rise of American Civilization* (New York: Macmillan, 1927).

Beaty, Jack, "The Exorbitant Anachronism," *Atlantic Monthly*, June 1989.

Beltz, Cynthia, *High-tech Maneuvers: Industrial Policy Lessons of HDTV* (Washington, DC: AEI Press, 1991).

Bendix, Reinhard, *Kings and People: Power and the Mandate to Rule* (Berkeley: University of California Press, 1978).

Benson, Lee, *Merchants, Farmers, and Railroads: Railroad Regulation and New York Politics, 1850–1887* (Cambridge: Harvard University Press, 1955).

Bergsten, Fred C. and William R. Cline, *The United States–Japan Economic Problem* (Washington, DC: Institute for International Economics, 1987).

Bernstein, Michael, *The Great Depression: Delayed Recovery and Economic Change in America, 1929–1939* (New York: Cambridge University Press, 1987).

Bhagwati, Jagdish, *Lectures: International Trade* (Cambridge, MA: MIT Press, 1983).

Bhagwati, Jagdish, *Protectionism* (Cambridge, MA: MIT Press, 1988).

Bhagwati, Jagdish and Hugh Patrick (eds), *Aggressive Unilateralism* (Ann Arbor: University of Michigan Press, 1990).

Bhagwati, Jagdish, *The World Trading System at Risk* (Princeton, NJ: Princeton University Press, 1991).

Bidwell, Peter, and John I. Falconer, *History of Agriculture in the Northern United States, 1620–1860* (Washington, DC: Carnegie Institute, 1925).

Bils, Mark, "Tariff Protection and Production in the Early US Cotton Textile Industry," *Journal of Economic History*, **44** (1984), pp. 1033–46.

Bjork, Gordon, "The Weaning of the American Economy: Independence, Market Changes, and Economic Development," *Journal of Economic History*, **24** (1964), pp. 541–60.

Blendon, R. J. and D. E. Altman, "Public Attitudes about Health Care Costs: A Lesson in National Schizophrenia," *New England Journal of Medicine*, **311** (1984) 613–16.

Blendon, Robert *et al.*, "Satisfaction with Health Care in Ten Nations," *Health Affairs*, **9** (1990).

Bluestone, Barry, and Bennett Harrison, *The Deindustrialization of America: Plant Closings, Community Abandonment, and the Dismantling of Basic Industries* (New York: Basic Industries, 1982).

Blum, John Morton, *V was for Victory: Politics and American Culture during World War II* (New York: Harcourt, Brace, and Jovanovich, 1976).

Bogart, Leo, *Silent Politics* (New York: John Wiley, 1972).

Boltuck, Richard, and Robert Litan (eds), *Down in the Dumps: Administration of Unfair Trade Laws* (Washington, DC: Brookings Institute, 1991).

Borden, William S., *The Pacific Alliance: United States Foreign Economic Policy and Trade Recovery, 1947–1955* (Madison: University of Wisconsin Press, 1984).

Borrus, Michael, James Millstein, and John Zysman, "US–Japanese Competition in the Semiconductor Industry," *Policy Papers in International Affairs*, **17** (Berkeley: Institute for International Studies, University of California, 1983).

Borrus, Michael, *Competing for Control: America's Stake in Microelectronics* (Cambridge, MA: Ballinger, 1988).

Borrus, Michael and Jeffrey Hart, "Display's the Thing: The Real Stakes in the Conflict over High-Resolution Display," *Brie Working Papers 52* (Berkeley, CA: Berkeley Roundtable on the International Economy, 1992).

Bowen, Catherine Drinker, *Miracle at Philadelphia* (Boston: Little, Brown, 1966.

Brander, James, and Barbara Spencer, "Export Subsidies and International Market Share Rivalry," *Journal of International Economics*, **18**, no. 1–2 (February 1985), pp. 85–100.

Brander, James A., "Rationales for Strategic Trade and Industrial Policy," in Paul Krugman (ed.), *Strategic Trade Policy and the New International Economics* (Cambridge, MA: MIT Press, 1986).

Brander, James A., "Shaping Comparative Advantage: Trade Policy, Industrial Policy, and Economic Performance," in R.G. Lipsey and W. Dobson (eds), *Shaping Comparative Advantage*, Policy Study no. 2 (Toronto: C.D. Howe Institute, 1987).

Brandes, Stuart D., *American Welfare Capitalism, 1880–1940* (Chicago: University of Chicago Press, 1976).

Brock, Leslie, *The Currency of the American Colonies, 1700–64* (New York: Arno Press, 1975).

Bromley, Alan, "US Technology Policy: The Path to Competitiveness," Address to the Technology 2000 Meeting (Washington, DC: November 27, 1990).

Brownlee, W. Elliot and Mary M. Brownlee (eds), *Women in the American Economy: A Documentary History, 1675–1929* (New Haven, CT: Yale University Press, 1976).

Bruchey, Stuart, *Roots of American Economic Growth, 1607–1861* (London: Hutchinson, 1965).

Bruchey, Stuart, *The Colonial Merchant: Sources and Readings* (New York: Harcourt, Brace and World, 1966).

Bruchey, Stuart, *Cotton and the Growth of the American Economy* (New York: Harcourt, Brace and World, 1967).

Bureau of Labor Statistics, US Congress, JEC, 88th Congress, 1st Session, Hearings, *Steel Prices, Unit Costs, and Foreign Competition* (Washington, DC: GPO, 1963).

Burner, David, *Herbert Hoover: A Public Life* (New York: Alfred A. Knopf, 1979).

Burrows, Edwin and Michael Wallace, "The American Revolution: The Ideology and Psychology of National Liberation," *Perspectives in American History*, **6** (1972), pp. 208–15.

Callender, Guy S., "The Early Transportation and Banking Enterprises of the States in Relation to the Growth of Corporations," *Quarterly Journal of Economics*, **17** (1902).

Calleo, David, *The Imperious Economy* (Cambridge, MA: Harvard University Press, 1982).

Calomiris, Charles, "Institutional Failure, Monetary Scarcity, and the Depreciation of the Continental," *Journal of Economic History*, **48** (1988) pp. 47–68.

Carman, Harry (ed.), *American Husbandry* (Port Washington, NY: Kennikat Press, 1964).

Carosso, Vincent P., *The Morgans: Private International Bankers, 1854–1913* (Cambridge, MA: Harvard University Press, 1987).

Carrol, S. L., "The Market for Commercial Aircraft," in R. E. Caves and

M. J. Roberts (eds), *Regulating the Market* (Cambridge, MA: Ballinger, 1975).

Cassady, James M., *Demography in Early America* (Cambridge, MA: Harvard University Press, 1969).

Cathell, D. W., *The Physician Himself* (Philadelphia: F. A. Davis, 1890).

Chandler, Alfred, *The Railroads: The Nation's First Big Business* (New York: Harcourt, Brace and World, 1965).

Chandler, Alfred, *The Visible Hand: The Managerial Revolution in American Business* (Cambridge: Belknap Press in Harvard University Press, 1977).

Chandler, Alfred A. and Stuart Bruchey (eds), *Giant Enterprise: Ford, General Motors, and the Automobile Industry* (New York: Arno Press, 1980).

Chandler, Lester, *America's Greatest Depression, 1929–1941* (New York: Harper and Row, 1970).

Chandler, Lester V., *American Monetary Policies, 1928–41* (New York: Harper & Row, 1971).

Chitwood, Oliver P., *A History of Colonial America* (New York: Harper & Bros., 1961).

Choate, Pat, *Agents of Influence: How Japan's Lobbyists in the United States Manipulate America's Political and Economic System* (New York: Alfred A. Knopf, 1990).

Clark, John Maurice, *The Cost of the World War to the American People* (New Haven, CT: Yale University Press, 1931).

Clark, Victor S., *History of Manufacturers in the United States*, 3 vols (New York: Peter Smith, 1949).

Clarkson, Grosvenor B., *Industrial America in the World War: The Strategy behind the Line, 1917–1918* (Boston, MA: Houghton Mifflin, 1923).

Cline, William, "US Trade and Industrial Policy: The Experience of Textiles, Steel, and Automobiles," in Paul Krugman (ed.), *Strategic Trade Policy and the New International Economics* (Cambridge, MA: MIT Press, 1986).

Clowse, Converse D., *Economic Beginnings in Colonial South Carolina, 1670–1730* (Columbia: University of South Carolina Press, 1971).

Coale, Ansley and Melvin Zelink, *New Estimates of Fertility and Population in the United States: A Study of Annual White Births from 1855 to 1960 and of Completeness of Ennumeration of Censuses from 1880 to 1960* (Princeton, NJ: Princeton University Press, 1963).

Cobb, James C., *The Selling of the South: The Southern Crusade for Industrial Development, 1936–1980* (Baton Rouge: Louisiana State University Press, 1982).

Cochran, Thomas C., *Railroad Leaders, 1845–1890: The Business Mind in Action* (Cambridge, MA: Harvard University Press, 1953).

Cochran, Thomas, "Did the Civil War Retard Industrialization?" in *The Economic Impact of the Civil War*, (ed.) Ralph Andreano (Cambridge, MA: Schenkman, 1862).

Cochrance, Rexmond C., *Measures for Progress: A History of the National Bureau of Standards* (Washington, DC: US Department of Commerce, GPO, 1966).

Coen, Robert M., "Labor Force and Unemployment in the 1920s and 1930s," *Review of Economics and Statistics*, **55** (1973), pp. 40–55.

Congressional Budget Office, *The Industrial Policy Debate* (Washington, DC: Government Printing Office, 1983).

Conrad, Alfred H. and John Meyer, "The Economics of Slavery in the Antebellum South," *Journal of Political Economy*, 66 (1958), pp. 95–122.

Cordtz, Dan, "Change Begins in the Doctor's Office," *Fortune*, 81 (January 1970).

Coulter, E. Merton, *The South during Reconstruction, 1865–1877* (Baton Rouge: Louisiana State University, 1947).

Crandall, Robert W., *The US Steel Industry in Recurrent Crisis* (Washington, DC: Brookings, 1981).

Crandall, Robert, "Investment and Productivity Growth in the Steel Industry: Some Implications for Industrial Policy," in Walter H. Goldberg (ed.), *Ailing Steel: The Transatlantic Quarrel* (New York: St Martin's Press, 1986).

Cremin, Lawrence A., *The Transformation of the School: Progressivism in American Education, 1876–1957* (New York: Alfred A. Knopf, 1961).

Cremin, Lawrence A., *American Education: The National Experience, 1783–1876* (New York: Harper and Row, 1980).

Cronin, Thomas, *The State of the Presidency* (Chicago: Scott, Foresman, 1980).

Cuff, Robert D., *The War Industries Board: Business–Government Relations During World War I* (Baltimore: Johns Hopkins Press, 1973).

Dahl, Robert, *Who Governs?* (New Haven, CT: Yale University Press, 1963).

David, Jules, *American Political and Economic Penetration of Mexico, 1877–1920* (New York: Arno Press, 1976).

David, Paul A., "Learning by Doing and Tariff Protection: A Reconsideration of the Case of the Antebellum United States Cotton Textile Industry," *Journal of Economic History*, 30 (1970), 521–601.

David, Paul A., *Technical Choice, Innovation and Economic Growth: Essays on American and British Experience in the Nineteenth Century* (Cambridge: Cambridge University Press, 1975).

David, Paul A., et al., *Reckoning with Slavery: A Critical Study of the Quantitative History of American Negro Slavery* (New York: Oxford University Press, 1976).

David, Henry, *The History of the Haymarket Affair* (New York: Russell & Russell, 1958).

Davis, Lance E., "Capital Formation in the United States during the Nineteenth Century," in *The Cambridge Economic History of Europe*, vol. 7 (Cambridge: Cambridge University Press).

Davis, Joseph S., *Essays in the Earlier History of American Corporations*, 2 vols (Cambridge, MA: Harvard University Press, 1917).

Davis, K. and D. Rowland, *Medicare Policy: New Directions for Health and Long-term Care* (Baltimore: Johns Hopkins University Press, 1986).

Davis, Lance E., "Banks and their Economic Effects," in *American Economic Growth: An Economist's History of the United States*, ed. Lance E. Davis et al. (New York: Harper and Row, 1972).

Deane, Phyllis, *The First Industrial Revolution* (Cambridge: Cambridge University Press, 1965).

DeCanio, Stephen J. and Joel Mokyr, "Inflation and the Wage Lag during the American Civil War," *Explorations in Economic History*, 14 (1977) pp. 311–36.

Defense Science Board Task Force, *Foreign Ownership and Control of US Industry* (Washington, DC: Defense Science Board, June 1990).

Defense Science Board Task Force, *Foreign Ownership and Control of US Industry*, released by the Office of Congressman Mel Levine (D-CA), May 13, 1991.

Degler, Carl N., *Out of our Past: The Forces that Shaped America* (New York: Harper & Row, 1959).

DeGrasses, Robert W., *Military Expansions, Economic Decline: The Impact of Military Spending on US Economic Performance* (New York: M. E. Sharpe, 1983).

Derian, Jean-Claude, *America's Struggle for Leadership in Technology* (Cambridge, MA: MIT Press, 1990).

Dewar, Mary (eds), *A Discourse of the Commoweal of this Realm of England, Attributed to Sir Thomas Smith* (Charlottesville: University Press of Virginia, 1973).

Dewey, Donald, *Monopoly in Economics and Law* (Chicago: Rand McNally, 1959).

Dickens, William and Kevin Lang, "Why It Matters What We Trade: A Case for an Active Trade Policy," in William Dickens, Laura D'Andrea Tyson, and John Zysman (eds), *The Dynamics of Trade and Employment* (Cambridge, MA: Ballinger, 1988), pp. 87–112.

Dickerson, Oliver M., *The Navigation Acts and the American Revolution* (New York: Octagon, 1978).

Divine, Robert A., *Eisenhower and the Cold War* (New York: Oxford University Press, 1981).

Dixit, Avinash K. and Albert S. Kyle, "The Use of Protection and Subsidies for Entry Promotion and Deterrence," *American Economic Review*, **75**, March 1985.

Dixit, Avinash, "Optimal Trade and Industrial Policy for the US Automobile Industry," in Robert Feenstra (ed.), *Empirical Methods for International Trade* (Cambridge, MA: MIT Press, 1988), pp. 141–65.

Donaldson, S., *Hold on, Mr. President!* (New York: Random House, 1987).

Dubovsky, Melvyn, *Industrialism and the American Worker, 1865–1920* (New York: Thomas Crowell, 1975).

Dyer, Davis, Malcom Salter and Alan Webber, *Changing Alliances* (Boston: Harvard Business School Press, 1987).

Easterlin, Richard A., *Population, Labor Force, and Long Swings in Economic Growth: The American Experience* (New York: Columbia University Press, 1968).

Eaton, Jonathan and Gene M. Grossman, "Optimal Trade and Industrial Policy under Oligopolly," *Quarterly Journal of Economics*, **101** (May 1986), pp. 383–406.

Eckstein, Otto and Gary Fromm, "Steel and Postwar Inflation," Study Paper no. 2, US Congress, JEC, 86th Congress, 1st Session, *Materials Prepared in Connection with the Study of Employment, Growth, and Prices Levels* (Washington, DC: GPO, 1959).

Eichengreen, Barry, *Golden Fetters: The Gold Standard and the Great Depression, 1919–1939* (New York: Oxford University Press, 1992).

Eisner, Robert, *How Real is the Federal Deficit?* (New York: Free Press, 1986).

Eldridge, Hope T. and Dorothy Swain Thomas, *Population Redistribution and Economic Growth*, 3 vols (Philadelphia: American Philosophical Society, 1964).

Eliot, Jared, *Essays upon Field Husbandry in New England, and other Papers, 1748–1762*, ed. Harry J. Carman and Rexford G. Tugwell (New York: Columbia University Press, 1934).

Elliott, J. H., *The Old World and the New, 1492–1650* (Cambridge: Cambridge University Press, 1970).

Endicott, Kenneth M. and Ernest M. Allen, "The Growth of Medical Research, 1941–1953 and the Role of the Public Health Service Research Grants," *Science*, 118 (September 25, 1953).

Engerman, Stanley L., "The Economic Impact of the Civil War," *Explorations in Economic History*, 3 (1955) pp. 176–199.

Erikson, Robert S., "Economic Conditions and the Presidential Vote," *American Political Science Review*, 83 (Spring 1989) pp. 567–73.

Ernst, Dieter and David O'Connor, *Competing in the Electronics Industry – The Experience of Newly Industrializing Economies* (London: Pinter, 1992).

Ernst, Joseph Albert, *Money and Politics in America, 1755–75: A Study in the Currency Act of 1764 and the Political Economy of Revolution* (Chapel Hill: University of North Carolina Press, 1973).

Evans, Peter B., Dietrich Rueschemeyer, and Theda Skocpol (eds), *Bringing the State Back In* (Cambridge: Cambridge University Press, 1985).

Evans, Robert G. and Morris L. Barer, "The American Predicament," in *Health Care Systems in Transition* (Paris: OECD, 1990).

Evans, Stephen Peter, *Dependent Development* (Princeton, NJ: Princeton University Press, 1979).

Eyenbach, Mary Locke, *American Manufactured Exports, 1879–1914* (New York: Arno Press, 1976).

Federal Trade Commission, *Report on Wartime Costs and Profits for Manufacturing Corporations, 1941 to 1945* (Washington, DC: Government Printing Office, 1947).

Feigenbaum, Susan, "Risk Bearing in Health Care Finance," in Carl Schramm (ed.), *Health Care and its Costs: Can the US Afford Adequate Health Care?* (New York: W. W. Norton, 1987).

Fenstermaker, J. Van, *The Development of American Commercial Banking: 1782–1837* (Kent, Ohio: Bureau of Economic and Business Research, 1965).

Ferguson, Charles H., "America's High Tech Decline," *Foreign Policy*, 74 (Spring 1989) pp. 123–44.

Ferguson, Charles H., and Charles R. Morris, *Computer Wars: How the West Can Win in a Post-IBM World* (New York: Times Books, 1993).

Ferguson, F. James, *The Power of the Purse* (Chapel Hill: University of North Carolina Press, 1961).

Ferguson, F. James, *The American Revolution: A General History, 1763–1790* (Homewood, IL: Dorsey Press, 1979).

Field, Albert, "The Magnetic Telegraph, Price, and Quantity Data, and the New Management of Capital," *Journal of Economic History*, 52 (1992): 401–13.

Fine, Sydney, *The Automobile under the Blue Label* (Ann Arbor: University of Michigan Press, 1963).

Fisher, Franklin M., James W. McKie, and Richard B. Mancke, *IBM and the US Data Processing Industry: An Economic History* (New York: Praeger, 1983).

Fishlow, Albert, *American Railroads and the Transformation of the Ante-Bellum Economy* (Cambridge: Harvard University Press, 1965).

Fishlow, Albert, "Internal Transportation," in *American Economic Growth*, ed. Lance Davis *et al.* (New York: Harper & Sons, 1972) pp. 468–547.

Fite, Gilbert C., *The Farmers Frontier, 1865–1900* (New York: Holt, Rinehart and Winston, 1966).

Fitzpatrick, John C. (ed.), *The Writings of George Washington, 1745–1799* (Washington, DC: Government Printing Office, 1934–44).

Flamm, Kenneth, *Targeting the Computer: Government Support and International Competition* (Washington, DC: Brookings Institute, 1987).

Flamm, Kenneth, *Creating the Government, Industry, and High Technology* (Washington, DC: Brookings Institute, 1988).

Fletcher, Stevenson W., *Pennsylvania Agriculture and Country Life, 1640–1840* (Harrisonburg: Pennsylvania Historical and Museum Commission, 1950).

Flisig, Heywood W., *Long-Term Capital Flows and the Great Depression: The Role of the United States, 1927–33* (Ithaca, NY: Cornell University Press, 1975).

Fogel, Robert W., *Railroads and American Economic Growth: Essays in Econometric History* (Baltimore: Johns Hopkins Press, 1964).

Fogel, Robert and Stanley Engerman, *Time on the Cross: The Economics of American Negro Slavery* (New York: Little, Brown, 1974).

Fogel, Robert W., *Without Consent or Contract: The Rise and Fall of American Slavery*, vol. 1 (New York: W. W. Norton, 1989).

Ford, Paul Leiscester (ed.), *The Writings of Thomas Jefferson* (New York: G.P. Putnam's Sons, 1892–9).

Frankel, Jeffrey, "The 1807–1809 Embargo Against Great Britain," *Journal of Economic History*, **42** (1982) pp. 291–308.

Free, Lloyd and Hadley Cantril, *The Political Beliefs of Americans* (New York: Simon and Schuster, 1968).

Frendreis, John and Raymond Tatalovich, *The Modern Presidency and Economic Policy* (Itasca, IL: F. E. Peacock Press, 1994).

Freshnock, L. J., *Physicians and Public Attitudes on Health Care Issues* (Chicago: American Medical Association, 1984).

Friedman, Benjamin, *Day of Reckoning: The Consequences of American Economic Policy under Reagan and After* (New York: Random House, 1988).

Friedman, Milton and Anna Schwartz, *A Monetary History of the United States, 1869–1960* (Princeton: Princeton University Press, 1963).

Fuchs, Victor, *Who Shall Live?* (New York: Basic Books, 1974).

Galbraith, John Kenneth, *The Great Crash: 1929* (Boston: Houghton Mifflin, 1954).

Galbraith, John Kenneth, *The Culture of Contentment* (Boston: Houghton Mifflin, 1992).

Galenson, David W., *White Servitude in Colonial America: An Economic Analysis* (Cambridge: Cambridge University Press, 1981).

Gallman, Robert E. and Edward S. Howle, "Trends in the Structure of the American Economy since 1840," in *The Reinterpretation of American Economic History*, ed. Robert W. Fogel and Stanley L. Engerman (New York: Harper & Row, 1971).

Gallman, Robert, "The Pace and Pattern of American Economic Growth," in *American Economic Growth*, ed. Lance Davis, Richard Easterlin and William Parker (New York: Harper & Row, 1972).

Garraty, John A., *The Great Depression: An Inquiry into the Causes, Course, and Consequences of the Worldwide Depression of the Nineteen-Thirties, as seen by Contemporaries in the Light of History* (New York: Harcourt, Brace, Jovanovich, 1986).

Garten, Jeffrey, *A Cold Peace: America, Japan, Germany and the Struggle for Supremacy* (New York: Times Books, 1992).

Gates, Paul W., *The Farmer's Age: Agriculture, 1815–1860* (New York: Holt, Rinehart, and Winston, 1960).

Gates, Paul W., *Agriculture and the Civil War* (New York: Alfred A. Knopf, 1965).

Gates, Paul, *History of Public Land Law Development* (Washington, DC: Government Printing Office, 1968).

Genovese, Eugene, *The Political Economy of Slavery: Studies in the Economy and Society of the Slave South* (New York: Pantheon, 1965).

Genovese, Eugene, *Roll, Jordan, Roll: The World the Slaves Made* (New York: Pantheon, 1974).

Gerster, Arpad, *Recollections of a New York Surgeon* (New York: Paul B. Hoeber, 1929).

Gervasi, Tom, *The Myth of Soviet Military Supremacy* (New York: Harper & Row, 1987.

Gilbert, Charles, *American Financing of World War I* (Westport, CT: Greenwood Press, 1970).

Gilpin, Robert, *The Political Economy of International Relations* (Princeton, NJ: Princeton, 1987).

Goldin, Claudia and Frank Lewis, "The Economic Cost of the American Civil War: Estimates and Implications," *Journal of Economic History*, **35** (1975) pp. 294–326.

Goldin, Claudia, *Urban Slavery in the American South, 1820–1860* (Chicago: University of Chicago Press, 1976).

Goldin, Claudia and Frank Lewis, "The Role of Exports in American Economic Growth during the Napoleonic Wars, 1793–1807," *Explorations in American History*, **17** (1980) pp. 291–308.

Goldstein, Judith, "Ideas, Institutions, and American Trade Policy," *International Organization*, **42**: 1 (Winter 1988) 179–217.

Good, H. G., *A History of American Education* (New York: Macmillan, 1956).

Goodrich, Carter, "The Revulsion against Internal Improvements," *Journal of Economic History*, **10** (1950) pp. 145–69.

Goodrich, Carter, *Government Promotion of American Canals and Railroads* (New York: Columbia University Press, 1960.

Goodrich, Carter, "Internal Improvements Reconsidered," *Journal of Economic History*, **30** (1970).

Gordon, Robert A., *Economic Instability and Growth: The American Record* (New York: Harper & Row, 1974).

Gordon, Robert J. and James A. Wilcox, "Monetary Interpretations: An Evaluation and Critique," in *The Great Depression Revisited*, ed. Karl Brunner (Boston: Martinus Nijhoff, 1980).

Gourevitch, Peter, "International Trade, Domestic Coalitions, and Liberty: Comparative Responses to the Crisis of 1873–1896," *Journal of Interdisciplinary Studies*, 8 (Autumn 1977).

Goven, Thomas P., *Nicholas Biddle, Nationalist and Public Banker, 1786–1844* (Chicago: University of Chicago Press, 1959).

Graham, Edward M. and Paul R. Krugman, *Foreign Direct Investment in the United States* (Washington, DC: Institute for International Economics, 1991).

Gray, Lewis C., *History of Agriculture in the Southern United States to 1860* (Washington, DC: Carnegie Institute, 1933).

Greene, Jack P., "An Uneasy Connection: An Analysis of the Preconditions of the American Revolution," in *Essays on the American Revolution*, ed. Stephen G. Kurtz and James H. Hutson (Chapel Hill: University of North Carolina Press, 1973).

Greenwald, Maurine Weiner, *Women, Work, and War: The Impact of World War I on Women Workers in the United States* (Westport, CT: Greenwood Press, 1980).

Greider, William "The Education of David Stockman," *Atlantic Monthly* (December 1981).

Greider, William, *The Education of David Stockman and other Americans* (New York: E. P. Dutton, 1986).

Greider, William, *Secrets of the Temple: How the Federal Reserve Runs the Country* (New York: Simon & Schuster, 1988).

Griffin, John I., *Strikes: A Study in Quantitative Economics* (New York: Columbia University Press, 1939).

Griffith, Robert K., *The Military–Industrial Complex: A Historical Perspective* (New York: Praeger, 1980).

Gross, Robert A., *The Minute Men and their World* (New York: Hill & Wang, 1976).

Gunderson, Gerald A., *A New Economic History of America* (New York: McGraw-Hill, 1976).

Haber, Samuel, "The Professions and Higher Education in America,' in *Higher Education and the Labor Market*, ed. Margaret Gordon (New York: McGraw-Hill, 1974).

Hacker, Louis, *The Triumph of American Capitalism* (New York: Columbia University Press, 1940).

Haites, Erik and Gary Walton, *Western River Transportation: The Era of Early Internal Development, 1810–1860* (Baltimore: Johns Hopkins University Press, 1975).

Hamilton, Alexander, "Report on a National Bank" (1790) in Jacob Cooke (ed.), *The Reports of Alexander Hamilton* (New York: Harper & Row, 1964).

Hamilton, Alexander, "Report on Manufactures, December 5, 1791," in Jacob Cooke (ed.), *The Reports of Alexander Hamilton* (New York: Harper & Row, 1964).

Hamilton, Alexander, "Report on the Subject of Manufactures" (1791), in H. C. Syrett (ed.), *The Papers of Alexander Hamilton*, vol. 10 (New

York: Columbia University Press, 1966).

Hammond, Bray, *Banks and Politics in America from the Revolution to the Civil War* (Princeton: Princeton University Press, 1957).

Handlin, Oscar and Mary F. Handlin, "Origins of the American Business Corporation," *Journal of Economic History*, **5** (1945).

Harley, C. Knick, "Transportation, the World Wheat Trade, and the Kuznets Cycle, 1850–1913," *Explorations in Economic History*, **17** (1980) pp. 224–25.

Harper, Lawrence, "Mercantilism and the American Revolution," *Canadian Historical Review*, **23** (1942) pp. 1–15.

Harper, Lawrence, "The Effect of the Navigation Acts on the Thirteen Colonies," in *The United States Economic History*, ed. Harry Scheiber (New York: Alfred A. Knopf, 1964) pp. 42–78.

Harris, Richard, *Trade, Industrial Policy, and International Competition* (Toronto: University of Toronto Press, 1985).

Hart, Jeffrey and Laura D'Andrea Tyson, "Responding to the Challenge of HDTV," *California Management Review*, **31**, no. 4 (Summer 1989) pp. 132–45.

Hartung, William D., *And Weapons for All: How America's Multi-billion Dollar Arms Trade Warps our Foreign Policy and Subverts Democracy at Home* (New York: HarperCollins, 1994).

Hartz, Louis, *The Liberal Tradition in America* (New York: Harcourt Brace, 1955).

Hawley, Ellis, "Herbert Hoover, the Commerce Secretariat, and the Vision of an 'Associative State,' 1921–1928," *Journal of American History*, **61** (1974) pp. 116–40.

Heckscher, Eli F., *Mercantilism*, 2 vols (London: Allen & Unwin, 1955).

Heclo, Hugh, "Industrial Policy and the Executive Capacities of Government," in Claude Barfield and William Schambra (eds), *The Politics of Industrial Policy* (Washington, DC: American Enterprise Institute for Public Policy Research, 1986).

Heilbroner, Robert, and Peter Bernstein, *The Debt and the Deficit: False Alarms/Real Possibilities* (New York: W. W. Norton, 1989).

Heller, Walter, *New Dimensions of Political Economy* (Cambridge, MA: Harvard University Press, 1966).

Henretta, James, *The Evolution of American Society, 1700–1815: An Interdisciplinary Analysis* (Lexington: D.C. Heath, 1973).

Hicks, John D., *The Populist Revolt* (Minneapolis: University of Minnesota Press, 1934).

Higgs, Robert, "Railroad Rates and the Populist Uprising," *Agricultural History*, **44** (1970).

Higgs, Robert, *The Transformation of the American Economy, 1865–1914* (New York: John Wiley, 1971).

Hill, Peter Jensen, *The Economic Impact of Immigration into the United States* (New York: Arno Press, 1975).

Hippel, Eric von, *The Sources of Innovation* (New York: Oxford University Press, 1988).

Hirschman, Albert, *National Power and the Structure of Foreign Trade* (Berkeley: University of California Press, 1945).

Hofstadter, Richard, *The American Political Tradition* (New York: Vintage, 1972).

Hogan, William T., *Economic History of the Iron and Steel Industry in the United States*, 5 vols (Lexington, MA: Lexington Books, 1971).

Holman, Mary, *The Political Economy of the Space Program* (Palo Alto, CA: Pacific Books, 1974).

Horlick, Gary, "The United States Anti-Dumping System," in John H. Jackson and Edwin A. Vermulst (eds), *Anti-Dumping Law and Practice: A Comparative Study* (Ann Arbor: University of Michigan Press, 1989).

Houndshell, David, *From the American System to Mass Production: The Development of Manufacturing in the United States, 1800–1932* (Baltimore: Johns Hopkins Press, 1984).

Howell, Thomas R. *et al.*, *Steel and the State: Government's Intervention and Steel's Structural Crisis* (Boulder, CO: Westview Press, 1988).

Howell, Thomas *et al.*, *The Microelectronics Race: The Impact of Government Policy on International Competition* (Boulder, CO: Westview Press, 1988).

Howell, Thomas, Brent L. Bartlett, and Warren Davis, *Creating Advantage: Semiconductors and Government Industrial Policy in the 1990s* (Santa Clara: Semiconductor Industry Association, 1992).

Hunter, Louis C., *Steamboats on the Western Rivers* (Cambridge: Harvard University Press, 1936).

Huntington, Samuel, *The Soldier and State: The Theory and Practice of Civil–Military Relations* (Cambridge, MA: The Belknap Press, 1957).

Hutchins, John G. B., *The American Maritime Industries and Public Policy, 1789–1914: An Economic History* (Cambridge, MA: Harvard University Press, 1941).

Ikenberry, G. John, "Conclusion: An Institutional Approach to American Foreign Economic Policy," *International Organization*, **42**: 1 (Winter 1988) pp. 219–43.

Inman, B. R. and Daniel F. Burton, "Technology and Competitiveness: The New Policy Frontier," *Foreign Affairs*, **69**: 2 (Spring 1990) pp. 116–34.

James, John A., *Money and Capital Markets in Postbellum America* (Princeton: Princeton University Press, 1978).

James, John A., "Public Debt Management Policy and Nineteenth Century American Economic Growth," *Explorations in Economic History*, **21** (1984) pp. 192–217.

Jameson, J. Franklin, *The American Revolution Considered as a Social Movement* (Princeton: Princeton University Press, 1967).

Janowitz, Morris, *The Professional Soldier: A Social and Political Portrait* (New York: Putnam, 1960).

Johnson, Chalmers, *Miti and the Japanese Miracle* (Stanford, CA: Stanford University, 1982).

Johnson, Chalmers (ed.), *The Industrial Policy Debate* (San Francisco, CA: Institute for Contemporary Studies, 1984).

Johnson, H. Thomas, "Postwar Optimism and the Rural Financial Crisis of the 1920's," *Explorations in Economic History*, 11 (1973).

Jones, Alice Hanson, *Wealth of a Nation To Be: The American Colonies on the Eve of the Revolution* (New York: Columbia University Press, 1980).

Jones, E. L., *Agriculture and the Industrial Revolution* (New York: John Wiley, 1974).

Jones, Lawrence A. and David Durand, *Mortgage Lending Experience in Agriculture* (Princeton: Princeton University Press, 1954).

Jordan, Winthrop D., *White over Black* (Chapel Hill: University of North Carolina Press, 1968).

Katz, Harold C., *The Decline of Competition in the Automobile Industry, 1920–1940* (New York: Arno Press, 1977).

Katz, Harold C., *Shifting Gears: Changing Labor Relations in the US Automobile Industry* (Cambridge, MA: MIT Press, 1985).

Katzenstein, Peter, "Conclusion: Domestic Structures and Strategies of Foreign Economic Policy," in Katzenstein (ed.), *Between Power and Plenty* (Madison: University of Wisconsin, 1978).

Katzenstein, Peter, *Small States in World Markets* (Ithaca, NY: Cornell University Press, 1986).

Keene, Karyn and Everett Ladd, "Government as Villain," *Government Executive*, 11 (January 1988) pp. 13–16.

Kennedy, Susan Estabrook, *The Banking Crisis of 1933* (Lexington: University Press of Kentucky, 1973).

Kennedy, William, *Rise and Fall of the Great Powers* (New York: Random House, 1987).

Keohane, Robert, "The Theory of Hegemonic Stability and Changes in International Economic Regimes," in Ole Hosti, R. Siverson, and Alexander George (eds), *Change in the International System* (Boulder, CO: Westview Press, 1980).

Keohane, Robert, "Reciprocity in International Relations," *International Organization*, 40 (Winter 1986) pp. 1–28.

Keohane, Robert and Joseph Nye, *Power and Interdependence* (Boston, MA: Little, Brown, 1977).

Keohane, Robert, and Joseph Nye, "Power and Interdependence Revisited," *International Organization*, 41: 4 (Autumn 1987) pp. 737–8.

Kerridge, Eric, *The Agricultural Revolution* (London: Allen & Unwin, 1967).

Key, V. O., *Public Opinion and American Democracy* (New York: Alfred A. Knopf, 1961).

Keynes, John Maynard, *The General Theory of Employment, Interest, and Money* (New York: Harcourt, Brace, 1936).

Kimmel, Lewis H., *Federal Budget and Fiscal Policy, 1789–1958* (Washington, D.C.: Brookings Institute, 1959).

Kindleberger, Charles (ed.), *The International Corporation* (Cambridge, MA: MIT Press, 1970).

Kindleberger, Charles P., *The World in Depression* (London: Penguin Books, 1973).

Kirkland, Edward C., *Industry Comes of Age: Business, Labor, and Public Policy* (New York: Holt, Rinehart & Winston, 1961).

Koistinin, Paul A. C. "The 'Industrial–Military Complex' in Historical Perspective: World War I," *Business History Review*, 41 (1967).

Krasner, Stephen, *Defending the National Interest* (Princeton, NJ: Princeton University, 1978).

Krasner, Stephen, *International Regimes* (Ithaca, NY: Cornell University Press, 1982).

Krueger, Anne, "Theory and Practice of Commercial Policy, 1945–1990," *NBER Working Papers 3569* (Cambridge, MA: National Bureau of Economic Research, 1991).

Krugman, Paul, "The US Response to Foreign Industrial Targeting," *Brookings Papers on Economic Activity*, **15**: 1 (1984).

Krugman, Paul (ed.), *Strategic Trade Policy and the New International Economics* (Cambridge, MA: MIT Press, 1986).

Krugman, Paul, *The Age of Diminished Expectations: US Economic Policy in the 1990* (Cambridge, MA: MIT Press, 1990).

Kuttner, Robert, "Economists Really Should Get Out More Often," *Business Week*, April 24, 1989.

Kuznets, Simon, *Shares of Upper Income Groups in Income and Saving* (New York: National Bureau of Economic Research, 1953).

Ladd, Everett Carl, "The Polls: Taxing and Spending," *Public Opinion Quarterly*, **43** (Spring 1979).

Lafeber, Walter, *The New Empire: American Expansion, 1860–1898* (Ithaca, NY: Cornell University Press, 1963).

Lake, David A., "International Economic Structures and American Foreign Economic Policy, 1887–1934," *World Politics*, **28** (April 1976) pp. 317–43.

Lake, David A., "The State and American Trade Strategy in the Pre-Hegemonic Era," *International Organization*, **42**: 1 (Winter 1988) pp. 51, 52.

Landes, David S., *The Unbound Prometheus* (Cambridge: Cambridge University Press, 1969).

Lauderbaugh, Richard A., *American Steel Makers and the Coming of the Second World War* (Ann Arbor: University of Michigan Research Press, 1980).

Lave, Judith and Lester, *The Hospital Construction Act: An Evaluation of the Hill-Burton Program, 1948–1973* (Washington, DC: American Enterprise Institute, 1974).

Laverge, Real P., *The Political Economy of US Tariffs* (New York: Academic Press, 1983).

Lebergott, Stanley, *Manpower in Economic Growth: The American Record since 1800* (New York: McGraw-Hill, 1964).

Lebergott, Stanley, "Labor Force and Employment, 1800–1960," in *Output, Employment, and Productivity in the United States After 1800*, ed. Dorothy Bradley, National Bureau of Economic Research, vol. 30: *Studies in Income and Wealth* (New York: Columbia University Press, 1966).

Lebergott, Stanley, "The Return to US Imperialism, 1890–1929," *Journal of Economic History*, **32** (1972).

Lebergott, Stanley, *The Americans* (New York: W. W. Norton, 1984).

Lee, Susan Previant, *The Westward Movement of the Cotton Economy, 1840–1860: Perceived Interests and Economic Realities* (New York: Arno Press, 1977).

Lee, Susan, "Antebellum Southern Land Expansion: A Second View," *Agricultural History*, **52** (1978) pp. 488–502.

Lester, Richard A., *Monetary Experiments: Early American and Recent Scandanavian* (New York: Augustus Kelly, 1939).

Lester, Richard, "Currency Issues to Overcome Depression in Delaware, New Jersey, New York, and Maryland, 1715–1737," *Journal of Political Economy*, 47 (1939).

Letwin, William, *Law and Economic Policy in America* (New York: Random House, 1965).

Letwin, William (ed.), *A Documentary History of American Economic Policy since 1789* (New York: W. W. Norton, 1972).

Leuchtenburg, William E., *The Perils of Prosperity* (Chicago: University of Chicago Press, 1959).

Leuchtenburg, William E., *Franklin D. Roosevelt and the New Deal, 1932–1940* (New York: Harper & Row, 1963).

Leuchtenberg, William E., "The New Deal and the Analogue of War," in *Change and Continuity in Twentieth Century America*, ed. John Braeman *et al.* (Athens: Ohio University Press, 1966).

Levin, Richard, "The Semiconductor Industry," in Richard R. Nelson (ed.), *Government and Technical Progress: a Cross-Industry Analysis* (New York: Pergamon, 1982).

Levinson, Phyllis *et al.*, *The Federal Entrepreneur: The Nation's Implicit Industrial Policy* (Washington, DC: The Urban Institute, 1982).

Levit, Katherine R. and Cathy A. Cowan, "Businesses, Households, and Governments: Health Care Costs, 1990," *Health Care Financing Review*, **13**: 2 (1991).

Lindert, Peter, "Long-Run Trends in American Farmland Values," *Agricultural History*, **62** (1988) pp. 45–86.

Lipcap, Gary P., *The Evolution of Private Mineral Rights: Nevada's Comstock Lode* (New York: Arno Press, 1978).

Lippman, Walter, *The Phantom Public* (New York: Macmillan, 1925).

Lipsey, Robert E., "Foreign Trade," in *American Economic Growth*, ed. Lance Davis *et al.* (New York: Harper & Row, 1972), 898–9.

List, Freidrich, *The National System of Political Economy* (London: Longmans, Green, 1885).

Littleton, A. C. and Basil C. Yamcy (eds), *Studies in the History of Accounting* (Homewood, Ill.: Richard D. Irwin, 1956).

Lively, Robert A., "The American System: A Review Article," *Business History Review*, **29** (1955).

Lockwood, William, *The Economic Development of Japan* (Princeton: Princeton University Press, 1954).

Long, Clarence B., *Wages and Earnings in the United States, 1860–90* (Princeton: Princeton University Press, 1960).

Loory, Stuart H., *Defeated: Inside America's Military Machine* (New York: Random House, 1973).

Lorant, John Herman, *The Role of Capital Improving Innovations in American Manufacturing During the 1920* (New York: Arno Press, 1975).

Lowi, Theodore, *The End of Liberalism* (New York: W. W. Norton, 1969).

Lubove, Roy, *The Struggle for Social Security, 1900–1935* (Cambridge, MA: Harvard University Press, 1968).

MacKuen, Michael B., Robert S. Erikson and James A. Stimson, "Peasants or Bankers," *American Political Science Review*, **86** (September 1992) pp. 597–611.

Main, Jackson Turner, *The Social Structure of Revolutionary America* (Princeton: Princeton University Press, 1965).

Manners, Gerald, *The Changing World Market for Iron Ore, 1950–1980* (Baltimore: Johns Hopkins Press, 1971).

Mansfield, Edwin, *Industrial Research and Technological Innovation* (New York: W.W. Norton, 1968).

March, James G. and Johan P. Olsen, "The New Institutionalism: Organizational Factors in Political Life," *American Political Science Review*, **78** (September 1984).

Markus, Gregory B., "The Impact of Personal and National Economic Conditions on Presidential Voting, 1956–1988," *American Journal of Political Science*, **36** (1992) pp. 829–34.

Markusen, Ann *et al.*, *The Rise of the Gunbelt: The Military Remapping of Industrial America* (New York: Oxford University Press, 1991).

Mathias, Peter, *The First Industrial Nation* (New York: Charles Scribner's Sons, 1969).

Matsushita, Mitsuo and Lawrence Repeta, "Restricting the Supply of Japanese Automobiles: Sovereign Collusion?," *Case Western Reserve Journal of International Law*, **14** (Winter 1982).

Mayhew, Anne, "A Reappraisal of the Causes of Farm Protest in the United States, 1879–1900," *Journal of Economic History*, **32** (1972) pp. 464–75.

McClelland, Peter, "The Cost to America of British Imperial Policy," *American Economic Review*, **59** (1969) pp. 370–81.

McClelland, Peter, "The New Economic History and the Burdens of the Navigation Acts: A Comment," *Economic History Review*, **26** (1973) pp. 679–86.

McCurdy, Charles M., "American Law and the Marketing Structure of the Large Corporation, 1875–1890," *Journal of Economic History*, **38** (1978) pp. 631–49.

McDonald, Forrest, *We the People: The Economic Origins of the Constitution* (Chicago: University of Chicago Press, 1958).

McCraw, Thomas, "Mercantilism and the Market: Antecedents of American Industrial Policy," in Claude Barfield and William Schambra (eds), *The Politics of Industrial Policy* (Washington, DC: American Enterprise Institute, 1986).

McFarland, Andrew, "Public Interest Lobbies vs. Minority Faction," in Cigler and Loomis (eds), *Interest Group Politics* (Washington, DC: Congressional Quarterly Press, 1983).

McFetridge, Donald, "The Economics of Industrial Policy," in D. G. McFetridge (ed.), *Canadian Industrial Policy in Action* (Toronto: University of Toronto Press, 1985).

McKenzie, Richard B., "National Industrial Policy: An Overview of the Debate," Heritage Foundation, *Backgrounder*, no. 275 (July 12, 1983).

McKeown, Timothy, "Firms and Tariff Regime Change: Explaining the Demand for Protection," *World Politics*, **36** (January 1984) pp. 215–33.

McQuire, Robert and Robert L. Ohsfeldt, "Economic Interests and the American Constitution: A Quantitative Rehabilitation of Charles A. Beard," *Journal of Economic History*, **44** (1984) pp. 509–20.

McQuire, Robert and Robert L. Ohsfeldt, "An Economic Model of Voting Behavior over Specific Issues at the Constitutional Convention of 1787," *Journal of Economic History*, **46** (1986) pp. 79–112.

Millis, Walter, *Arms and Men: A Study in American Military History* (New York: Putnam, 1956).

Mills, C. Wright, *The Power Elite* (New York: Oxford University Press, 1956).

Milner, Helen V. and David B. Yoffie, "Between Free Trade and Protectionism: Strategic Trade Policy and a Theory of Corporate Trade Demands," *International Organization*, **43**: 2 (Spring 1989), pp. 239–73.

Mingos, Harry, "Birth of an Industry," in G. R. Simonson (ed.), *The History of the American Aircraft Industry* (Cambridge: MIT Press, 1968) pp. 43–4.

Monroe, Paul, *The Founding of the American Public School System: A History of Education in the United States*, vol. 1 (New York: Macmillan, 1940).

Morgan, Edmund, *Birth of the Republic, 1763–1789* (Chicago: University of Chicago Press, 1977).

Morris, Richard, *Government and Labor in Early America* (New York: Columbia University Press, 1946).

Mowery, David, and Nathan Rosenberg, "The Commercial Aircraft Industry," in Richard Nelson (ed.), *Government and Technical Progress: A Cross-Industry Analysis* (New York: Pergamon Press, 1982) pp. 101–61

Mowery, David, and Nathan Rosenberg, "New Developments in US Technology Policy: Implications of Competitiveness and International Trade Policy," *California Management Review*, **32**: no. 1 (Fall 1989) pp. 107–24.

Myers, Margaret, *A Financial History of the United States* (New York: Columbia University Press, 1970).

Nash, Gary B., *The Urban Crucible: Social Change, Political Consciousness, and the Origin of the American Revolution* (Cambridge, MA: Harvard University Press, 1979).

National Advisory Committee on Semiconductors, *Toward a National Semiconductor Strategy: Regaining Markets in High-Volume Electronics* (Washington, DC: National Advisory Committee on Electronics, 1991).

Neal, Larry, "Interpreting Power and Profit in Economic History: A Case Study of the Seven Years' War," *Journal of Economic History*, **37** (1977) pp. 20–35.

Nelson, Daniel, *Managers and Workers: Origins of the New Factory System in the United States, 1880–1920* (Madison: University of Wisconsin Press, 1975).

Nelson, Donald M., *Arsenal of Democracy* (New York: Harcourt, Brace, 1946).

Nelson, Ralph, *Merger Movements in American Industry, 1895–1956* (National Bureau of Economic Research, General Series, no. 66 (Princeton: Princeton University Press, 1959).

Nelson, Richard, "U.S. Technological Leadership: Where Did It Come from and Where Did It Go?", *Research Policy*, **19**, pp. 117–32.

Nester, William, *Japanese Industrial Targeting: The Neomercantilist Path to Economic Superpower* (New York: St Martin's Press, 1991).

Nester, William, *American Power, The New World Order, and the Japanese Challenge* (New York: St Martin's Press, 1993).

Nester, William R., *International Relations: Geopolitical and Geoeconomic Continuities and Changes* (New York: HarperCollins, 1995).

Neustadt, Richard, *Presidential Power* (New York: John Wiley, 1960).

Nettels, Curtis P., *The Emergence of a National Economy, 1775–1815* (New York: Holt, Rinehart & Winston, 1962).

Nettels, Curtis P., *The Roots of American Civilization* (New York: Appleton, Century, Crofts, 1963).

Nocera, Joseph, *A Piece of the Action: How the Middle Class Joined the Money Class* (New York: Simon and Schuster, 1994).

North, Douglass C., "The United States Balance of Payments, 1790–1860," in National Bureau of Economic Research, *Trends in the American Economy in the 19th Century*, Studies in Income and Wealth, vol. 24 (Princeton: Princeton University Press, 1960) pp. 573–627.

North, Douglass C., *The Economic Growth of the United States, 1790 to 1860* (Englewood Cliffs, NJ: Prentice Hall, 1961).

North, Douglass C. and Robert Paul Thomas, *The Rise of the Western World: A New Economic History* (Cambridge: Cambridge University Press, 1973).

Norton, Hugh S., *The Employment Act and the Council of Economic Advisors, 1946–1976* (Columbia, SC: University of South Carolina Press, 1977).

Odell, John, *US International Monetary Policy: Markets, Power, and Ideas as Sources of Change* (Princeton, NJ: Princeton University Press, 1982).

Office of Technology Assessment, *Competing Economies: America, Europe, and the Pacific Rim* (Washington, DC: GPO, October 1991).

Office of the US Trade Representative, *Procedures to Introduce Supercomputers* (Washington, DC: GPO, 1990).

Oleson, Alexandra and John Voss (ed.), *The Organization of Knowledge in the United States* (Baltimore: Johns Hopkins University Press, 1979).

Olson, James, *Herbert Hoover and the Reconstruction Finance Corporation, 1931–33* (Ames: University of Iowa Press, 1977).

Olson, Mancur, "Supply-Side Economics, Industrial Policy, and Rational Ignorance," in Claude E. Barfield and William A. Schambra (eds), *The Politics of Industrial Policy* (Washington, DC: American Enterprise Institute, 1986).

Palmer, John L. and Isabel V. Sawhill (eds), *The Reagan Experiment: An Examination of Economic and Social Policies under the Reagan Administration* (Washington, DC: Urban Institute, 1982).

Parker, William M., "Slavery and Southern Economic Development: An Hypothesis and Some Evidence," *Agricultural History*, **44** (1970) pp. 115–25.

Parmet, Herbert S., *Eisenhower and the American Crusades* (New York: Macmillan, 1972).

Parry, J. H., "Colonial Development and International Rivalries Outside Europe," in *The New Cambridge Modern History*.

Pearce, Joan and John Sutton, *Protection and Industrial Policy in Europe* (London: Routledge & Kegan Paul, 1986).

Pelzer, Louis, *The Cattlemen's Frontier: A Record of the Trans-Mississippi Cattle Industry from Open Times to Pooling Companies, 1850–1890* (New York: Russell & Russell, 1969).

Pennick, James *et al.*, *The Politics of American Science: 1939 to the Present* (Cambridge, MA: MIT Press, 1972).

Peretz, Paul, "Economic Policy in the 1980s," in *The Politics of American Economic Policy Making*, ed. Peretz (Armonk, NY: M.E. Sharpe, 1986).

Perkins, Edwin J., *The Economy of Colonial America* (New York: Columbia University Press, 1980).

Peters, B. Guy, *American Public Policy: Promise and Performance* (Chatham, NJ: Chatham House, 1993).

Phillips, Robert Kevin, *Boiling Point: Republicans, Democrats, and the Decline of the Middle-Class* (New York: Random House, 1993).

Pincus, Jonathan, *Pressure Groups and Politics in Antebellum Tariffs* (New York: Columbia University Press, 1977).

Poggi, Gianfranco, *The Development of the Modern State* (Stanford, CA: Stanford University Press, 1978).

Polenberg, Richard, *War and Society: The United States, 1941–1945* (Philadelphia: J. B. Lippincott, 1972).

Pollard, Robert A., *European Security and the Origins of the Cold War, 1945–1950* (New York: Columbia University Press, 1985).

Pope, Daniel, *The Making of Modern Advertizing* (New York: Basic Books, 1983).

Porter, James, "The Growth of Population in America, 1700–1860," in *Population in History*, ed. D. V. Glass and D. E. C. Eversley (London: Edward Arnold, 1965).

Porter, Michael, "The Structure within Industries and Companies' Performance," *Review of Economics and Statistics*, **61** (May 1979).

Porter, Michael, *The Competitive Advantage of Nations* (New York: Free Press, 1990).

Preliminary Report of the Special Committee on Investigation of the Munitions Industry, *Senate Report*, 74 Congress, 1 Session, no. 944, Part I (Serial 9881).

Prestowitz, Clyde, Alan Tonelson, and Robert Jerome, "The Last Gasp of GATTism," *Harvard Business Review*, March–April 1991.

Price, Jacob M., "Economic Function and the Growth of American Port Towns in the 18th Century," *Perspectives in American History*, **8** (1974).

Primack, Martin, *Farm Formed Capital in Agriculture, 1850 to 1910* (New York: Arno Press, 1977).

Pursell, Carroll W. (ed.), *The Military–Industrial Complex* (New York: Harper & Row, 1972).

Puth, Robert C., *American Economic History* (Chicago: Dryden Press, 1982).

Pye, Lucian, *Politics, Personality, and Nation Building* (New Haven, CT: Yale University Press, 1962).

Pye, Lucian (ed.), *Political Culture and Political Development* (Princeton: Princeton University Press, 1965).

Rae, John, *The American Automobile Industry* (Boston, MA: Twyane Publishers, 1984).

Ransom, Roger, "British Policy and Colonial Growth: Some Implications of the Burden from the Navigation Acts," *Journal of Economic History*, **28** (1968) pp. 427–35.

Ransom, Roger and Richard Sutch, *One Kind of Freedom: The Economic*

Consequences of Emancipation (Cambridge: Cambridge University Press, 1977).

Ransom, Roger, *Conflict and Compromise: The Political Economy of Slavery, Emancipation, and the American Civil War* (New York: Cambridge University Press, 1989).

Rastatter, Edward S., "Nineteenth-Century Public Land Policy: The Case for the Speculator," in *Essays in Nineteenth-Century Economic History: The Old Northwest*, ed. David C. Klingaman and Richard K. Vedder (Athens: Ohio University Press, 1975).

Rees, Albert, *Real Wages in Manufacturing, 1890–1914* (Princeton: Princeton University Press, 1961).

Reich, Robert, "Making Industrial Policy," *Foreign Affairs*, Spring 1982.

Reich, Robert B., *The Next American Frontier* (New York: Times Books, 1983).

Relman, Arnold S., "The New Medical–Industrial Complex," *New England Journal of Medicine*, **303** (October 23, 1980) pp. 963–70.

Remini, Robert, *Andrew Jackson and the Bank War* (New York: W. W. Norton, 1967).

Renn, Steven, "The Structure and Financing of the Health Care Delivery System of the 1980s," in Carl J. Schramm (ed.), *Health Care and its Costs: Can the US Afford Adequate Health Care?* (New York: W. W. Norton, 1987).

"Report and Recommendations of the Senate Republican Task Force on Industrial Competitiveness and International Trade," March 16, 1983, 1.

Rettig, Richard A., *Cancer Crusade: The Story of the National Cancer Act of 1971* (Princeton: Princeton University Press, 1977).

Rice, John R., *HDTV: The Politics, Policies, and Economics of Tomorrow's Television* (New York: Union Square Press, 1990).

Richardson, David J., "The Political Economy of Strategic Trade Policy," *International Organization*, **44** (Winter 1990) pp. 107–35.

Riis, Jacob, *How the Other Half Lives* (New York: Scribner's, 1890).

Ripley, William Z., *Railroads, Finance, and Organization* (New York: Longman, Green, 1915).

Roberts, Paul Craig, *The Supply-Side Revolution: An Insider's Account of Policymaking in Washington* (Cambridge, MA: Harvard University Press, 1984).

Rockman, Bert, *The Leadership Question: The Presidency and the American System* (New York: Praeger, 1984).

Rockoff, Hugh, "The Free Banking Era: A Reexamination," *Journal of Money, Credit, and Banking*, **6**: 2 (May 1974).

Rodman, Paul, *Mining Frontiers of the Far West: 1848–1880* (New York: Holt, Rinehart & Winston, 1963).

Rogin, Leo, *The Introduction of Farm Machinery and its Relation to the Productivity of Labor in the Agriculture of the United States during the Nineteenth Century* (Berkeley: University of California Press, 1931).

Rohrlich, Paul Egon, "Economic Culture and Foreign Policy: the Cognitive Analysis of Economic Policy Making," *International Organization*, **41**: I (Winter 1987) pp. 61–91.

Rollins, George W., *The Struggle of the Cattlemen, Sheepman, and Settler for Control of Lands in Wyoming* (New York: Arno Press, 1979).

Romasco, Albert U., *The Poverty of Abundance: Hoover, the Nation, the Depression* (New York: Oxford University Press, 1965).

Romasco, Albert U., "Herbert Hoover's Policies for Dealing with the Great Depression: The End of the Old Order or the Beginning of the New?," in *The Hoover Presidency: A Reappraisal*, ed. Martin L. Fausol and George T. Mazuzam (Albany: State University of New York Press, 1974).

Romasco, Albert U., *The Politics of Recovery: Roosevelt's New Deal* (New York: Oxford University Press, 1983).

Rose, Willie Lee (ed.), *A Documentary History of Slavery in North America* (New York: Oxford University Press, 1976).

Rosen, Steven (ed.), *Testing the Theory of the Military–Industrial Complex* (Lexington, MA: D.C. Heath, 1973).

Rosenberg, Nathan, "Technological Change in the Machine Tool Industry, 1840–1910," *Journal of Economic History*, **23** (1963).

Rosenberg, Nathan, *The American System of Manufactures* (Edinburgh: Edinburgh University Press, 1969).

Rosenberg, Nathan, *Technology and American Economic Growth* (New York: Harper & Row, 1972).

Rosenberg, Nathan, "Selection and Adaptation in the Transfer of Technology: Steam and Iron in America, 1800–1870," in *Perspectives on Technology*, ed. Nathan Rosenberg (Cambridge: Cambridge University Press, 1976).

Rosenberg, Nathan, "Innovative Responses to Materials Shortages," in *Perspectives on Technology*, ed. Nathan Rosenberg (Cambridge: Cambridge University Press, 1976).

Rosenbloom, Richard and Michael Cusamano, "Technological Pioneering and Competitive Advantage: The Birth of the VCR Industry," *California Management Review*, **29**: 4 (Summer 1987) pp. 51–76.

Rossiter, Clinton, *The American Presidency* (New York: Harcourt, Brace, Jovanovich, 1984).

Rostow, W. W., *The Stages of Economic Growth: A Non-Communist Manifesto* (Cambridge: Cambridge University Press, 1960).

Russett, Bruce, "The Mysterious Case of Vanishing Hegemony; Or Is Mark Twain Really Dead?," *International Organization*, **39** (Spring 1985).

Russell, Robert W., "Congress and the Proposed Industrial Policy Structures," in Claude Barfield and William Schambra (eds), *The Politics of Industrial Policy* (Washington, DC: American Enterprise Institute, 1986).

Salisbury, Harrison E., *A Time of Change* (New York: Harpers & Row, 1988).

Samuelson, Paul, and Everett E. Hagen, *After the War, 1918–1920: Military and Economic Demobilization of the United States, its Effect on Employment and Income* (Washington, DC: National Resources Planning Board, 1943).

Sandholtz, Wayne, Michael Borrus, and John Zysman (eds), *The Highest Stakes: The Economic Foundations of the Next Security System* (London: Oxford University Press, 1992).

Sarkesian, Sam C. (ed.), *The Military–Industrial Complex: a Reassessment* (Beverly Hills, CA: Sage, 1972).

Saunders, C. T. (ed.), *Industrial Policies and Structural Change* (London: Macmillan, 1987).

Savelle, Max and Robert Middlekauff, *A History of Colonial America* (New York: Holt, Rinehart & Winston, 1964).

Schattschneider, E. E., *Politics, Pressures, and the Tariff* (New York: Prentice Hall, 1935).

Scheiber, George, Jean-Pierre Poullier, and Leslie Greenwald, "Health Care Systems in Twenty-four Countries," *Health Affairs*, **10**: 3 (1991).

Scheiber, Harry N., *Ohio Canal Era: A Case Study of Government and the Economy, 1821–1861* (Athens: Ohio University Press, 1969),

Scheurman, William, *The Steel Crisis: The Economics and Politics of a Declining Industry* (Westport, CT: Greenwood Press, 1986).

Schiltz, Michael, *Public Attitudes Toward a Social Security, 1935–1965* (Washington, DC: US Government Printing Office, 1970).

Schlosstein, Barry Stephen, *Trade War: Greed, Power, and Industrial Policy on Opposite Sides of the Pacific* (New York: Congdon and Weed, 1984).

Scholten, Catherine M., "On the Importance of the Obstetrick Art: Changing Customs of Childbirth in America, 1760 to 1825," *William and Mary Quarterly* (Summer 1977) pp. 427–45.

Schumacher, Max G., *The Northern Farmer and his Markets during the Late Colonial Period* (New York: Arno Press, 1975).

Schur, Leon M., "The Second Bank of the United States and the Inflation after the War of 1812," *Journal of Political Economy*, **68** (1960) pp. 119–120.

Schultze, Charles L., "Industrial Policy: A Dissent," *Brookings Review*, **2**: 1 (Fall 1983) pp. 3–12.

Schultze, Charles L., "Cars, Quotas, and Inflation," *Brookings Bulletin*, **17**: 3 (1983) pp. 3–4.

Seagal, Harvey, "Canals and Economic Development," in *Canals and American Economic Development*, ed. Carter Goodrich (New York: Columbia University Press, 1961) pp. 216–48.

Seager, Henry R. and Charles A. Gulick, *Trust and Corporation Problems* (New York: Harper, 1929).

Sellers, Leilla, *Charleston Business on the Eve of the American Revolution* (Chapel Hill: University of North Carolina Press, 1934).

Sellers, James, "The Economic Incidence of the Civil War on the South," in *The Economic Impact of the Civil War*, ed. Ralph Andreano (Cambridge, MA: Shenkman, 1962) pp. 57–62.

Shannon, Fred, *The Farmer's Last Frontier: Agriculture, 1860–1897* (New York: Farrar & Rinehart, 1945).

Shaw, Ronald E., *Erie Water West: A History of the Erie Canal, 1792–1854* (Lexington: University of Kentucky Press, 1966).

Shear, Jeff, *The Keys to the Kingdom: The FSX Deal and the Selling of America's Future* (New York: Doubleday, 1994).

Shepherd, James T. and Gary M. Walton, *Shipping, Maritime Trade, and the Economic Development of Colonial America* (Cambridge: Cambridge University Press, 1972).

Shryock, Richard, *American Medical Research* (New York: Commonwealth Fund, 1947).

Shuman, Howard, *Politics and the Budget: The Struggle Between the President and the Congress* (Englewood Cliffs, NJ: Prentice-Hall, 1992).

Smaller War Plants Corp., "Economic Concentration and World War II," 79 Congress, 2 session, S. Doc. 206 (1946) pp. 21, 54.

Smith, Adam, *The Wealth of Nations* (New York: Modern Library, 1937).

Smith, Abbott Emerson, *Colonists in Bondage: White Servitude and Convict Labor in America, 1607–1776* (Chapel Hill: University of North Carolina Press, 1968).

Smith, R. Elberton, *The Army and Economic Mobilization* (Washington, DC: Government Printing Office, 1959).

Smith, J. Russell, *North America: Its People and the Resources, Development, and Prospects of the Continent as an Agricultural, Individual, and Commercial Area* (New York: Harcourt, Brace, 1925).

Smith, Walter B., *Economic Aspects of the Second Bank of the United States* (Cambridge, MA: Harvard University Press, 1953).

Snidal, Duncan, "The Limits of Hegemonic Stability Theory," *International Organization*, **39** (Autumn 1985) pp. 579–614.

Somers, Herman and Anne, *Doctors, Patients, and Health Insurance* (Washington, DC: Brookings Institute, 1961).

Spar, Deborah and Ray Vernon, *Beyond Globalism: Remaking American Foreign Economic Policy* (New York: Free Press, 1989).

Spencer, Linda, *Foreign Investment in the United States: Unencumbered Access* (Washington, DC: Economic Strategy Institute, 1991).

Spencer, Linda, *High Technology Acquisitions: Summary Charts, October 1988– April 1992* (Washington, DC: Economic Strategy Institute, 1992).

Sonnefeld, Sally, *et al.*, "Projections of National Health Expenditures through the Year 2000," *Health Care Financing Review*, **13**: 1 (1991).

Soule, George, *The Prosperity Decade, 1917–1929* (New York: Holt, Rinehart, and Winston, 1947).

Speakes, Larry, with Robert Pack, *Speaking Out* (New York: Scribners & Sons, 1988).

Stampp, Kenneth, *The Peculiar Institution* (New York: Alfred A. Knopf, 1956).

Starr, Paul, *The Social Transformation of American Medicine* (New York: Basic Books, 1982).

Starr, Paul, *The Logic of Health Care Reform: Why and How the President's Plan Will Work* (New York: Whittle Books, 1994).

Stegemann, Klaus, "Policy Rivalry among Industrial States: What Can We Learn from Models of Strategic Trade Policy," *International Organization*, **43**: 1 (Winter 1989).

Stein, Herbert, *The Fiscal Revolution in America* (Chicago: University of Chicago Press, 1969).

Stein, Herbert, *Presidential Economics: The Making of Economic Policy from Roosevelt to Reagan and Beyond* (New York: Simon & Schuster, 1984).

Stockfish, J. A., *Plowshares into Swords: Managing the Defense Establishment* (New York: Mason and Lipscomb, 1973).

Stover, John F., *American Railroads* (Chicago: University of Chicago Press, 1961).

Strassmann, W. Paul, *Risk and Technological Innovation: American Manu-facturing Methods during the Nineteenth Century* (Ithaca, NY: Cornell University, 1959).

Strauss, Frederick and Louis H. Bean, *Gross Farm Income and Indices of Farm Production and Prices in the United States, 1869–1937*, US Department of Agriculture, Technical Bulletin no. 703 (Washington, DC: Government Printing Office, 1940).

Strickland, Stephen, *Politics, Science, and Dread Disease: A Short History of United States Medical Research Policy* (Cambridge, MA: Harvard University Press, 1972).

Stubbing, Richard and Richard Mendel, "How to Save $50 Billion a Year," *Atlantic Monthly*, June 1989.

Studenski, Paul, and Herman Krooss, *Financial History of the United States* (New York: McGraw-Hill, 1965).

Summers, Colonel Harry, "A Bankrupt Military Strategy: Our Military Assets No Longer Cover our Foreign Policy Liabilities," *Atlantic Monthly*, June 1989.

Swank, James S., *The Industrial Policies of Great Britain and the United States* (Philadelphia: American Iron and Steel Foundation, 1876).

Swisher, Carl B., *Roger B. Taney* (Hamden, CT: Archon Books, 1935).

Talbott, Strobe, "Rethinking the Red Menance," *Time*, January 1, 1990.

Taussig, F. W. (ed.), *State Papers and Speeches on the Tariff* (Cambridge, MA: Harvard University Press, 1892).

Taylor, George Rogers, *The Transportation Revolution, 1815–1860* (New York: Western Holt, Rinehart, & Winston, 1951).

Taylor, George Rogers (ed.), *The Early Development of the American Cotton Textile Industry* (New York: Harper & Row, 1969).

Taylor, Roger and Bonnie Newton, "Can Managed Care Reduce Employers' Retiree Medical Liability," *Benefits Quarterly*, 7: 4 (1991).

Temin, Peter, *Iron and Steel in Nineteenth-Century America* (Cambridge, MA: MIT Press, 1964).

Thomas, Keith, *Religion and the Decline of Magic* (New York: Scribner, 1971).

Thomas, Robert, "A Quantitative Approach to the Study of the Effects of British Imperial Policy on Colonial Welfare: Some Preliminary Findings," *Journal of Economic History*, 25 (1965) pp. 615–38.

Thomas, Robert, *An Analysis of the Pattern of Growth in the Automobile Industry* (New York: Ayer, 1977).

Thorelli, Hans B., *The Federal Antitrust Policy: Origination of an American Tradition* (Baltimore: Johns Hopkins Press, 1955).

Thurow, Lester, *Head to Head: The Coming Economic Battle among Japan, Europe, and America* (New York: Morrow, 1992).

Tiffany, Paul A., *The Decline of American Steel: How Management, Labor, and Government Went Wrong* (New York: Oxford University Press, 1988).

Timberlake, Richard H., *The Origins of Central Banking in the United States* (Cambridge, MA: Harvard University Press, 1978).

Tolchin, Martin and Susan, *Selling our Security: The Erosion of America's Assets* (New York: Alfred A. Knopf, 1992).

Toynbee, Arnold, *The Industrial Revolution* (Boston, MA: Beacon Press, 1956).

Trescott, Paul B., *Financing American Enterprise: The Story of Commercial Banking* (New York: Harper & Row, 1963).

Truman, David, *The Government Process: Political Interests and Public Opinion* (New York: Alfred A. Knopf, 1951).

Tucker, Robert W. and David C. Hendrickson, "Thomas Jefferson and American Foreign Policy," *Foreign Affairs*, **69**: 2 (Spring 1990).

Tyson, Laura D'Andrea, "They are not US: Why American Ownership Still Matters," *The American Prospect*, **4** (Winter 1991) pp. 37–48.

Tyson, Laura D'Andrea, *Who's Bashing Whom? Trade Conflict in High-Technology Industries* (Washington, DC: Institute for International Economics, 1992).

Ullman, Harlan, *In Irons: US Military Might in the New Century* (Washington, DC: National Defense University Press, 1995).

US Bureau of the Census, *Historical Statistics of the United States, Colonial Times to 1970* (Washington, DC: Department of Commerce, 1975).

US Congress, House Energy and Commerce Committee, Report on HR 4360, reprinted as *House Report* 98–697, part 2, 23.

US Congress, JEC, 88th Congress, 1st Session, Hearings, *Steel Prices, Unit Costs, Profits, and Foreign Competition* (Washington, DC: GPO, 1963).

US Federal Trade Commission, *Report on the Motor Vehicle Industry* (Washington, DC: GPO, 1939).

US General Accounting Office, National Security and International Affairs Division, *US Business Access to Certain Foreign State-of-the-Art Technology* (Washington, DC: US General Accounting Office, September 1991).

US International Trade Commission, *Foreign Industrial Targeting and its Effects on US Industries: Phase I, Japan* (Washington, DC: USITC Publication 1437, 1983).

US Steel Corporation, *Steel and Inflation: Fact vs. Fiction* (New York: US Steel Corporation, 1958).

Vatter, Harold G., *The US Economy in World War II* (New York: Columbia University Press, 1985).

Viner, Jacob, *Dumping: A Problem in International Trade* (Chicago: University of Chicago Press, 1923).

Viner, Jacob, "Mercantilist Thought," *International Encyclopedia of the Social Sciences* (New York: Macmillan, 1968) pp. 435–43.

Wallerstein, Immanuel, *The Modern World System* (New York: Academic Press, 1974).

Walsh, Mary, *"Doctors Wanted: No Women Need Apply"* (New Haven, CT: Yale University Press, 1977).

Walton, Gary, "The New Economic History and the Burdens of the Navigation Acts," *Economic History Review*, **24** (1971) pp. 533–42.

Walton, Gary and James F. Shepherd, *The Economic Rise of Early America* (New York: Cambridge University Press, 1979).

Walton, Mark and Gary Walton, "Steamboats and the Great Productivity Surge in River Transportation," *Journal of Economic History*, **32** (1972) pp. 619–40.

Watch, Richard, "A Note on the Cochran Thesis and Small Arms Industry in the Civil War," *Explorations in Entrepreneurial History*, **4** (1966) pp. 57–62.

Wachter, Michael and Susan, *Toward a New US Industrial Policy?* (Philadelphia: University of Pennsylvania Press, 1981).

Warren, Kenneth, *The American Steel Industry, 1950–1970: A Geographical Interpretation* (London: Oxford University Press, 1973).

Weaver, Paul H., "The New Journalism and the Old–Thoughts after Watergate," *Public Interest*, no. 35 (Spring 1974) pp. 67–88.

Webb, Walter P., *The Great Plains* (Boston, MA: Ginn, 1931).

Weigley, Russell, *The American Way of War: A History of the United States Military Strategy and Policy* (New York: Macmillan, 1973).

Well, Joseph Frazier, *Andrew Carnegie* (New York: Oxford University Press, 1970).

White, Gerald T., *Billions for Defense: Government Financing by the Defense Plant Corporation during World War II* (Tuscaloosa: University of Alabama Press, 1980).

White, Lynn, *Medieval Technology and Social Change* (Oxford: Clarendon Press, 1962).

Wicker, Elmus L., "A Reconsideration of Federal Reserve Policy during the 1920–21 Depression," *Journal of Economic History*, **26** (1966).

Wilburn, Jean, *Biddle's Bank: The Crucial Years* (New York: Columbia University Press, 1967).

Wilcox, Walter W., *The Farmer in the Second World War* (Ames: Iowa State University Press, 1947).

Wildavsky, Aaron, "Industrial Policies in American Political Culture," in Claude Barfield and William Schambra (eds), *The Politics of Industrial Policy* (Washington, DC: American Enterprise Institute for Public Policy Research, 1986).

Wildavsky, Aaron, *The New Politics of the Budgetary Process* (Glenview, IL: Scott, Foresman, 1988).

Wilkins, Mira, *The Emergence of Multinational Enterprise: American Business Abroad from the Colonial Era to 1914* (Cambridge, MA: Harvard University Press, 1970).

Wilkins, Mira, "Multinational Automobile Enterprises and Regulation: An Historical Overview," in Douglas H. Ginsberg and William J. Abernathy (eds), *Government, Technology, and the Future of the American Automobile* (New York: McGraw-Hill, 1980) pp. 224–228.

Williams, Ralph C., *The United States Public Health Service, 1798–1950* (Richmond, VA: Whittet and Shepperson, 1951).

Williamson, Jeffrey G., *Late Nineteenth-Century American Development: A General Equilibrium History* (Cambridge: Cambridge University Press, 1974).

Williamson, Jeffrey, "Watersheds and Turning Points: Conjectures on the Long-term Impact of Civil War Financing," *Journal of Economic History*, **34** (1974) pp. 631–61.

Winter, Sidney, "Knowledge and Competence as Strategic Assets," in David Teece (ed.), *The Competitive Challenge* (Cambridge, MA: Ballinger, 1987).

Winthrop, John, "Sermon on the Arbella," in Stuart Bruchey (ed.), *The Colonial Merchant: Sources and Reading* (New York: Harcourt, Brace, and World, 1966).

Wolfe, Tom, *The Right Stuff* (New York: Farrar, Straus, & Giroux, 1979).

Woodward, C. Van, *Origins of the New South, 1877–1913* (Baton Rouge: Louisiana State University, 1951).

Woodward, C. Van, *The Burden of Southern History* (Baton Rouge: Louisiana State University Press, 1960).

Wright, Gavin, "New and Old Views on the Economics of Slavery," *Journal of Economic History*, **33** (1973) pp. 452–66.

Wright, Gavin, *Political Economy of the Cotton South: Households, Markets, and Wealth in the Nineteenth Century* (New York: W. W. Norton, 1978).

Wright, Gavin, "The Strange Career of the New Southern Economic History," in *The Promise of American History: Progress and Prospects*, ed. Stanley I. Kutler and Stanley N. Katz (Baltimore: Johns Hopkins Press, 1982).

Wright, Gavin, "American Agriculture and the Labor Market: What Happened to Proletarization?" *Agricultural History*, **62** (1988) pp. 182–209.

Wyllie, Irwin G., *The Self-Made Man in America: The Myth of Rags to Riches* (New Brunswick, NJ: Rutgers University Press, 1954).

Yamamura, Kozo and Jan Vandenberg, "Japan's Rapid Growth Policy on Trial: The Television Case," in Gary Saxonhouse and Kozo Yamamura (eds), *Law and Trade Issues of the Japanese Economy* (Seattle: University of Washington, 1986).

Zysman, John, "US Power, Trade, and Technology," *International Affairs*, **67**: 1 (1991) pp. 81–106.

Index